The
Astonishing
World

Also by Barbara Grizzuti Harrison

Unlearning the Lie: Sexism in School

*Visions of Glory: A History
and a Memory of Jehovah's Witnesses*

Off Center

Foreign Bodies (a novel)

Italian Days

The Islands of Italy

BARBARA GRIZZUTI HARRISON

The Astonishing World

✦ E S S A Y S ✦

TICKNOR & FIELDS ✦ NEW YORK ✦ 1992

For information about permission to reproduce selections
from this book, write to Permissions, Ticknor & Fields,
215 Park Avenue South, New York, NY 10003.

Library of Congress Cataloging-in-Publication Data

Harrison, Barbara Grizzuti.
The astonishing world : essays / Barbara Grizzuti Harrison.
p.   cm.
ISBN 0-395-59105-8
I. Title.
AC8.H36697 1992   91-46278
814'.54—dc20   CIP

Printed in the United States of America

MP 10 9 8 7 6 5 4 3 2 1

"My Brother, Myself" first appeared in *GQ;* "In the Name of the Father" first
appeared in *Partisan Review;* "Twins" and "Secret Thoughts of a Married Woman"
first appeared in *Mademoiselle;* "Women and Blacks and Bensonhurst" first
appeared in *Harper's Magazine;* "Glimpses of Morocco" and "Dubrovnik: Spell of
the Moonflower" first appeared in *Condé Nast Traveler;* "The Hill Towns of Tuscany"
first appeared in *European Travel and Life;* "Pure Gore" first appeared in the *Los Angeles
Times Magazine;* "The Godfather" and "Nadia Comaneci" first appeared in *Life;*
"Budapest, Winter 1989" first appeared in the *New York Times;* "Mary: The Stars in
Her Crown" first appeared in *Long Island Monthly;* "Horror at Island Pond" first
appeared in *New England Monthly;* "Prayer" first appeared in *Commonweal;*
and "White Curtains" first appeared in *Ms.*
The author is grateful for permission to quote from the following material: *We Are
Three: New Rumi Poems* by Coleman Barks. Reprinted by permission of Maypop
Books, 196 Westview Drive, Athens, GA 30606. *War in Val d'Orcia* by Iris Origo.
Reprinted by permission of David R. Godine, Publisher. "Gulshan-i-raz" ("The
Garden of Mystery") by Mahmud Shabistavi, in *Sufi* by Laleh Bakhtiar. Reprinted by
permission of Thames and Hudson, Inc., 1987. Excerpt of "Burnt Norton" from *Four
Quartets* by T. S. Eliot. Copyright 1943 by T. S. Eliot and renewed 1971 by Esme
Valerie Eliot. Reprinted by permission of Harcourt Brace Jovanovich, Inc.

Contents

✦ ✦ ✦

The world, this palpable world, which we were wont to treat with the boredom and disrespect with which we habitually regard places with no sacred association for us, is in truth a holy place, and we did not know it. *Venite, adoremus.*

— Teilhard de Chardin, *The Divine Milieu*

The Astonishing World

Introduction

✦ ✦ ✦

*W*hile I was assembling stories and essays for this collection, I spent — in an apparently unrelated activity — the better part of a morning in a shop called Second-Hand Rose, avidly poring over books and books of old wallpaper — botanically incorrect white and yellow lilies on dull black backgrounds; fat red roses on shiny silver; harsh red-and-black geometrical squiggles on blank white; borders, ribbons, stripes; colors that — like certain diseases, lumbago, for example — have gone out of style: cerise, fuchsia, magenta, teal. They all seemed silly to me and they all seemed wonderful to me.

I missed the smell of glue.

They took me right back: There was Daddy (the lumbago in his shoulder notwithstanding), naked to the waist, papering the wall of the bedroom which, ever so oddly, I shared with my mother. And there she was, too, instructing, correcting, despairing of his ever getting it right (despairing of his ever getting anything right).

The samples were sad as well as wonderful, and not silly at all.

I was looking for something I remembered imperfectly but with an electric jolt of emotion: the exact wallpaper that covered that bedroom wall. I thought I was shopping for wallpaper for the foyer of my high-in-the-sky apartment, an apartment that I love (this morning a migrating cloud of orange monarch butterflies flew past my uncurtained windows, giving me very great joy). I had halfway convinced myself that early fifties wallpaper would complement a Josef Hoffman chair when I realized that I was searching, not for wallpaper, but for memories. Something — something beyond the considerable powers of my memory, which, in moments of vanity, I tell myself is a perfect recording instrument — happened in that bedroom, I don't know what (I search for clues).

I brought home samples. They were close to the wallpaper I remembered; they weren't the same. I'd have thought — I looked at sample books for hours — that the identical wallpaper would have leapt out at me; it was a common pattern.

The samples are in a closet now, having served their purpose.

In fact the wallpaper I brought home, botanically incorrect and only tangentially related to the wallpaper of that bedroom on Seventy-fifth Street in Bensonhurst, released a flood of memories — and not those I'd been courting.

Well, memory isn't an exact science. And storytelling isn't, either. One gets as close to the truth as one can.

It's for that reason I've mixed some fiction in with essays, or reporting, or, if you will, journalism: in my case — I don't say in every writer's case — these categories sometimes overlap. I don't, by this, mean to suggest that facts are unimportant or interchangeable or disposable. They're not. But facts aren't truth; they are — though well to be honored — only facts.

I don't — may God forbid it — mean that I would ever feel justified in playing fast and loose with facts; I have never consciously misquoted anyone or attributed to anyone words that he or she did not actually say. I mean only that the slightest nuance has the power to modify the most obdurate fact; and writers deal in nuance. In fiction, almost nothing I say is the literal truth; in nonfiction, everything I say is the truth as I perceive it — and it comes out, as far as I can see, pretty much the same, take it or leave it.

There is, for example, in this collection, a story, a report, about a cult that thrives in Island Pond. Nobody from Island Pond or anywhere else has ever disputed a single fact in that story as it was published. But, had I not myself been raised in a sect, as one of Jehovah's Witnesses, I would have written that story very differently — I would have seen and felt and understood it differently (perhaps with less horror for the lost lives of the children of the cult). The facts are objective; the writer can't be — to rejoice in objectivity is to rejoice in divesting one's self of self; to lay claim to objectivity is to lie. One can strive for fairness — although in the face of extreme evil (a cult that deprives children of their childhood, for example), or in the case of extreme beauty (certain streets in Rome, for example), even fairness seems a bland, if not a negative, virtue. (I recognize the danger implicit in saying — thinking — this.)

Disinterestedness is an excellent thing in a Supreme Court justice — perhaps even in a great painter (the art of Piero della Francesca always seems to me sublime precisely because its magnanimity is disinterestedness carried logically to complete acceptance of a given world); but a disinterested writer? I couldn't be one — why would one choose to spend a lifetime writing about subjects that didn't excite one's passions? — I'd be bored.

Like E. B. White, who writes so beautifully, I'm suspicious of anyone who claims to be an objective journalist. . . . Speaking of White, I once spent a day in the company of a novelist with this question held between us: Who do you think is as sane — on the written evidence — in his life as he is in his work, the work and the worker not (with often confounding results) being the same? At the end of the day we came up with one writer, one name: E. B. White. Sanity, of course, is indivisible from truth (which is why romanticizing insanity is wicked); and it's interesting that the one writer we reckoned to be absolutely sane is the writer who never for a moment believed in "objective" journalism.

For these reasons it makes little sense to me to speak of "personal journalism," or "personal essays." What other kind — unless it's an AP dispatch — is there? How, for example, could my response to Morocco, or to Mario Cuomo, or to the events that surrounded the killing of Yusuf Hawkins in Bensonhurst be anything but personal and idiosyncratic? The context in which I hold the facts is different from (say) the context in which Spike Lee holds the facts.

Am I belaboring the obvious?

When people inveigh against personal journalism (they are less likely to inveigh against personal essays, because, I'd like to think, of the patent absurdity of doing so), they may, with justification, be responding to self-absorption or narcissism or self-centeredness, parochialism and smug narrowness of mind. While there may be no such thing as writing that is not personal, there is writing that is self-indulgent and writing that is not self-indulgent. There is writing about the self that elevates and stops at the self and loves the self unbecomingly; and, on the other hand, there are writers who go in — to the core — in order to move out — to the things of this world which love calls us back to (if we listen). The ultimate reality is experienced and understood in the deepest center of the writer, the spiritual core; that is where the meaningful connections are made.

The universe, Teilhard de Chardin, scientist and Jesuit, wrote, is

> in a continual tension of organic doubling-back upon itself, and thus of interiorization. . . . It is worth while performing the salutary exercise which consists in starting with those elements of our conscious life in which our awareness of ourselves as persons is most fully developed, and moving out from these. . . . We shall be astonished at the extent and the intimacy of our relationship with the universe. . . . We know ourselves and set our own course but within an incredibly small radius of light. Immediately beyond lies impenetrable darkness, though it is full of presences — the night of everything that is within us and around us, without us and in spite of us. . . . In fact, everything beyond a certain distance is dark, and yet everything is full of being around us.

Writers are not social workers. The task of writing, I think, is to discern the presences in the dark, bearing in mind that "there are as many partial universes as there are individuals, . . . that if *per impossibile* we could migrate from one consciousness into another we should each time change our world." Or: We go in in order — our wish is desperate, and sincere — to go out, to "migrate from one consciousness into another." We go into the self to escape the prison of self. We are aware of the perils — both to ourselves and to our hapless readers — but we wish to love the world; and the world is terrible for those who do not know themselves.

I like to interview, more properly speaking, to talk with people (I used, for my sins, to interview starlets when I first started writing; no more); and I like to write essays — I seldom know the end from the beginning when I do so, it is a process of discovery (and to those editors who have trusted me enough to set me on this voyage, I am grateful). And — I came to this late — I love to write travel essays, for, as Italo Calvino wrote, "The more one was lost in unfamiliar quarters of distant cities, the more one understood the other cities he had crossed to arrive there. . . . Arriving at each new city, the traveler finds again a past of his that he did not know he had." We seek the strange to find the familiar. We go to be changed. These are apparent, not real, contradictions. When we travel, Camus says,

> we are feverish but also porous, so that the slightest touch makes us quiver to the depths of our being. We come across a cascade of light, and there is eternity. That is why we should not say that we travel for pleasure. There is no pleasure in traveling, and I look upon it more as an occasion for spiritual testing. . . . Pleasure takes us away from ourselves in the same way as distraction, in Pascal's use of the word, takes us away from God. Travel, which is like a greater and a graver science, brings us back to ourselves.

I somewhat disagree with Camus, whose own journey was toward the light, toward God: traveling for me is pleasure — joy. But with his essential point (as I understand it), that travel brings us back to ourselves, and, as a consequence, to God, I do agree. There is that doubling-back again: in: in order to move out; out: in order to move in . . . an arabesque, a dance.

Certain phrases and ideas crop up repetitiously in these stories; perhaps only I notice them — but I have decided not to alter the text on their account: I think it's fair, if I'm going to publish a collection at all, to leave my obsessions and compulsions on parade.

My Brother, Myself (1990)

✦ ✦ ✦

WHEN MY BABY BROTHER was brought home from the hospital, I sat on him. I bounced. I wanted to kill him. I was five years old; this is the earliest memory in which I am the initiator of an action, the earliest dimensional memory I own, the first memory I can lay claim to that is not picture-flat. The unassailable logic of remembered emotion tells me that the vivid dimension of passion entered my life when my brother entered my life, and a singularly uncomplicated passion it was: I was usurped, he was the usurper. I hated him.

How I managed not to kill him I can't imagine, nor do I remember who rescued him, a squalling dark bundle in the middle of my parents' bed, surrounded by a sea of pillows and overcoats. In my memory, I bounce and merrily bounce: the rage I feel is inseparable from the glee I feel.

"Rub my back, Ricky," I say. We are in my bedroom watching television, my brother, my sister-in-law, and I. "Lie down," he commands: he straddles me and his fingers knead my shoulders till splinters of light form behind my eyes. Every muscle in my body relaxes, my consciousness unknots; how nice. Nobody does this better than my brother. "Remember when I bounced on you and tried to kill you?" I ask, my mind forsaking logic. My brother's only answer is to bounce gently on his knees, and to laugh. "All you Grizzutis are crazy," my sister-in-law, Carole, says, her good-natured common sense — our shenanigans bore her — bringing me back into the present: soon they go home, but I don't feel the emptiness of

*being the last at the party, I don't feel lonely, I feel full, full of the past,
full of love, full of my brother. . . .*

I don't know when the hate turned into love (or if the one had
always been contained in the other). I remember sandbox fights in
which we championed each other. Once my brother hit a little boy
on the head with a toy shovel; I covered the kid's head with mud
to hide the blood. Sometimes my love ran cold: he was clumsy
when he was little, and he'd run after me to school, and his crayon
box would fall, and his pencils, and he'd cry, "Bobbie! Bobbie!"
and I'd harden my heart, which was set on being teacher's pet, my
mother and father having fallen down on the job, and I'd turn icy-
mean because *he* was part of *Them.* I snitched on him, too — to
Them and particularly to Her, my mother.

When I was nine and Ricky four, she turned herself into
a Jehovah's Witness. At first, faced with this new mother in
whom rapture and wrath were mixed and with a father rendered
impotent by bewilderment, we were each other's comforters.
We would, obedient to Mama and wary, trudge from door to
door, hand in hand, selling "Watchtower" literature — which my
brother hadn't yet learned to read. We were two precocious little
mouthpieces for apocalypse, and our freakishness was apparent
even to us. We were all of the time tired — tired of trudging and
of people's stony or incredulous looks (only their condescending
kindness was harder to bear), tired of Their fights, of our vigilance,
of not even knowing what it was that we were guarding ourselves
against or for. We had no friends.

*Ricky is six years old. I am eleven. He has hauled suitcases out of the attic
room, and while I watch, he is putting into them my father's shirts, ties,
pants, shoes. We exchange no words; there is no need. His face is covered
with snot and tears. Our father threatens to leave home all the time, but
he never does; he stays, only to fight with my mother some more. My
brother, battle-weary, doesn't understand the reasons for the grown-up
war; he wants to precipitate some violent explosion of feeling and action.
He wants our father to go if he is going to go away from us and not to talk,
talk, talk about it. When They don't have bitter fights, Ricky and I share a
room with twin maple beds. (There is nothing to remember of those sleep-*

filled nights; there is only our mingled quiet breathing.) When They do have bitter fights, my mother takes my brother's place in his bed; Ricky moves into our parents' room.

When Ricky is done packing, he climbs into the armchair from which I have been watching, scared. We hold each other, rock each other, our tears wetting each other's face. . . .

Our paths diverged. My brother acquired a genius for self-preservation. He stopped living according to my mother's design. He stopped going from door to door. Just stopped. I could never have done that. I thought — I knew — that if I stopped, my mother would die. Or I would. I became my mother's daughter, her double, her dependent (and she mine). Ricky became:

A street kid.

My father's son.

My mother's son, too (still), his falling away from faith notwithstanding; he was, to the end of her life, my mother's boy, her darling child. He was the boy, and then the man, she loved. I forgive him for this, although there is nothing to forgive.

He stayed out past suppertime, playing with the toughest kids, the ones who grew up to be criminals, three-time losers, or cops. I was sent to look for him. "Ricky! Ricky!" I called, feeling both mournful and put-upon. I would never find him.

Is charm enough to sustain a life? I don't know what else kept him afloat. He was very smart, but he acted — and given the company he kept, one could see why — as if this were not a quality one would wish to exploit. He exuded a careless, sensual charm to which both men and women responded. He seemed the most open, the most accessible, the most carefree of boys. In fact he was none of those things, but when he became withdrawn, when he went into one of his silences, the force of his charm — which people, for lack of a better word, call earthy — was such that everyone around him wanted to enter his silence, because to jolly him out of it was clearly impossible. (I have come to think that charm — his — is a form of grace. It functions like love; it draws people to its source.)

I willed myself to become impervious to his charm; I could not will myself to become unaffected by his silences, the sudden reticence like a storm cloud on a perfect day.

*

In the fifties, he did everything fifties-right: doo-wop, gang wars, zoot suit, ducktail haircut, toothpick permanently between his teeth — his life reads almost as if he were prescient for nostalgia. He even had an Edsel, which was so wrong it was right. And he had Carole.

I am in my early twenties, not yet married. I am having the sweetness-and-angst time of my unchaperoned life. My brother lives at home — where I, by all the laws of my tribe, should be living, too. He is engaged to Carole. Carole does not approve of me, my black-leotard uniform, my black jazz-musician lover, my not-in-Bensonhurst East Village apartment. I am contemptuous of Carole: she lives at home, she will rejoice to cook and clean for my brother. She lives in a mold, I think.

Today, we are in the right-field stands of Ebbets Field, my brother, Carole, and I; this outing is meant to signify détente. Carole sits on one side of my brother, I on the other. I am holding his hand. Whether he is holding mine is a good question.

It is impossible for a spectator to be self-conscious in a ballpark on a summer afternoon; I am self-conscious. I regard my emotions and understand that I am experiencing jealousy and a numbing sense of loss. I am jealous of Carole.

Duke Snider hits a home run, bases loaded, and my brother — I used to take him to the ballpark when we were kids — turns to me and hugs me first. Me first! Me first!

In the fifties, I left my mother's religion, stopped going from door to door, took a lover. Ricky said, "You're gonna kill your mother, Bob." In retaliation for which, I never once went to see him when he went to Fort Dix for basic training. I got snooty. We became polite strangers. (These are surfaces.) Two decades passed.

I am at the movies with Robert, who is gay. We are seeing The Godfather. *Every time James Caan appears on the screen, Robert clutches my thigh; he is hot for Sonny, charming, larger-than-life, ba-dee-ba-dop-ba-dee-ba-dop-da-doom sexy Sonny. Every time Sonny appears on the screen, I clutch Robert's knee. Sonny reminds me of my brother. Minus the machine gun and the connections. My brother is a handsome man. I miss my brother. . . .*

*

They'd give up their planned lives and live in Staten Island with plastic rhododendrons and plastic slipcovers and they'd go to Atlantic City every weekend with him, with my brother, if they could marry my brother, someone like my brother (there is no one like my brother), that's what my friends say. He's sexy.

He's male. He's as much my complement and other as anyone has ever been.

I have never kept company with a man who resembled, in any way my intelligence could grasp, my brother. There is an Italian actor I meet sometimes at parties — he always scolds me. There is an Italian writer I sometimes see — I pick fights with him. I always think they are telling me to go back into the kitchen, where good Italian women belong. It is difficult for me to tell whether this thought comes from them or from me.

I have never gone to bed with an Italian man. This may be my way of remaining faithful to my brother, I don't know.

My brother has always been bewildered by my choices. But then so have I. It occurs to me that if I were to choose a man my brother liked and comprehended, I would be home free. I somehow doubt that I ever will.

In the early days of the women's liberation movement, when sexual politics was the name of the game and rage governed thought and action, my brother was never far from my heart and mind. My anger — to which I had a right — was tempered by the thought of him; it never escalated into hatred. (I am grateful to him for this.) And yet this was at a time when we were strangers to each other.

It was after a family funeral. Carole, whom I'd once been so foolish as to despise, came back with him to my house for amaretto, anisette. "Okay," Carole said to us, "talk." We talked.

My brother is more charitable than I. That's one way of putting it. Another way of putting it is that my brother won't allow himself to remember the bad past. That's my job; I asked for it. He lets me do it. That's what I did the night of the funeral. He looked, at first — we were, after all, polite strangers, and remote — like a man awaiting execution. But slowly, and jointly, we pieced together a life. Our life.

We don't do that too much anymore, we don't talk about the bad past. We play poker. We have enormous family meals. (Enormous family, and enormous meals.) Our kids hang out together. We listen to Sinatra (". . . there used to be a ballpark . . ."). We tell each other dumb jokes. The ease I feel with him I feel with no one else; it is the ease of animal comprehension.

He does not remember, but he knows. He is my past. He and I know about the dirty pictures in the attic room, about the night my father developed hysterical blindness driving on a mountain road, about my mother's wailing in the night — he knows why. He knows all the silly things too, all those chance and seemingly incidental things that, joined to our genes and chromosomes, make us who we are. He knows what Johnny-boy yelled from his bedroom window, why Frankie was on the front page of the *World-Telegram and Sun*, what happened on Bay 8 in Coney Island every summer. We talk about these things in code. We read each other's slightest gesture. We laugh. We trust each other forever.

On some level where politics count for nothing and style for less, we are twins, and we are each other's keeper; I keep his history, he keeps mine. Insofar as anyone can be said to know, we know the genesis of each other's flaws. His flaws seem to me not like failures but inevitabilities; in his company I feel almost as if there had never been original sin. I feel completely natural. I am not myself without him.

In the Name of the
Father (1988)

❖ ❖ ❖

ALL HOSPITALS, she had thought, were alike; but in some respects this was not so. In this hospital, the one in which he lay dying, the wall behind her father's head was bright orange. This wall he could not see, tied, as he was, to his bed — to what remained of his life — by bottles and tubes that were indeed like all the other bottles and tubes that had bound him precariously to his life in all the other hospitals. The door to his room was bright yellow.

The nursery-room colors reminded Clara of a playground she had seen somewhere in the South long ago: orange slides and yellow swings and green monkey bars next to an old church in the middle of a graveyard. Clara had cherished that image of life in the midst of death, children sailing high above the tombstones on their yellow swings into the clean blue sky; what could be, if you thought about it, more natural? Of course the smell in this room was awful, hothouse flowers and something else — something swampy, rancid. The playground must have been connected to a school, she thought idly, a church school. And the kneebone is connected to the ankle bone, the ankle bone. . . . What nonsense one thought in the presence of the dying. Silly rhymes kept coming into her head. In this room they talked neither of life nor of death. They hardly talked at all. Occasionally someone murmured, "It's a sin"; voices murmured in assent: "It's a sin."

The old man, who was stubborn, had not allowed the nurses to remove his contact lenses — what a fuss there had been when

Clara's mother found out — and now there was a milky film over his eyes. Under the film, his caged pupils burned bright with fever. When Clara's son was in the hospital after his skiing accident, wrapped like a mummy in a body cast, he'd had to wear a loin cloth. But he always managed to take it off. One day she'd come in to find him crying; his loin cloth was on. "The nurse said, 'Where's your modesty?'" the child said, "so I have to wear my modesty now." Old enough to have a skiing accident and not old enough to know the word *modesty*, imagine. One is never old enough, Clara thought; and then she thought, Old enough for what?

From the window next to the old man's bed there was a view of tenements and backyards, laundry flapping in the wind. Black smoke billowed in the far distance. Clara saw fire engines tiny as a child's toy. Where are the flames? Clara wondered. "Where there's smoke, there's fire," she said out loud. "Now, now," the nurse — who was removing the old man's contact lenses with a tiny rubber suction cup — said. The old man was wearing a light-blue hospital gown; paper slippers were placed neatly at the foot of his bed. Like that painting of Saint Ursula in Venice: slippers near her bed while the angel trumpets and she sleeps, the slippers so obdurately themselves. The physical world doesn't change at all, how odd, Clara thought. Nothing shares our grief.

Clara and her brother held hands. "Are you frightened, Daddy?" Clara said. "What a question," her mother said. The old man raised his left arm and made a clenched fist. They all looked to see for whom the salute was intended, all but Clara's brother, who said, "It's all right, Old Man, your heart's okay," which was not true. Clara felt an accustomed jealousy; how like her brother to understand their father so well, how unfair. How kind. In a spasm of attention, the old man sought his grandson's eyes: "Doing your homework?" he said. "Yes, Grandpa," Clara's son said. The boy's left leg was shorter because of the skiing accident; only Clara ever seemed to notice. "Good," the old man said, after which he subsided into random tremors and said no more. His daughter-in-law rearranged the flowers in the vases. Clara's daughter cradled and kissed the old man's forehead, crooning, "Grandpa." "Now wash your hands," her grandmother said. Clara always called her father *Daddy*; she called her mother *Mother*, although she'd always wanted Clara to call her Sadie. "No, Nana," the child replied, "I won't."

"I want to talk about money," Sadie said. "Not in the room with Daddy," Clara said. "Not now, Ma," her brother said. "You're a good girl," the old man said; it was not clear for whom his words were intended.

Riding home in the car they passed Sunset Park. "Remember when we used to swim here?" Clara said. "Yeah," her brother said; "you were always scared some jigaboo would drown you."

"My friend Marie got raped here last year," Clara said; "she was on her way to the daycare center."

"Don't talk about things like that," Sadie said. "I'm sensitive. It hurts me."

"It hurt Marie a lot more," Clara said.

"I wouldn't worry, Ma," Clara's brother said. "She probably asked for it." His shoulders were trembling with suppressed laughter. In the back seat Clara and her sister-in-law squeezed each other's hands to keep from laughing out loud.

They stopped at a red light. "Why are we parking?" Sadie said. Clara and her sister-in-law snorted with laughter, gagged on it. The grandchildren stared straight ahead.

"The Old Man's threatening to walk."

"Walk? He's got 104 fever."

"Yeah. He pulled a tube out of his arm. He said it hurt. He said they were trying to kill him."

"The fever must be down."

"He wouldn't make it to the door. Ma made me take his clothes away so he couldn't walk."

The last time he'd been in the hospital, the old man had walked out, an overcoat over his striped pajamas, and hitchhiked home. "We want to do an exploratory operation," the doctors had said. "You're not Columbus and I'm not a continent, and nobody's doing any exploring around here," the old man said; then he walked.

"Is Grandpa really dying this time?"

"He's threatening to walk."

"What will Nana say?"

"Probably what she said last time he walked — 'What are you doing in my kitchen? You're killing me.'"

"That's what she said?"

"That's what she said."

"She's a jerk."

Oh God let him walk, Clara prayed. She felt as if there were deep fissures running through her body. ("*Fishes?*" her psychiatrist asked.) But when her brother called, she said, "It's really bad this time. He's got to stay."

"Yeah. You gotta admire him. He's making Ma sick. He won't listen to what's good for him."

Oh good, Clara thought, remembering her father's raised arm, his clenched fist; *good.*

The fever left, no one knew why. No one knew why it had come. The next time the family went to see him, he was sitting up in bed, complaining about the food. "Why didn't you come to see me?" he said, fixing his clouded eyes on Clara and her daughter.

"Oh, Daddy, we did."

"We did, Grandpa."

"*You* did," he said to his son. "You're a good boy," he said to his grandson.

His granddaughter turned her face away and cried. His grandson cried too. The Christmas he gave me fifty dollars he gave my brother an Edsel, Clara thought; never mind.

"I never had a heart attack," the old man said.

"That's right, dear," Sadie said.

"How come I saw that machine with all the blips on it, Daddy?" Clara said. When he was hooked to that machine he had called her an angel of light. "Send the angel of darkness away," he'd said. ("Why do you think the angel of darkness was your mother?" Clara's psychiatrist asked. "It's not what I think, it's what he thinks." "He might have meant the angel of death?" "No.")

"I never had a heart attack. They have doctors back there twisting dials behind the machine. Like a television set."

"So what did you have, Daddy?"

"Gas." He never remembered seeing Clara in the hospital.

"When am I going home?"

"Soon, Old Man," his son said.

"Be good, dear," his wife said.

"We love you, Grandpa," his granddaughter said.

"The food stinks."

The next time Clara called him at the hospital, the old man spoke to her in Italian, which she only dimly understood. He spoke in a guttural whisper: "They want to kill me."

"Can't you tell me in English, Daddy?"

"They don't want me to leave here," he said. "They're listening."

"They can't want to kill you if they want to keep you here forever, Daddy," Clara said. But he had hung up.

"Pull the drapes," the old man said. He meant the hospital curtains. "They're doing terrible things in here," he said. "That guy there. Terrible." He nodded weakly in the direction of the man who shared his room, rubbing his throat to his chin with his index finger, a gesture that meant: *Words can't say. . . . If words could say. . . . Ooooh. . . .* The man in the next bed was dying of cancer; no one ever came to see him. "Animals," the old man said. Clara's brother looked puzzled; for once Clara understood first: sex. He meant they were doing sex. "I see it," he said. "I know. They take him down for x-rays and he doesn't come back. I know. Nuns. They think I don't know. Creeping around all night long." It was a Methodist hospital, there were no nuns.

"Daddy's talking about sex," Clara said.

"You know you got a dirty mind?" her brother said.

What if my brother should die? Clara thought. Drunk, she saw her brother's car in flames, his charred body. She allowed her son to comfort her: "Grandpa will be all right, Ma." *Poor little boy.* She meant her son. She meant her brother. Her son, weeping, held her as she wept. *Daddy,* she said, *Daddy,* deceiving her son, who loved her. *My brother,* she thought; *my brother.* She saw her brother in an airplane, spiraling down into oily waters. She closed her eyes against the sound of the crash.

The man in the next bed died. Clara's mother, alert with greed, asked the Filipino nurse to tell her all about it. "Can it, Ma," Clara's brother said. *Well, what do you know?* Clara thought; *he told Sadie to can it.* "I'm only trying to express an interest," Sadie said. *Like unto Job's comforters,* Clara thought; *my mother's getting fat.* She giggled. "Can it, Clara," her brother said.

"Terrible things, terrible things," the old man said.

"The man who was doing terrible things isn't here anymore, Daddy. There's somebody else here now." The old man shouted a curse in Italian; who would have thought he could summon up such strength?

"Get the nurse," Sadie said.

"What for, Mother?"

Sadie bit her hand. "This is killing me," she said, her hand muffling her words.

"You're killing your mother," Clara's brother said.

"Who, me? What did I do?" *I never do nothing and I never do much,* Clara thought.

"You talk too much," her brother said.

The old man was asleep now, his toothless mouth open. Clara thought she could smell his breath across the room.

After they dropped Sadie at home, Clara and her brother went to a bar.

"Remember that Edsel the old man bought me?"

"I remember."

"I paid him back. A hundred a month."

"I never knew that."

"Now you know."

"I talk too much," Clara said.

"Yeah. But you got the charm in this family."

"I do?"

"Yeah."

"Do me a favor? Take my side more often."

"Hey. There aren't any sides. We're all on the same side."

That's his charm, Clara thought; he believes it.

The old man hadn't spoken to his sister for years. Not since their mother — Clara's grandmother — had died. Really such a silly will to quarrel over — a couple of acres on a highway and a ramshackle summer cottage was all she'd left. And after all, the old man's sister deserved it: she'd nursed the mean-tempered woman all through her final illness; she'd never married. But the old man was unable to forget that he'd pruned the pear trees that were the only glory of the summer place; he felt entitled. The business stuck in his craw: "What does an old maid want with pear trees?" he asked, a constant refrain. It had become a joke between Clara and her brother: "What does an old maid want with pear trees?" they chanted whenever events confounded them, whenever they met after long separations; when Clara married, her brother startled the priest by saying, "What does an old maid want with pear trees?" Once when they were playing poker, Clara's brother said "What does an old maid want with pear trees?" just before the last raise, and Clara laughed so hard she wet her pants, and lost the hand even though she had aces over kings.

Now the old man was calling his sister every day. Sadie suspected Clara of having given him her phone number to foment trouble — Sadie saw any possible reconciliation as trouble, it hurt her, she was sensitive — but the fact was that the old man had, over all the intervening years, remembered. He talked to his sister in Italian: "They're trying to kill me. Get me out. They do terrible things." So now Sadie and the old man's sister called each other every day, Sadie tearfully pleading that the doctors knew best; she couldn't handle him at home, it was killing her, the old man's sister snapping that *she* had taken care of *her* mother, a wife was *supposed* to take care of her husband, that was what marriage was *about*, "after *all*."

"I want Daddy out," Clara said.

"It's killing Ma," Clara's brother said.

"Why can't he die at home?"

"Are you gonna change his diapers? Ma can't."

"I'll hire a nurse."

"I love you, Clara, you're my sister, but you never knew anything about money."

"I don't think money is what this fight is about. What does a nurse cost?"

"Hey. What fight? We're not fighting. The old man's sister knows how to give orders, but I don't see her coming to the hospital."

"What's that got to do with anything?"

"Hey, come on, your kids are getting upset."

"Why shouldn't they get upset? Somebody's dying."

"You gotta say dying in front of the kids?"

"They know life's not a candy store."

"Yeah. They live with you."

"Don't disturb the doctor," Sadie said; "don't call him up."

"Why not?" Clara said.

"He's a kind man," Sadie said.

"I notice he doesn't answer my phone calls."

"He's busy, dear."

"Do you understand that Daddy's dying?"

"Don't say *dying*," Sadie wailed, amazing how she could wail and whine at the same time; Clara felt a shudder that seemed to come straight from the bowels of her childhood.

"Are you going to take care of him?" Sadie said. "I'm an old woman."

Clara stiffened her heart against her mother's tears; she looked up *rubber hygienic goods* and *practical nurses* in the Yellow Pages. It was a wife's business to take care of her husband. After *all*. Clara told herself she shrank from that intimate contact — how could she, his daughter, change her father's diapers? Or is it really the smell I'm afraid of? she wondered; it is the smell. His flesh, slippery now, against the bones, was still sweet to her; but she couldn't bear the smell. Like rotting orchids, bat dung. Were poisonous gases escaping through all those bottles and tubes?

"Jesus, the smell," Clara's brother said, and hugged her.

"Does it bother you too?"

"Jesus," he said, and kissed her.

The old man was leaning against the yellow door; he was wearing blue paper slippers. "We're taking you home, Daddy," Clara said.

"Possibly," the old man said.

"Not 'possibly,' *really*. Don't you believe me?"

"Possibly," the old man said; "could be."

But when Clara's brother walked in, he said, "Good boy, good boy," and grinned. He had shrunk so much they had to tie his belt around his pants with a double knot to keep them up.

When they rolled him past the nurses' station in the wheel-

chair, he waved — "Hey, Old Man, you look like the pope blessing the crowds," Clara's brother said. He waved and he sang out,
pleasantly as spring, "Fuck you, fuck you." "You gotta hand it to
the old guy," Clara's brother said. Clara's hand rested on her
brother's as he wheeled the old man to the elevator. A woman
shuffled toward them. Her hair was hennaed bright red, there was
a bald spot the size of a quarter on the top of her head. She wore a
shiny pink nylon robe, a red nylon feather boa, and blue paper
slippers. She bent over to whisper something in the old man's ear.
Clara could have sworn she bit it. The old man grinned and patted
the woman's thigh. In the elevator, Clara's brother said, "I got my
own ideas about who's been doing terrible things in this hospital."
"Just what I was thinking," Clara said. They laughed so hard the
old man bounced in his wheelchair. "Nice to see you children
happy," he said. They laughed harder. "What does an old maid
want with a pear tree?" Clara's brother said.

Riding in the car, Clara felt as if she were going on a picnic.
The old man's head, on its stalk of a neck, made quick, birdlike
movements, side to side, taking the world in like a child. He slept
for a while.

Then: "Pop's dead," he said.

"Yeah, Old Man."

"It's a sin."

"Yeah, it's a sin."

"When did Mama die?"

"Grandma died twenty years ago, Daddy."

"It's a sin." The old man was crying, and singing:

> "Oh Hel —
> Oh Hel —
> Oh Helen please be mine.
> Your count —
> Your count —
> Your country is divine.
> For cu —
> For cu —
> For curiosity
> Oh Hel —
> Oh Hel —
> Oh Helen please love me."

"Clara?"

"I'm sitting right behind you, Daddy."

"Be sure to sing that one to the kids, Old Man," Clara's brother said.

"It'll kill Ma," Clara said. Her brother caught her eye in the rearview mirror and winked.

Sadie didn't want to rent a hospital bed: "What for?" she said. "It's just a matter of time," Clara's brother said. Sadie didn't want to hire a practical nurse: "I can't afford it," she said. "But if it's just a matter of time?" Clara said. "Don't say *dying*," Sadie said to Clara, who hadn't said dying. Clara's sister-in-law rattled the dishes in the sink: "Shit!" she said. Clara exchanged looks with her daughter, who rolled her eyes. Clara's son sat in the small room off the kitchen, holding the old man's hand.

Sadie's Barcalounger stood in the doorway to the old man's room, which was really the second parlor. He lay on a foam-rubber couch that had doubled for a bed — such a narrow bed — ever since Clara could remember. The couch and the bolsters were covered in slipcovers that Clara coveted — cerise cabbage roses against pale gray-and-lime stripes, Deco delight. In the first parlor, the one in which no one ever sat, the sofas were red velvet covered with heavy perforated plastic; the wood was white, trimmed with gold. The couch-bed in the second parlor was covered with heavy plastic too. And now with a rubber sheet. Where are all the doilies Sadie crocheted when we were young? Clara wondered. That morning, before her brother and his wife arrived, while Sadie napped, she had gone through all of Sadie's kitchen cabinets, removing all the 1940s glasses, which she put in a large shopping bag. Also a Depression-glass sugar pitcher and creamer. "Mommy, what are you doing?" her daughter asked; the child had sounded frightened. "Sadie will never miss them," Clara said; "we'll buy her new ones." Clara's son said, "Mommy, don't." But Clara plundered nonetheless.

The Barcalounger was covered with shiny green slipcovers. "You wouldn't think you could get slipcovers for a Barcalounger," Clara said; "wouldn't you think they'd interfere with the machinery? Trust my mother." Clara's son poured her a drink. "What I really want is a cigarette," she said. Sadie — who could sleep through earthquakes, but who'd always heard the key turn in the lock when Clara came home from dates, to this house, years ago — called from the bedroom: "No cigarettes! That's what's killing your father!" "Don't say *killing*," Clara said.

Now Clara said, "Why don't you put the Barcalounger in the room with Daddy, next to his bed? He likes somebody to hold his hand." "*You* hold his hand," Sadie said; "I can't stand his moaning. I'm too compassionate, it hurts me."

"Ma can't sleep," Clara's brother said.

"It's only a matter of time," Clara said, while her sister-in-law banged the pots in the sink, and her daughter said, "Oh Mommy!"

"Hey!" her brother said.

Clara wondered how she was going to get the shopping bag with the Depression glass and the Deco juice glasses out of the house.

The stench in the old man's room overwhelmed all of Clara's sympathy, all of Clara's love. She could think of nothing else. She could not remember what the old man had looked like before he looked like this — shrunken, bent, fierce, skin like crinkled crepe. His breathing was shallow and fast. Once in a while he spoke: "Give me a cigarette," he said. "No, Daddy," Clara said; she was afraid of Sadie, who had found three cigarettes in his pajama top. The cigarettes had come from Clara's son, who was not afraid of Sadie, and who did not mind the smell.

"Who are all these men?" the old man said, his fire-bright eyes scanning the dark, empty room.

"There's no one here, Daddy, just shadows," Clara said.

"Who are all these men?" he said.

"Shhh. It's okay."

The old man began to cry.

From the kitchen, Sadie said: "He imagines things all the time. He thinks there are men in there. Tell him they're shadows."

"Do the men bother you, Daddy? Do you want me to tell them to go away?" Clara said.

"No."

"Are they kind?"

"They're good guys."

"Good."

"It's that other guy I can't stand. The one that was with me when I was born, the one that looks like me. The one who does terrible things. Always did terrible things."

"Oh, Daddy," Clara said. "I don't think he ever meant to do terrible things. I don't think he's bad. I know he's not bad." She held her father's hand. She knelt at his bed and pressed her cheek against his, happy, absolving.

"You don't know shit!" the old man yelled. "Give me a cigarette," he whispered.

Clara thought: God, the smell.

"Don't trust that Clara," the old man said, "she's not so nice."

"It's me, Daddy, Clara, I'm here."

"Oh."

Clara, who was drunk, told her daughter, "Grandpa said he couldn't trust me."

"He meant because you wouldn't give him a cigarette."

"That's not what he meant. My brother wouldn't give him a cigarette either."

"You know Grandpa loves you, Mommy."

But that was exactly what Clara didn't know. She arranged all the proofs in her mind, she remembered endearments, reconciliations. But she could not connect the proofs, the endearments, the reconciliations, with the man who lay burning, dying. Perhaps the fever has burned away all that is false in him, she thought; in which case, he does not love me.

She drank.

The old man's father had died whistling a bird-call. The old man's mother had died with the words *veal cutlets* on her lips. What do these things mean. If only she could remember what he'd looked like before he'd become this thing. Clara no longer knew for whom she cried. She dreaded her visits to the airless, phantomed room. Maybe there's a point to Sadie after all, she thought, and then she wrenched her sympathy away from her mother. But she could not find the father she loved, even in her dreams. Orphaned, she wept.

One day Clara arrived to find her father sitting at the kitchen table. He was slurping lentil soup while Sadie hovered with a dishcloth, a napkin. He asked for peppers and eggs, most of which he ate. "I got a joke for you," he said to Clara. "A very religious man was sitting in the park. A pretty woman walked by with a baby. The baby was doing terrible things. It was ugly. So the man said, ''Scuse me, lady, but how come such a pretty woman like you has such an ugly baby? Who was the father?' So the woman said, 'Well, there was no father. I had artificial insemination.' So the man said, 'That's what the Bible means when it says spare the rod and spoil the child.' Get it? Spare the rod and spoil the child?"

"I love you, Daddy," Clara said.

"Sure you do," he said, "we know that. Tell her to go away." He meant Sadie.

Sadie took a cuticle scissors from the pocket of her house-dress, dipped a dishcloth in a glass of water, snipped off two edges of the cloth, and stuffed them in her ears: "I can't stand the moaning," she said.

"Who's moaning?" the old man said. Clara mopped his face, his chest. "No more talk about dying around here," he said. "She says she's here all the time, but she goes away." He meant Sadie. "I'm here, Daddy," Clara said. "Of course," he said. When he rose to go to the bathroom, Sadie jumped up to help him. "You tell her, Clara," he said, "tell her I can do it alone. You know I can do it. You know I'm good."

"He'll fall and kill himself," Sadie wailed. She seemed to be hearing all right, in spite of her earplugs. Clara thought he might very well fall and kill himself; she willed him across the room. "Shut up," she said to Sadie, who shrieked, "You're killing me!" He made it to the bathroom, and then to bed. "I feel good," he said. "Do you love me, Daddy?" He patted Clara's hand. He fell asleep. Sadie went into her bedroom and turned the television on, "The Price Is Right." Clara could hear her crying. She sat at the kitchen table and lit a cigarette. She finished her father's peppers and eggs.

The next day Clara's brother phoned: "He's gone."

"Gone where?"

"Gone."

"Where are you?"

"I'm at Ma's house."

"Gone where?"

Clara's sister-in-law got on the phone: "Cla? He passed away an hour ago."

The terrible thing has happened.

Clara woke her children up. "Never," she said; "never never never." What had she ever understood. "Never." Her son held her. Her daughter kissed her. She felt — she dressed — like a widow in her grief. She arrived too late to see her father's body taken away. "What were his last words?" Clara said. But Sadie had been on the phone when the old man died.

She stretched her body on the old man's bed, rested her face on his pillow. She pressed her flesh hard against the narrow bed. The windows were open and the summer cries of children filled the air: *Hide and Seek!*

Kneeling, she made the sign of the cross. She remembered only her father's outstretched hand, she could not summon up an image of his face. When she was young — she had not thought of this in years — she had seen graffiti on the posters of their subway stop, words she was not supposed to know; she'd thought she recognized her father's spiky handwriting. *In the name of the Father, the Son and the Holy Ghost.* Are the stories of our lives the real stories of our lives or are they stories about stories? She remembered his spiky handwriting, but she could not remember his face. She said the Lord's Prayer, stumbling over the word *trespasses; sin* came to her lips, it always had, more easily than trespasses.

In the kitchen they were having coffee. Sadie was in her Barcalounger: "Kiss me," she said. Clara lit a cigarette, observed the dandruff on the undertaker's jacket. She felt as if she had been carried a long distance — this was her own voice, sighing — to a place of no rest. She felt the future enter into her, darkly: "Kiss me," Sadie said.

Twins (1987)

✦ ✦ ✦

WHEN I WAS GROWING UP, there were two girls my age who lived in the apartment building next to mine; they were called Barbara and Violet, and I never tired of looking at them, and the reason I was smitten with them — with both the idea and the actual fact and literal presence of them — was that they were twins.

I was a lonely child. My mother was a religious fanatic, she was strange, she was not like other mothers; and my father was, as a consequence, largely absent. Over the years, my parents perfected an odd mating ritual: My mother would do something surpassingly strange, and my father would flee; then, drawn home by what conjugal mysteries I cannot imagine, he would return home. He loved my brother and me, and came back home in part to be with us, to be a dutiful father; but his essential transaction was with my mother — I cannot remember a time when I did not understand this.

Children are protective of their parents, even when — perhaps especially when — their parents are not protective of them. (The circle cannot be broken, and it is the frightened child who holds it together.) I wanted desperately to shield my mother; I wanted no one to know intimately just how strange she was. Of course she defeated my purposes: she walked across streets in bright sunlight carrying a red umbrella so that the cars she could not see would not strike her — her nearsightedness was being "healed" by a religious "doctor" at the time; she tried to make a bonfire of the aluminum pots her religion taught her were the source of cancer; she succeeded in making a bonfire of religious statues and pictures and calendars she considered "demonic"; and she went from door to door to tell people the world was coming to an end.

If I could not protect her from scorn, I could at least not allow people to see the effect her strangeness had on me; trying to shield her, I succeeded brilliantly in defending myself — I built a wall around myself, I let no one approach me in friendship or in curiosity. Friends were a luxury I could not afford.

To separate myself from my mother was unthinkable, so frightening my imagination could not entertain the idea . . . for if I were to look at her entirely objectively, her strangeness would — this was my conviction — somehow kill me, eradicate me, destroy me. Her strangeness had to be familiar, not alien, in order for me to survive.

I looked at Barbara and Violet, each other's familiar. I thought, They are never lonely; wherever they look, they find themselves. I could not imagine anything lovelier than having a twin; having a twin would mean you always had objective proof that you existed in the flesh (it was like carrying a magic mirror) and assurance that you could not be obliterated: *You* were two. You were also one — and that was the absolute charm of this relationship, in which one was separate/not separate, different/the same.

Many young girls fantasize that they are one of twins, the other lost. I approach this fact with my imagination, not as a scholar, unarmed with statistics. I think girls to whom the idea of twinning appeals are girls who are not easy in their lives, girls who struggle to find their proper place in a world of strangers. A twin defines you; she not only proves that you have the right to exist, she *obliges* you to exist: you owe it to her to be a twin so that *she* can be the twin she is. A twin is both an external manifestation of and a solution to the problem of separating from one's biological double — one's mother. In the *films noirs* of the forties about identical twins (films with Olivia de Havilland and Bette Davis), there was always a Good Twin and a Bad Twin — and this was psychologically adroit, an acting out of the psychodrama of the (good) girl who loves her mother who is the same (bad) girl who cannot be reconciled to her mother.

It has occurred to me that given my intense fascination with and love for Barbara and Violet, it might have been a logical progression for me to love women instead of men. I know as little as anyone else does how sexual identities are formed or chosen; I do know that all of the women who speak to me of their fascination with twins are heterosexual women. ("I *am* Heathcliff," they say; *Wuthering Heights* is about twinship between a man and a woman.) Each time I have been in love, I have said/he has said: *"You are me, I am you. . . . We are twins."* Men and women in love intuit each other's deepest (and darkest) needs. When I am gentled, it is my twin (my other/not other) who gentles me; when I am hurt, it is my twin (my other/not other) who hurts me . . . And somewhere, in all of this, is my mother and her red umbrella.

*W*hen, after the slaying of Yusuf Hawkins, I told my daughter, Anna Harrison, that I was going to write about Bensonhurst, where he was killed and I was raised, she said: "Oh God, *Moonstruck* all over again!" What interests me so much is that she might very well have been right: I could have chosen — which is to say my memory could have dictated to me — a story about big warm vulgar meals, a big warm vulgar family, mellow togetherness — that which we now in shorthand call "family values." (Just today, I read in the *New York Times* a charming story about the good people of Bensonhurst and the backyards in which they planted zucchini, and the pleasure with which they took the zucchini to friends and restaurants — images of bounty and goodwill.) I could have written what Anna (who shouldn't be misapprehended: she loves Italy and Italians) refers to as a macaroni-and-mandolin story. And if I had, I would not have been lying. I didn't write that story. That's not what my conscience — and, more importantly, I think, my unconscious — required and delivered up to me. Ewart Cousins, one of Anna's professors at Fordham, speaks of the coincidence of opposites (which is to say, how two apparently irreconcilable things can both be true): *Moonstruck* was true (*la famiglia!* love and wine and hugs and spontaneity); it made me cry, and the tears were, in part, tears of recognition . . . and, in part, tears of abject longing for what I never fully owned. For just as a bad marriage teaches you how good a good marriage might be, an anomalous upbringing teaches you how good a conventional (tribal) upbringing might, under certain circumstances, be. So: *Moonstruck* was true. But so, although it presents an almost violently opposed picture of Italian Americans, is *Women and Blacks and Bensonhurst*. A coincidence of opposites. . . . Ever since I learned this very helpful phrase, which literally changed my perception of reality, I've learned not to defend my truth so hard; at the same time, I claim it as my truth with fewer apologies.

A woman, presumably black, wrote to *Harper's*, where this piece was published, to ask what the hell I was about — she said I carried on more about my childhood than about the death of a black kid. I saw her point; but I didn't, as a result, regret having written as I did: there are certain essays that derive from necessity and invite criticism and dialogue; that's what you hope for.

I'm grateful to Lewis Lapham, editor of *Harper's*. He never bullies me into a point of view — he'd have printed, I bet, a macaroni-and-mandolin piece if it had internal logic, and was well written; he never uses the writer as a spokesperson for his point of view. That's rarer than one might think.

Women and Blacks
and Bensonhurst (1990)

✦ ✦ ✦

ON AUGUST 23, 1989, a sixteen-year-old black youth, Yusuf K. Hawkins, was shot to death in Bensonhurst, an almost entirely white section of Brooklyn, allegedly by Joseph Fama, a brain-damaged, neurologically impaired high school dropout with a "low normal" IQ of 72 and the academic achievement of a sec-ond- to fifth-grade child. According to the prosecution, Hawkins was confronted by about thirty white youths, some of them car-rying baseball bats. Fama, eighteen, and Keith Mondello, nine-teen, have been charged with intentional murder. Four other whites are charged with "depraved indifference to human life" and "acting in concert with other persons" to kill Yusuf Hawkins. On September 18, pleas of Not Guilty were entered for all defen-dants.

Keith Mondello was once the boyfriend of eighteen-year-old Gina Feliciano, whose father, no longer living, was Puerto Rican. Feliciano, who is under round-the-clock police protection and is expected to be a key witness for the prosecution, favored black and Hispanic boyfriends; interviewed on "60 Minutes," she was not at all reluctant to talk about her preferences.

One of the defense attorneys, Benjamin Brafman, questioned why the district attorney's office had not sought to indict Feliciano, whom he called an "instigating force" in the attack.

"Was she down there and did she fire a shot? Was she armed with a baseball bat?" Judge Thaddeus Owens asked. She wasn't; but it is more than a defense strategy to implicate Feliciano: it is

31

the prevailing feeling in Bensonhurst that she was responsible for the killing of a man.

My friend Biagio, who was brought up there, as was I, says the thing he misses most about Bensonhurst is the honeysuckle. "And pig's rind," he says. Pig's skin, pink-white and waxy, is stuffed with pine nuts and raisins and garlic and parsley, and rolled and tied with string and put — along with sweet and hot sausages, fresh pork shoulder, chuck beef, and chicken — into the "gravy," the tomato sauce for pasta. . . . Of course we never used the food-trendy word *pasta* in Bensonhurst; *macaronies* was our generic term, macaronies and gravy our Sunday ritual. . . . The pork rind gets gelatinous in the gravy, chewy, fragrant. . . .

Sometimes Biagio and I go back to Bensonhurst to buy the ingredients for gravy (nostalgia takes strange forms). Biagio patronizes a pork store on Avenue P. I like to shop on Eighteenth Avenue. I grew up in "the numbers"; Biagio grew up in "the letters"; each of us has trouble believing the other grew up in the heart of the heart of Italian Brooklyn. Bensonhurst is about territory, territory strictly defined and fiercely defended.

Besides "the numbers" and "the letters," there are "the Bays," those streets that stretch toward the Narrows. The girl who was to become my brother's wife lived on a pie-shaped block where "the letters" and "the numbers" converged; he met her at a dance in "the Bays." These facts of geography seemed to him liberating. He drove his Edsel to get to Carole's house and regarded their courtship as an event not unlike the Yalta Conference.

It isn't possible to overestimate the importance of the Sunday gravy; the amount of meat one ate was the most significant measure of affluence in Bensonhurst in the forties and fifties. You could live above a store, but if you ate meat six days a week, you counted yourself prosperous. And hospitality and generosity — character — were measured by the amount of meat you served your guests. "The kind of woman your mother was," my Uncle Pat said, summarily and succinctly defining my mother's nature, "was if four people came to dinner, there would be four pork chops." My mother was not prodigal, she was unnaturally frugal. Luigi Barzini had it that Italians in postwar Italy ate poorly, preferring to wear their money on their backs, where it showed, in the form of clothes, so as to make a *bel' figura*. But Barzini was a north-

ern Italian. Bensonhurst's Italian immigrants came from the pov-
erty-stricken South — from Naples and Calabria and Abruzzo —
and food was both comfort and tangible proof of success, as well
as justification and revenge, a way to show off to one's friends and
neighbors, and a perceived way of assimilating, just as the Host
(the "Communion cookie") was the way to God. We processed the
world through our digestive systems. My mother served organ
meat a lot, and appendages — heart stew and chicken-feet soup,
many things rubbery and many things slippery; and she went
comparison shopping for broccoli and fought with my maternal
grandmother over whether to use the dandelions that grew in an
empty lot next to us for salad or (as my grandmother wished) for
wine. From such evidence I tried to assess our relative position in
the world. . . . When there are internecine fights in Bensonhurst — when, for example, the new immigrants, not so impoverished as my grandparents, who came to America at the turn of
the century at the time of the *grande immigrazione,* are made objects
of scorn or become the source of bewilderment, Italians of my
generation use the understood language of food to express uneas-
iness. In 1974, there was a race riot at my high school, New
Utrecht, blacks having been brought in from other neighborhoods
to attend. When my brother and I went back to the old neighborhood to talk to some of his friends about it, one of them said: "We
got this big influx of Italians from the old country — geeps.
They're not like us. They got a chip on their shoulder. Mouthy.
They say, 'Blacks have been here for a hundred years and they
couldn't make it; now it's our turn.' It was a geep who beat up on
a black kid at Utrecht. The geeps are here three years and they got
money to buy a four-family house. That's all they think of is
money. They never heard of going to the movies. They never
heard of anisette. They never even heard of *coffee.* What kind of
Italian is that? They work two jobs, and they eat macaroni every
night — pasta lenticci, pasta fazool, that's it. We're here eating
steaks and drinking highballs and we hear them every night crack-
ing macaroni into the pot — unbelievable." Food is used to signify
opprobrium: a dope is called a *zhadrool,* slang for a cucumber or a
squash. . . .

I am skipping rope, double-dutch, in the magic dusk. "Come in,
the chicken's ready," my brother yells out the window. "Don't let

the Jews down the street know what we're having for dinner," one of my aunts calls out. . . .

So embattled. The Indians were always circling around the wagons. It was that way in the Old Country, where only silence brought a measure of peace — *don't interfere* — if not of economic freedom; and it was that way in America, too. Italian immigrants of my grandparents' and my parents' generation lived in the conviction that *they* — the "Americans," the Jews, the *others* — were out to get them, cheat them, kill them. *Don't let them know anything. What they don't know can't hurt you.* In the days of his senile dementia, my grandfather believed he'd flown with Lindbergh across the Atlantic — but that *they*, the Americans, wouldn't give an Italian credit for it. When Grandpa got cancer, it was "a sin" (not "what a shame," but "what a sin"), the greater sin being to tell anybody about it. The world was malevolent, it existed to be held off and thus controlled.

As for the honeysuckle: Perhaps honeysuckle grows somewhere else in New York; if it does, I don't know about it. Or maybe — this heretical thought has occurred to me — what Biagio and I both think of as honeysuckle is the flower of the privet hedges that decorously contain Bensonhurst's tidy one- and two- and four-family houses. But I am prepared to swear that it was the sweetness of honeysuckle that threaded its way through my waking and sleeping dreams when I was young and tempestuously in love — years and years of invalidated love — in Bensonhurst.

The first man I loved was a Jew.

My first lover was a black man.

It'll kill Mommy and Daddy, I thought (not without a delicate thrill of pleasure); Mommy and Daddy will kill me, I thought (feeling what I had never felt before: a sense of latent power absurdly coupled with ennui and a sense of hopelessness).

There was a honeysuckle bush on the corner of Sixty-sixth Street and Nineteenth Avenue; its perfume restored me to a love of an enlarged world when I was desperately unhappy — and simultaneously fed the unlicensed ardors that were a source of my unhappiness.

Now I dream, not of those lost loves, but of the honeysuckle bush, which has itself become an object of intense love, flowering in my reveries.

Yusuf Hawkins was shot dead on Sixty-eighth Street and Twentieth Avenue, two blocks away from the building my parents lived in till they died. Hawkins, together with three black friends, came to Bensonhurst to look at a used car. It was an act of singular naïveté, and the timing was deadly.

Eighteen-year-old Gina Feliciano's birthday fell on August 23. The young woman had invited black and Spanish friends to celebrate with her, and she told her ex-boyfriend, Keith Mondello; perhaps she taunted him with it. According to Feliciano, Mondello and his friends called her a "spic lover," told her her "nigger friends don't belong in the neighborhood" — "stay with your own kind."

Feliciano called the celebration off. According to her, while she and her mother and a girlfriend ate potato chips and pretzels in her apartment, white kids milled around her house on the night of her birthday. By horrible accident of fate, Hawkins and his friends, unrelated in friendship to Feliciano, walked by. The white kids chased them with bats they got from a nearby schoolyard; Hawkins was killed with a shot from a .32-caliber pistol.

White residents of Bensonhurst who talked to reporters claimed that Feliciano tried to frighten them — that she said black guys were coming into the neighborhood to beat them up. She denies this. She says she knows she's being called "a prostitute, a crackhead and a liar," and she says she was "with black guys in Coney Island — a couple of them" (the implication is that she was "with" them sexually) — but that it's nobody's business, especially not the business of the "Guidos" who "wear sixty chains and have hairspray in one hand and a mirror in the other" and use "jumper cables" to style their spiked hair: "They ain't paying my rent, they ain't puttin' clothes on my back and they ain't feedin' me" — and she's not sleeping with them, she said.

Bensonhurst's response to the tragedy in their community is not monolithic. But when I hear Gina Feliciano say that they tell her she "brought Bensonhurst down," I hear a chorus of voices from the past — the immediate past, and the mythological past: *The woman made me do it.*

According to Ms. Feliciano, there is a $100,000 contract out on her life.

I ran away — as fast and as hard and as far as I could (across the bridge, to Manhattan, the emancipating city of calculated dreams);

I fled from insularity and provincialism and suspicion of all that was not *us* and from familial love that was both careless and claustrophobic. I fled; and now I grieve. One cannot separate oneself from the landscape of earliest desire, the crucible, the wellspring, the source. I still want what I owned and what owned me — the honeysuckle bush on the corner. In memory I walk those streets; I look for clues, for the stuff that binds me to Yusuf Hawkins . . . and to his killers.

It is an established fact in my family that I am crazy. My Aunt Mary, who loves me, dissents — but as she is Sicilian, her word does not count for much among my Calabrian and Abruzzese aunts and uncles. Italians are tribal. Bensonhurst is tribal. My family called Aunt Mary "the Arab," Sicilians not being regarded as properly Italian.

My mother had a friend called Rosie-the-Spic. One day I answered the doorbell when Rosie-the-Spic came to visit (I can remember when doors in Bensonhurst were never locked, and so can generations of Italians. That was before, they say, "the element" moved among them). "ROSIE THE SPIC IS HERE," I shouted, having no idea whatsoever that "Thespic" was not her proper name. I didn't know about racial enmities then. I was four. Naturally Rosie-the-Spic never came back, and naturally (for whatever seemed unreasonable to me also seemed natural to me, though I made myself ill with temper tantrums trying to understand) I got a beating.

Once, lying in bed, I heard scrabbling and moaning and hoarse sounds coming from the bedroom of the apartment next door. I intuited that something I needed to know about and wanted to know about and wasn't going to be allowed to know about was going on, and, knowing also that the question was perverse, I asked my mother what the (exciting) noises were; her silence effectively anesthetized my genitals for years. . . . I wonder what questions Gina Feliciano asked her mother, and what answers she received.

Zhadrool had quasi-affectionate overtones. Blacks were called *mulanyam* — a corruption of *melanzane,* eggplant, and in that there is no affection at all — only blackness so opaque as to defy comprehension.

*

Sometimes we went to Prospect Park. I used — this is how, very early, I established my craziness — to run up to black people and touch their skin and tell them they were beautiful. This was an aesthetic, not an ideology. I was five years old; I don't know how or why I came to it. One of my aunts gave me a black doll and told me I could play with it if I never ever again touched a black person. It was a Little Black Sambo doll; I hated it. We never went to Prospect Park again, only to the Botanical Gardens, because the park was "full of *them*."

It did not surprise me when black protest marchers in Bensonhurst were greeted with cries of *nigger go home,* and with watermelons. Of course the kids we used to call "gees," the kids Gina Feliciano calls "Guidos," would use the language of food.

When I went to New Utrecht High School in Bensonhurst, there was only one black student, Joan Smith. She never spoke to anyone and no one ever spoke to her. At the end of her senior year, she was nominated for most popular. I have told this story so often I believe it to be wholly true; but if it is not true, it will, as they say in Italy, "serve." It is to the point.

It is not true that Joan Smith never spoke to anyone and no one ever spoke to her. I spoke to her. I spoke to her because I was a Jehovah's Witness, and it was my (hated and hateful) duty to proselytize. I tried to convert Joan Smith. It didn't take. (I did convert Fatima Ouida, though, an Egyptian girl who kept snakes in the apartment underneath the elevated train line where she lived; Fatima used to invite people over to watch her father pray to Mecca — he became known as "the guy who prays to the West End train.") In the lunchroom at New Utrecht, I sat with a girl who had one eye, her father having knocked the other one out of her head with a broomstick; and I sat with a girl whose makeup was puddled all over her face (she was mad); and I sat with the class slut, who was stupid. I tried to convert them all. In any case no one else would have much to do with me, my religion having made me an outsider and a freak.

There are of course voyeuristic advantages to being an outsider and a freak.

I was an outsider and a freak, but I was smart. (I was pretty, too, but I didn't know that; I didn't know what my father meant

when he said, "The world eats up pretty, smart girls like you."
Eats them up and spits them out, he meant; he meant *Beware*.)
One day a teacher approached me in the hallway of Utrecht and
said — genuinely bewildered, I think — "Why do you have an
Italian last name?" "Because I'm Italian," I said. He did not know
what to do with this. Jews were smart — they took academic
college-preparatory courses. Italians were dumb — or going immediately to be married (Jewish girls wore charm bracelets, Italian
girls wore engagement rings). They took commercial or vocational
courses. I took hold of this view of my world early — we all did. I
can remember when Miss Silver, my third-grade teacher, a chunky
woman who wore chunky Mexican silver jewelry (which jewelry I
associated with lesbians, perhaps because of Miss Silver's interest
in me, which my father considered untoward) came to my house
rustling with sibilant *s*'s when I had viral pneumonia; she came to
tell my mother I was going to skip a grade. My mother took a dim
view of what she regarded as interference. Actually Miss Silver
came really, I think, to say, *Look at your daughter, pay attention to her*
(she held my fevered hand); and this is what my mother, who
introduced herself as "Barbara's relative" and dwelt in the clouds
with Jehovah, having heavenly fish to fry, took a dim view of.

In junior high school there was one black kid; and my brother, at
the time of the race riots at Utrecht, said: "That kid was lucky. He
was bright and good-looking. If he was just a regular black kid,
he'd have had bad trouble. Every time teachers talked about black
history or slavery, my word of honor I felt sorry for the kid. If
they'd have talked about Italian history, there'd have been thirty
of us Italians, we wouldn't be embarrassed . . . not that they ever
talked about Italian history."

In high school Italian was offered as a second language. Everybody took French.

My brother got beat up bad when some kids in the Bays mouthed
him and Carole, and he, gallant, answered them back. He got in
his Edsel and drove to the station house all bloody, his nose
broken, and several ribs. "Were the kids white or colored?" the
desk sergeant asked. "White." "Go home and forget about it," the
sergeant said.

*

The flowers in the gardens were all old-fashioned: sweet peas and sweet williams and rambling roses. Mint. Fig trees swathed in tar paper and crowned with a tin bucket all winter, undressed at the first sign of spring.

I roller-skated for my life, maintaining a difficult, thrilling balance; overhead, the winy maple trees. Alone. At sunset we were safely gathered in. We were allowed to eat ice cream only from the Good Humor truck, it was good for us, like escarole. This was before my mother became a Jehovah's Witness, before I was nine years old. Afterward, my father said, marking and ruing the day, "She never made muffins anymore."

The first day of freshman English, Utrecht: David Zeiger is our teacher; he says: "Everyone with blue eyes has to do homework." Our world is divided into three parts, Italian, Jewish, and "American." The Americans have blue eyes. They protest. "It isn't fair" . . . making his point for him. David Zeiger spent a forty-minute English period, in 1948, telling freshman English students in Bensonhurst — many of whom had never seen a Negro — why it was wrong to judge people by the color of their eyes, or their skin.

According to the dogma by which I lived, Jehovah was a god of justice and mercy, and whatever happened — including the drowning of infants in their own blood at an imminent Armageddon — was by definition fair. But I knew — I viscerally knew, I was laceratingly divided — that my world was governed by caprice, that punishments and rewards were arbitrary. I lived after all with my mother. . . .

My mother, who was beautiful, had blue eyes, like an American; she was very nearly blind. She went to a doctor, a quack, who gave her eye exercises to do; one of them involved resting her head on the windowsill while she rolled her eyes in her head. A passing motorist saw her and thought she was convulsing. I came home to a fire-engine rescue team. "Why didn't you tell them I was doing eye exercises?" she asked me, her need to place the blame a rigorous passion. I must assume that given her voracious and discordant needs she was mad; and that her religion accommodated her madness. Mad. Sad. Of course the eye exercises didn't work. Thereafter, rain or shine, she carried a red umbrella so cars could see her when she crossed the street. A beautiful woman with blue eyes carrying a red umbrella.

My mother was incapable of dual allegiances. After she fell in love with Jehovah, she no longer wanted to sleep with my father. She made me tell him so. I was ten. He cried. But he slept in the mahogany double bed with my brother and my mother slept in the twin bed next to mine. She cried. One Christmas Eve my mother went out, against my father's protests, to proselytize from door to door. My father got drunk. I washed the dishes. The doors of all the kitchen cupboards flew open and everything in them — cups, saucers, pots — came flying out. For years I remembered that poltergeist phenomenon without remembering what had directly preceded it: my father put a dish towel around my neck and, yanking it, started to strangle me; then he fell in a wet heap on the floor, and then the cupboards flew open and everything in them flew out. I was twelve. The downstairs neighbors heard the noise. Weeks later they said to me: "We mind our business." All of our neighbors minded their business. They wouldn't have heard the sound of a shot and if they had they wouldn't have done anything about it.

No matter what happened, my father needed profoundly to keep up appearances.

In particular my father hated an uncle of mine who, after coming home from the war with a Purple Heart, had been converted by my mother. This uncle worked in a doll factory. At dinner my father would say: "Did you stuff dolls today?" This is how it was: the house was hot with sex; but nobody talked about sex. "What's Tampax?" I asked my mother. She left the room.

My aunts, my godmother among them, knew that my mother and my father did not sleep together. They blamed this on "the Jehovahs." But they maintained a stony silence; it was important for them to believe that they were "nice," and "nice" people — like the "Americans" — didn't talk about sex. When I was an adult, my godmother told me that Daddy had wanted to leave my mother to marry a woman who worked in the Bargain Hats department of Gimbel's Department Store. She talked her brother out of it, my godmother said, there never having been a divorce in the family. Italians didn't get divorced and Italians didn't talk about sex.

Which was what made it possible for my mother to have a romantic affair without a guilty conscience. After the war, the Witnesses who had been imprisoned for not serving in the armed forces came home. One of them, Louis, fell in love with my beautiful mother. They went from door to door together, holding hands. They considered, having consulted various Bible concordances, that they were married in the eyes of God, the pledge being as good as the deed; they would celebrate their marriage in Jehovah's "New World," after Armageddon had disposed of my father. Future-sex. Louis painted her toenails. I'm sure they never talked about sex. They talked about the New World, when the lion and the lamb would lie down together. I was told to regard Louis, whom I loathed, as my proper father-in-the-Lord. At dinner one night: "You were seen walking *mano a mano* with that Louis," my father said, "the one who stuffs dolls with your brother." My mother cried all night long in the twin bed next to mine: "What did you tell him, oh what did you tell him?" she cried. I hadn't told him anything. Everybody in "the numbers" knew. Word gets around. What you don't want known in Bensonhurst you don't do. "You've ruined my life," my mother said.

So all in all it wasn't race relations I learned from David Zeiger (or "tolerance," which was the word we used back then) so much as the idea, new to me and radical, that lives could and should exemplify fairness, that justice wasn't exercised only by God but by human beings.

David Zeiger is still my friend, though it is hard for me to change his place in the story of my life; in reveries, he belongs to the past — the runic past I spend the present reading, the past that contains Arnold Horowitz, who is dead.

Arnold Horowitz was David Zeiger's best friend and he was my English teacher when I was fifteen. A lot of the girls — the smart girls, the point of him not being obvious to the dumb girls — had a crush on Arnold Horowitz. I myself didn't see the point of him until he wrote this sentence on the blackboard: *The beautiful girl with hair the color of ripe wheat* . . . That's as far as I got in the sentence, and then I fell in love and could not believe there was a time I hadn't been in love with Arnold Horowitz.

Almost all of my Italian neighbors were casually antisemitic; it wasn't a matter of creed. Some of my neighbors and some of my family members were virulently antisemitic. My brother brought home a loaf of Arnold's Bread from the market one day; my mother threw it out the kitchen window — but that was not so much because Arnold was Jewish but because Arnold, like Miss Silver, paid attention to me. He was more dangerous than Miss Silver. Miss Silver only taught me I was smart. Arnold told me I was good. (I have loved him all my life.)

He sent pepperoni to the gees (the hoods, the hard guys) in jail. In 1945, ahead of his time, he co-edited a book for young adults called *This Way to Unity: For the Promotion of Goodwill and Tolerance Among Races, Religions, and National Groups.* (He published it under a pseudonym, Arnold Herrick, bland and Wasp — and also Gather Ye Rosebuds While Ye May; the Board of Education banned it — it contained the word *womb.*) Jehovah's Witnesses are forbidden to salute the flag. Arnold came into the school auditorium at assembly time during the flag salute and held my hand; how could I not have loved him? I met a black teacher in his house on the Bays one hot summer night. It was awkward in that big living room with the window seat and the blond Danish furniture and the Picasso prints. The others — David Zeiger and his wife, Lila, and some people whose faces I cannot recall — had very little conversation. We blamed it on the heat. One treated a black person as one treated an invalid — with courtesy and caution.

Antisemitism seemed a most peculiar thing to me. The halls of all our buildings smelled ecumenically of chicken fat and gravy. The girls I had talked dirty with before talking dirty became a sin were Italian and Jewish and equally inventive and equally ignorant of sex. The girls I'd played the Ouija board with under the stairs of apartment buildings were Jewish and Italian and equally titillated (the Ouija board said I was going to marry DICK, which was my father's name) and equally scared. I'd jumped across roofs with Jewish and with Italian girls and ridden up and down dumbwaiters with Jewish and Italian girls, and what was the difference?

When the world became full of catalogued sin, both Jewish and Italian girls were remote to me, equally to be envied because they had, it seemed to me, two gifts that I had not: the freedom to play and, within limits, to choose.

On Friday evenings my Jewish neighbors gave me two cents — they gave boys three — to turn on the stove and the lights for Sabbath.

Sometimes my family and my neighbors counted the number of Jews on the subway train. They were afraid of being overwhelmed.

On Bay Parkway a self-possessed smiling young woman

walked to the elevated line every morning in a silk dress underneath which there was no bra. (This was in an era when the single
most potent image of freedom I cherished was that of a girl with
long blond hair sitting at a lunch counter in a raincoat, her daringly
unstockinged feet out of her shoes.) "She must be Jewish," the
Italians said. They were afraid of sexual perdition and contagion.
They wanted their daughters pink and white and girdled and
pure.

Angela, one of Arnold's students, got a scholarship to Radcliffe. *The New Yorker* published Harold Brodkey's short story about
the love affair of a Harvard boy and a Radcliffe girl. Angela bought
every copy of *The New Yorker* to be had in Bensonhurst. That was
what Angela's family feared: that they *did it* there. Angela was the
only Italian girl from Bensonhurst I knew who went to college.
Italians didn't believe in college, it threatened family authority.
(And this has not changed.)

When I was twenty-two and Arnold had not married me or asked
me to marry him or for that matter declared his love for me, I fell
in love — at Minton's, on 128th Street in Harlem, with a jazz drum-
mer. It was a clever thing for me to have done; I had left my childhood religion but not the bed in the room where my mother cried
at night. I wanted a baptism of fire into the world and I got it.

I had never once seen a black man walk the streets of Bensonhurst.

I loved the nights.

In those days it was safe to take the subway late at night; and
full of love, replete, I'd walk at dawn to the apartment house . . .
where in the lobby my father, longing for proof of what he most
feared, my sexual indiscretion, lurked. (I always harbored a suspicion that the lady in the Bargain Hats department was black.) Even
in Manhattan it was hard for me and G., my musician, to walk in
safety; even in Birdland it was dicey to hold hands.

Once at Minton's an angry black man asked me who the Mau
Mau were. "Kenyan terrorists," I said promptly. I was ignorant
and innocent and did not suspect black people of laying traps. (G.
laughed and laughed because I couldn't say the word *nigger*, which
word he and his friends used all the time; he made me say it; I
cried.) The angry black man scolded me up and down and all
around. (G. was busy playing a set.) "Don't you call her no

names," a whiskey voice said. "She's a woman, she's a nigger — she can be raped." The voice belonged to Billie Holiday, whom as a consequence I loved.

It would not have occurred to me to walk the streets of Bensonhurst with G. Sometimes, to test me, and, I suppose, himself, he'd stop me on a busy Manhattan street and kiss me on the lips; but it would not have occurred to him to walk the streets of Bensonhurst with me — he was very much dedicated to his own survival. Once or twice he came to my door in a car or a cab — laughing his husky laugh (Coward's Violets pastilles and Camels cigarettes), amused, defiant, proud, to think of my father waiting there. My father took to following us around Harlem. He'd crouch beneath the areaways of brownstones that housed after-hours clubs; surely there was an illicit thrill in his determined vigilance.

Arnold said: "Are you happy?"

G. was married. Three years after I fell in love with him I married a white man, a man I could take home to Bensonhurst but never took to my heart.

The thing about taking G. to Bensonhurst was: he would have been killed. That was what we understood.

Arnold taught us, echoing Camus, that people were not so much good or bad as ignorant. I don't know. I believe in good and evil; and I believe in forgiveness. What I have written here, torn from a bloody past, is not the whole truth. In the whole truth belongs the safety of the stoops in the friendly dark; trips to Ebbets Field; my growing to love my sister-in-law, Carole; the steadfast love of my grandmother Concetta who prayed for me even when I despised her Catholic prayers; "Jack Armstrong" and "The Inner Sanctum" and a linen closet full of sugar cubes that smelled of lavender; the smell of glue and new paper and old books in the library in Gravesend; Mrs. Scalia, the junior high school teacher who wanted more than anything else to see my Italian name inscribed on the marble honor roll; my meanness to my brother and his to me and the restoration of our love for each other (and the time when he hit a kid on the head with a shovel — he was four — and I packed the bleeding wound with mud); the time Mike Collura drove me to my job in the Secretariat Building of the UN in his ice truck — right to the door; the bakeries and the lemon ices and the fish carts and the kosher butchers; the bike rides to Coney Island and the parachute ride; my maternal grandfather's grapevine, the yeasty smell of his wine pervading the house; the sun room my paternal grandfather built, and Aunt Louise's tailor's dummy and the big radio, which were in it; trips to the rodeo (I cried) and the circus and to the World's Fair (I shook hands with Johnny Weissmuller); Miss Isaacs, who would not let Shirley Gottlieb play with me in eighth grade because I might convert her; Aunt Louise's death when she was twenty-three, and Dr. Greenberg, who could not bring himself to present the family with a bill; the kindness I received from strangers — all those people, Italians and Jews, whose doorbells I rang in Bensonhurst with my message of superiority and doom; the goodness of teachers and nuns and priests who listened to a wild, unhappy girl preach; the high school girls I thought despised me and who now, when I meet them, say, We remember you, you were nice. I think it is a sin to have left out all the good things and not to have told all the truth. . . . But I am thinking of Yusuf Hawkins — and of Gina Feliciano.

"It was the woman's fault." The first lie, the lie the serpent told.

Bensonhurst is full of coffee bars now — social clubs for men, they really are; and I've tried to sit in them; and I've been — even with my brother and my son and my nephews — scared. Because they don't belong to us. Bensonhurst was territorial when I grew up. It is more territorial now. It is more defended, and more frightened.

If I had told the whole truth — if I had given equal time to what is good and what I loved — I would still not feel welcome there. If I spoke of their broken dreams, of their hard working-class lives, their economic nightmares, their fear of dope and crime and invasion and change — and their guts and their love — I would still not be welcome there. Because the first survival lesson, the first thing you have to understand to live in Bensonhurst, is to honor "the blood." And when family warmth and tribal feeling have been perverted by fear and alienation, corrupted to form an incubator for hatred, the duty of "the blood" to "the blood" is silence: it is held true that even a single reproach pollutes the stream of love. "We mind our own business."

I am afraid of black men now and I am afraid of being afraid but cannot reason my way out of fear. I am different from the murderers of Yusuf Hawkins; but perhaps not so different from the people who have spun a net of protection, a net of silence, around them. All the time I have been writing this, I have fought the inclination to do the same. I have fought my will to silence.

I loved the way the girls receiving First Communion looked. I envied them. I did not understand how I would ever be married if I didn't first become a child-bride in this ceremony that prefigured marriage and looked so much like it. I loved the way their missals smelled and looked, white leather and onionskin paper; I wanted flowers in my hair. It seemed to me a kind of doom that I could not join them, a prefiguration of spinsterish loneliness.

A special mass was said for Yusuf Hawkins in Bensonhurst. Priests led their parishioners, who looked solemn, grave, frightened, in a march to protest the killing, a march to express solidarity with the people of a child shot dead. They looked as if they were in shock; count-me-among-the-just/I-am-not-worthy, their looks said. They were brave.

You'd have to have lived in Bensonhurst to know how brave. You'd have to have lived in Bensonhurst, an outsider and a freak like I was, to know how good their goodness feels.

My brother says: "Thirty years ago, honest to God, I would've been with the guys with the bats. In August, I swear to God, I would have been with the protestors." I can't tell you how hopeful that makes me feel.

On an Alitalia flight from Rome a few weeks after the killing, I sat next to an immigrant from Calabria who lived in the Bays. I asked him if he'd heard about the trouble in Bensonhurst. "You mean the Chinese?" he said. "It hasn't been the same since Chinks came to live in the Bays, making trouble."

What can you do with a man like that?

I called a friend who lives on West Fifth Street and Avenue S — "the letters." "Bensonhurst . . ." I began. "I don't live in Bensonhurst," she said, "I live in Gravesend." "All your life you've said you lived in Bensonhurst!" I said. "No more," she said. And, with what I have come to think of as characteristic Italian logic, she added: "I never lived in Bensonhurst."

Then we talked about food.

Secret Thoughts of a Married Woman (1985)

◆ ◆ ◆

SHE WAS SO TIRED she couldn't remember the Italian word for milk. She hadn't slept at all on the train from Paris to Milan. So here she was, waiting for the train to Rome, drinking her coffee black. How could she tell him that she wanted a divorce? He would say, *Why?* She would say, *Because I don't love you.* He would say, *When did you stop loving me?* She would say, *I never loved you.* Then there would be more questions. When she thought of him as she had last seen him, planting perennials in the garden of their villa (though everything about their life abroad was temporary, at any moment they might be transferred from North Africa to another post), she could not imagine telling him the truth. How, remembering his sunburned neck, his naked shoulder blades, could she think of telling him the truth? *I have never loved your body. I want to go home.* In fact she often kissed the back of his neck; in fact she loved their villa. She even loved the smell of the kerosene that clung to their clothes during the Mediterranean winter when all the stoves were lit; even the mistral, the wild, hot wind that blew in from the Sahara, depositing a fine layer of gritty dust on everything — furniture, bodies, toothbrushes, flowers — the mistral, too, she liked.

On the other hand, perhaps he would ask no questions at all. Perhaps he would just say, *Yes.* After all, he never seemed sad to see her go: the thought of him, self-sufficient in the villa during their frequent separations, when she sailed, alone, to Italy — for clothes, she said, for art, in fact for the comfortable thrill of being

47

alone, not one of two — made her wonder if it would not be he who would ask for a divorce. This last time, when her ship pulled out from Tripoli for Siracusa, leaving him behind, he had cried. So, for that matter, had she.

But if he asked no questions, if he said, *Yes, I'll give you a divorce,* what would she tell her mother, who was waiting for them in Rome? She hadn't seen her mother in three years, and her mother had flown all the way from home, had predicated this reunion, with every reason in the world, on a belief in her married happiness. All her letters home had been happy, the letters of a woman living contentedly with a kind husband (he was kind) in a beautiful house by the sea: *Tonight we're sitting near the fireplace — you've never smelled a good fire until you've burned eucalyptus logs — listening to* Carmina Burana. *Mark always played Ethel Merman after* Carmina Burana, *don't you think that's funny? Sweet. Tomorrow I leave for Siracusa, and then to Capri, and then to Paris. We can't wait to meet you in Rome . . . Mark is planting perennials. . . .* And, the odd thing was, everything she wrote was true. She didn't write about the nights. Every day, in her walled garden, she thought about the nights. Every night: Would he? Wouldn't he? If he did, would it be better than the time before? It never was. And if he didn't — well, what was their marriage about? So she didn't know, she never knew, whether she wanted him to or didn't want him to, and she was tired of the burden of decision, though in fact the decision was always his. Yet (she would smother, she thought, under the weight of her own contradictions), she loved the way his body smelled. Like yeast. It was also true that she was bored.

The platform was crowded. She should have known better than to travel on Holy Thursday. Every Sicilian in Milan was going home for Easter; she would never get a seat. She had a car number and a seat number, but (someone jostled her, and coffee spilled, scalding her thigh), she knew just how little that would count for. She could as easily arrange a place for herself in heaven as on a train bound for Palermo on Holy Thursday. If heaven were a larger version of Tuscany, Purgatory, she thought, must look like this: a railroad station in Milan. A nun passed her and she smiled. The nun did not return her smile. Italian nuns never smiled.

The crowd was becoming aggressive. Surely the train could not accommodate all these pushing, eager people. She wrapped herself in thoughts of her villa. She knew, with prescient nostalgia, that someday she would remember her walled garden with such tenderness as ought to be reserved for the child Mark did not want to have. All her life she had wanted to live in a walled garden. A suitcase banged her shins, bringing quick tears to her eyes, and she thought of that cloistered amplitude: a twelve-foot-high white-washed wall, a profusion of purple bougainvillea spilling over it; a sandy approach to the wall, lined with spiky cactus blooming with pale orange pears; a door of fretted wood, painted green, set in the high white wall; and, inside the door, date palms and pomegran-ate trees, grapevines and lemon trees, morning glories, pansies, a riot of sunflowers, zinnias large as dinner plates, homely mari-golds with their astringent, weedy smell, starbursts of yellow jasmine, and nasturtiums and anemones; and, over all, the unam-biguous Mediterranean light. She wanted a child. She thought of the silky white moonflowers that she often caressed: closed and shriveled by day, open like pearly trumpets and fragrant by night. Was it true, what the Arabs said? To sleep with a moonflower under your pillow is to sleep without dreams; to sip their nectar is to sleep forever.

The train was late, and she was pushed farther away from the edge of the platform, deep into a tangle of bodies and bundles. Sometimes Arab women knocked on the fretted-wood door set in the villa's garden wall. She never knew what they wanted. Shrouded in black barracans, they stood there without words; they seemed only to want to look at her — and so much of her foreign flesh was available to their one-eyed gaze. Almost always they carried babies in their arms. When flies settled on the babies' kohl-lined eyes, they didn't even blink. Once she had tried to brush the flies away, but the women had giggled and retreated, disappear-ing into a curve of the sandy road. In the garden there was a tree laden with great misshapen hybrid red fruit, tumorous and too heavy for the slender branches, swollen against the glistening green leaves.

When the train pulled in, people ran up and down the length of the platform, throwing suitcases into the open windows of the moving train. When the train stopped, they ran up and down again, looking into windows for their suitcases and bags. A man addressed her in English: "We are an unruly people," he said, raising his hands to the sky, taking pleasure, she could see, in the unruliness of his countrymen. Inside the cars, men were ripping RESERVED signs off seats. When she boarded, all the compartments were filled; there was barely enough room in the aisle for her to place her luggage, hardly room enough for her to stand. How in the world would she manage to make her way through this wall of flesh when they came to Rome? She fought off dizziness. I'll cry, she thought; that always works in Italy. Amazed at her control, she saw her reflection in a window: a pretty young woman, crying. *"Chè cosa?"* a man asked. "I'm pregnant," she heard herself say in Italian. She said it with the conviction of truth. They made room for her in the nearest compartment, and she sat, crying, thinking, Well, it's only fair.

She closed her eyes. The compartment smelled of garlic, and of sweat, and of her perfume — "like vanilla," her first lover had said it was; why hadn't she married him? And why did women never marry men like the men they loved in the movies? She fell asleep.

When she woke up, there was a hand on her thigh. The hand belonged to the man who had arranged for her to sit; what to do? She didn't want to appear ungrateful. Her stomach was hard and flat; perhaps he hadn't believed her lie — which was strange, because she had, during the space of time it had taken her to say it, believed it herself. Perhaps I am going to ask for a divorce, she thought; how easy it is to lie, she thought: "I'm pregnant." She offered the man the smoked chicken she'd brought from Paris; she ate his bread and cheese. He looked as if he thought she had gotten the better part of the bargain. Why did she and Mark never talk about sex?

A man asked her why she was going to Rome. To ask my husband for a divorce, she thought; to tell my mother the truth. "Because of all the cities of the world I love Rome best," she said, which was true. The man — a Milanesi — said: "Rome is a sewer. A pestilence. Even the Romans hate their city. You see it written all over — SPQR: *Sono porchi questi Romani* — 'They are pigs, these Romans.' A city for animals. Have a fig." How she loved Italians, so unruly.

"How do you know," the man from Milan asked (he was speaking now in Italian), "that your husband will be waiting for you in Rome? In your country you believe in divorce. So . . .?" He shrugged.

"I know," she said, fearing, of all things, the evil eye (why had he spoken of divorce?), "because he said so." Biting into the fig, which was sweet and ripe, she thought, He will be there. He has never broken a promise. What if I should never see the villa again? Who will live in the walled garden after I am gone? She had said: "I'm pregnant." She wished the nun had smiled at her.

The questions — would her husband be there? would he not? — became a game in which she played no part. She wondered, at first idly, about her physical presence. Was it as irrelevant to Mark as it appeared now to be to these men? She listened to them debate all the nuances of possibility. Even the man who had placed his hand on her thigh discussed her husband — would he be there? would he not? — as if her flesh had no part in the equation. A baby wailed in the next compartment. She slept again.

When the train stopped outside of Rome, a nun glided by. Emerging from sleep, she did not know if the nun had been real, or a figure in her dreams. Of course, she thought, apparitions are not real, but they are real apparitions. The look on the nun's face reminded her of the inward look she had seen on the faces of pregnant women. She understood how one might become, in some beautifully protected way, invisible — the floating garments of nuns, the floating garments of pregnant women: an integrity of flesh. She thought of the women in barracans who had come to inspect her. She smiled, thinking, I don't exist for these people, now, except as a metaphor; they believe I am pregnant.

They were all, as the train came into the station, crowded at the windows. When Mark ran up, calling her name, they cheered. They cheered him. *Bravo! Bravo!* they shouted. They made a path for her.

She thought of the invisibility of nuns, the invisibility of pregnant women. She walked toward his smile in a cloud of perfume; and her clothes, in her mind's eye, floated around her.

I lived in Libya for nineteen months. My son, Joshua, was born in the hospital of Wheelus Air Force Base in Tripoli — at that time (twenty-eight years ago) the largest extraterritorial United States military base in the world. I had very few close friends. That is not true. I had no close friends in Libya — my life was filled with strangers, some kinder than others. I remember now with acute distaste my feelings of superiority, which were in fact disguised feelings of alienation and pain: I had bemused contempt for the Americans who, disdaining the produce of the Mediterranean, would wait for wilted lettuce to arrive at the base, scorning the luscious tomatoes and figs and olives and wine of Libya and of Sicily (the wine came over in beautiful hand-blown green bottles, taller than I). The woman across the road from me washed her hands over and over, compulsively — she came from Texas, she had never before been out of Texas; and she was scared . . . as — lacking the grace to admit it, however — was I. I wasn't scared of Libya. I was scared because I was in a marriage I didn't understand, and I thought I would be in it forever. I felt hateful, futureless, unmoored. The birth of my son ameliorated these feelings. But even that event could not reconcile me to a sterile marriage. It is terrible to be in a beautiful place and to find nothing in it to love. My garden was beautiful. The rocky sea — down a sandy path from my cloistered villa — was beautiful. I was miserable. By the time I left Libya, I was convinced — being unable to tell the truth to myself (and unable, consequently, to write) — that I loathed

Libya. In fact I did not. My loathing was a chosen mask. Very little of this was clear to me until I went to Morocco. Things work out strangely. I didn't love Morocco. But I remembered all kinds of lovable things about Libya while I was in that neighboring North African land. Unhappiness anesthetizes one. I must have loved Libya — aspects of Libya — all along. It took a shocking visit to Morocco, and the passage of twenty-seven years, to recall me to this love. Morocco revivified landscapes and people and events of that long-ago time for me; I reclaimed Libya, and loved it much more than I ever knew I had. I wish I could go back.

Glimpses of Morocco (1990)

✦ ✦ ✦

IN THE EXOTIC and terrifyingly familiar landscape of dreams —
in which the impossible is the inevitable and the alien is one's
brother; in which the dreamer is simultaneously visible and invisible, caressed and assaulted in her dreaming flesh which is disem-
bodied matter — rivers run through deserts, flowers bloom along
paths where seductive dangers lurk, houses are caves through
which the dreamer's tunneled unconscious searches and stum-
bles. In this territory, where the known and the unknown are
identical twins and what happens in the heart resounds in the
receptive universe, objects and events form a unity that is more
perilous than chaos; stasis and flow, monotony and variety are
indistinguishable, as is the prince from the toad . . . and from this
country no one returns undisturbed.

Travelers, whether of wholesome disposition like Edith Wharton, or of decadent disposition like Paul Bowles, tend to perceive
and describe Morocco in terms of dreams. In this place, Wharton
writes, "Buildings, people, customs, seem all about to crumble
and fall of their own weight: the present is a perpetually prolonged
past. To touch the past with one's hands is realized only in dreams;
and in Morocco the dream-feeling envelops one at every stage."
For Bowles, who perversely rejoiced in decay, Morocco came as a
gift: he rose from a dream with "a residue of ineffable sweetness
and calm," and in the late-afternoon sunlight "walked slowly
through complex and tunneled streets. . . . I realized with a jolt
that the magic city really existed. . . . My heart accelerated, and
memories of other courtyards and stairways flooded in, still
fresh. . . ."

Of course Morocco is not, though it often seems to be, part of what Jung called the imaginal (real/unreal) world, that world which is not delusory but not susceptible of rational proof, either; but Morocco exists, one sometimes thinks, in its very own light, which Wharton describes as a light of "preternatural purity which gives a foretaste of mirage . . . the light in which magic becomes real; . . . to people living in such an atmosphere, the boundary between fact and dream perpetually fluctuates."

It comes as a surprise to me, now that I have been to Morocco, that dreams are not permeated with palpable fragrance, the sense of smell being, we are told, the most evocative of all the senses. Morocco smells better than any place I have ever been. It also smells worse.

The time is too short. I feel sometimes, driving through Morocco, as if I am hurtling through a museum of impressionist and cubist paintings in a wheelchair; and sometimes as if I am (out-of-body) flying; I never feel quite relaxed (one is never so alert as in a dream). I am in the midst of dazzling confusion.

In my dream I make my way through dun-colored honeycombed rooms so low I have to crawl from one to the other. Sometimes a green door punctuates my journey, which has no end. The tunneled rooms are brilliantly lit, and full of wondrous things — hands made of gold and milk-white cats and carpets of edible colors and warriors in silken robes. Will somebody be cruel to me? Why is nobody cruel to me? When I wake from this dream I am sad.

Before I went to Morocco I thought this dream was about Libya, where I once lived, although the *souk* of my dreams only dimly resembled the streets and shops of the Libyan souk — not dun-colored, but white and blue; not darkly tunneled but latticed, light, and airy — where I bought copper hands of Fatima to keep away the evil eye and camel bags with lozenges of color (like jujubes) and where once, in impenetrable alleys, my favorite cat got lost (and later found); and cruelty came from unforeseen directions. After I went to Morocco, I was inclined to believe that the dream was prescient and prefigured it. And now it doesn't matter anymore whether the dream belonged to the past or to the future, whether it prefigured Morocco or harked back to Libya. It closed a circle: in Morocco I found a great deal not to like; nevertheless I am beholden to it — it helped me to reclaim Libya, which my memory had chosen to misplace and thereby to malign. Without Morocco I would not have grasped the measure of love I entertained for that other time and other place. *"We shall not cease from exploration / And the end of all our exploring / Will be to arrive where we started / And know the place for the first time."*

The bodies of the Moroccan women boarding Royal Air Maroc tell us they think of themselves very differently from the way we think of ourselves. The older women have abandoned their bodies, or slumped comfortably into them (slop-slop in their run-down shoes; shoes seem never to be important, even to a well-dressed Moroccan woman, even to a stewardess; one doesn't know why). The progression is girl–mother–grandmother. I look in vain for someone I might categorize as sister, as *woman*, sexual, proud, full of ripe being. I begin immediately to feel anomalous. I think of the tourist guidebook that exhorts the woman traveler to "play one of the stereotyped but recognizable 'unavailable' roles: the wife, the mother, the intellectual, etc. . . . though traveling with a companion or a man would be more relaxing." I feel a little tug of dread. "Men are superior to women," the Koran says, "wiser." Morocco is not a country in which a woman can take her femaleness for granted.

One sometimes wonders what discernible mark the French — whose "protectorate" Morocco was between 1912 and World War II — had on this country placed between the desert and the sea. They left behind a language, a taste for sleazy satin; and they created a network of superbly serviceable roads. There were no roads in Morocco as late as the first decade of the present century; according to some writers, even the wheel was unknown. That was the time when, as Edith Wharton writes, "the 'Christian' [whom Moroccans, when they are not calling him "infidel," call "Nazarene"] might enjoy the transient joy of wandering unmolested in cities of ancient mystery and hostility, whose inhabitants seemed hardly aware of his intrusion."

The road we take through the fertile lowlands from Casablanca (no longer glamorous, if in real life it ever was) to the imperial city of Fez is narrow but splendid. And the men and

women sitting on their haunches along the roadside among ancient wells and hand plows seem hardly aware of our intrusion.

Four men in long white cotton gowns sit, with biblical simplicity and intensity, under a date palm, turbans wound around their
heads. No one could ask more of them but to keep their unselfconscious pose. A young girl carrying reeds and sweet grasses
emerges from the shadow of a nearby glade, papyrus rustling; a
glance at us and she is gone with the grace of a gazelle, leaving us
to wonder if she was ever there.

A profusion of red poppies, vivid and frail, among the green
wheat, the amber wheat with silvered plumes; an olive tree bearing both flower and nascent fruit, a metaphor for bounty; carpets
of wildflowers, sapphire, violet, purple, pale buttercup yellow,
acid-lemon yellow, alternate with aggressively tidy fields of grass-
hopper green lined with neat rows of olive trees. A woman
dressed in black, friendly and candid, next to an ancient Berber-
painted bridge, waves to me (a coolie's conical hat; Cleopatra's
face); a riot of poppies sways among onions whose long slender
stalks culminate in many-headed white blossoms emerging from
vellum jackets. The astringent smell of onions is added to the mint-
scented air, and yeasty-smelling milk is sold in plastic orange
buckets under eucalyptus trees in the heat of day.

P.L., the photographer traveling with me, says the wheat "is
like propaganda for goodness."

A Sufi poet says, "The world is a mirror. . . . In every atom
are a hundred blazing suns. . . . If you examine closely each grain
of sand, a thousand Adams may be seen in it. . . . A world dwells
in the heart of a millet seed."

In this purified, translucent light, soft and fresh, and in these
luminous shadows, Matisse learned to reconcile abstraction and
decoration with realism, and his paintings became tender, fluid —
"fire," one of his critics says, "filtered through water," the red of
Fauvism yielding to sap green and cameo pink, pale ocher, peri-
winkle, all as cool "as a freshly opened almond."

A viaduct of warm red-gold stone carries a train over a sluggish brown river in which an orange truck and a black Mercedes
are being washed and little girls bathe. Sheep's wool, not pretty
and white as in fairy tales but oily and brown, waits for its river-
bath among squatters' huts and cypresses and palm trees and a

senseless square of watered and manicured lawn ringed about with century trees, their stalks like giant asparagus; dumb sheep wander on the banks. Dogs wallow like pigs in the swampy brown water; an old man in a silver djellabah stands on the viaduct to survey the scene; the raggedy children chatter and touch. . . . This makes me happy.

Boys along the side of the road hold up strange artifacts — a hairy turtle? — for sale.

And all the while our car is going so fast it startles the birds.

We stop in a generic third-world café along a street of yellow-white and dirty arcades. Carcasses of animals, their tails and feet and privates intact, hang from hooks above the wooden tables where we sit, and from these indecipherable animals meat is carelessly hacked — it is lamb, and very good — and placed on a brazier fanned with cardboard. We eat our succulent charred lamb with mint tea, a garden in a glass. There are no women in the café, there never are. We suck the fragrant tea through sugar cubes. It tastes like the spearmint gum we used to chew to sweeten our breath on adolescent dates.

What lies behind that clutch and huddle of whitewashed houses on tangled sandy lanes? (The smell of woodfires and of musk and of the distant sea and orange blossoms makes me restless with indefinable longing and at the same time comforts me.) That little village is not a secret to me; I lived in it once; but that was in (pre-Qaddafi) Libya. . . . Let me bring your baby to the doctor, I said to the Arab woman down the road, the witch who knew when I was pregnant before I did but whose sorcery could not heal her child. No, she said. Your baby is dying, I said. It is Allah's will, she said; and then, relenting: When my husband comes home from the oilfields we will go, she said — she could not leave her hovel without his permission. *When?* He will be back in six months. In two weeks the baby was dead. I thought thereafter that she wanted my baby; and I made the sign to take away the evil eye.

In the dry hills above the old city of Fez, children romp among Merinid tombs, the detritus of a golden age of Berber kings.

The hills are dun-colored; the houses and terraces, ramparts and fortresses of the medina — the old city — that stretch below my hotel balcony are a dull-dun gloss on a tawny plateau, tumbling toward a brown river that used once to separate Arabs from Andalusians — but the buildings are frozen in their fall as if arrested by a squinting god who saw them in the pearly haze of dawn, when they take on the stylized enameled look of a Persian miniature. Fez, the oldest Islamic medieval city of the world, home of the oldest university, was the prototype of the just and ordered city communally minded Moslems aspire to create. It is dirty now, it crumbles; but it is alive, and its thrills are not vestigial. Pale mountains surround and cradle it.

The medina is a labyrinth within an enclosure — an enclosure, however, without psychological closure if you are a stranger to it: a scary maze.

In London, where I went from Morocco to recover from a multiplicity of impressions, I met an Englishwoman whose mother had lived an expatriate life in the medina of Tangiers. She wore a haik — the enveloping blanketlike garment of purdah — so as to pass through the streets unnoticed and undisturbed; and for good measure she ordered a rubber gorilla mask from London and wore that too. What a nice idea. It is impossible to walk through the winding streets of the medina without a guide; if you do not hire a guide, young men, old men, and ragamuffins will attach themselves to you offering their services — in either case, you are never ever alone. No experience is unmediated by another human being.

I might have loved Morocco had I been invisible.

> *The more one was lost in unfamiliar quarters of distant cities, the more one understood the other cities he had crossed to arrive there; and he retraced the stages of his journeys, and he came to know the port from which he had set sail. . . . What he sought was always something lying ahead, and even if it was a matter of the past it was a past that changed gradually as he advanced on his journey. . . . Arriving at each new city, the traveler finds again a past of his that he did not know he had: the foreignness of what you no longer are or no longer possess lies in wait for you in foreign, unpossessed places.* — Italo Calvino, Invisible Cities*

Honey sweetheart darling madam, my guide calls me; his name is Ismail. He is unctuous, bossy, full of veiled but risible contempt.

Balak! Balak! the donkey herders cry: Beware! One donkey and his burden and a pedestrian in any threadlike street of the medina create a traffic jam — a camel cannot go through the eye of a needle. In blank façades beautiful iron-bossed doors tantalize: that there are gorgeous gardens behind these endless tall walls one must take on faith; there is nothing visibly flowery here. In fact the stench suggests dead meat. Dead skins. We are nearing the tanneries. Ismail, whose sadism percolates through his fawning smiles, says, unanswerably: "If you had a tannery in your country, darling madam, it would smell even more, I am sure." In round pits of dried earth, animal skins are washed and dyed. The brilliant colors of the dye — in which men, their skirts hiked above their knees, are trampling — are supposed, one assumes, to compensate the tourist for the horrid smell of cows' urine and excrement, which is part of the curing process.

If Ismail were kind he would have provided me with a sprig of mint to hold under my nostrils to mitigate the nauseating smell and earned my gratitude forever. Naturally he did not. He grabs my hand with his sweating one to haul me up deep, slimy steps to a rooftop observation post, making no effort to disguise the disgust he feels at having to touch my alien flesh — touch made necessary by economic considerations which rob us both of dignity. ("They call foreigners *berraniyin* — outsiders," Peter Mayne writes, "regarding them as laughable and also pathetic. They are so safe themselves in the Muslim world that Allah has created for them that they can afford to patronize the poor, simple, underprivileged souls born outside it.") On a terrace above the pits — it shames me to watch men do this work — I wander among skins dyed poppy red, and skins dyed indigo. Small skins spread out as if for crucifixion look like giant bats covered with swarming flies. ("The soul is a newly-skinned hide," the Sufi mystic Rumi writes, "bloody and gross. / Work on it with manual discipline / and the bitter tanning-acid of grief, / and you'll become lovely, and *very strong*.") Garbage burns on the river, which is an oily rainbow of vegetable dyes and animal and toxic wastes. Sheep and goats meander and low. On projecting balconies Fassians have planted flowers; I want to like the flowers but they seem to me to possess malignity; how else would they flourish in this touristed hell? . . . Which Ismail appears to believe is the epiphany of a walk through Fez.

At my importuning we stop at the gate of the great Kairouan mosque, closed, as are all mosques in Morocco, to non-Moslems, "because," Ismail says, "the French soldiers broke beer bottles in our mosques, honey madam, and pissed" — for which French sin there is no historical evidence. I stop at one of the fourteen doors, where I glimpse rush matting, men performing ritual ablutions at a fountain, jute-covered white columns, green pitched roofs.

And now all my impressions are confused; I have been wandering in a maze with an uncongenial companion too long, cypress beams and reed matting overhead, donkey shit underfoot. There are 238 quarters, or neighborhoods, in the Old City, each with its own bakery, its own fountain, and its own Koranic school. To the inhabitants of those quarters I have traversed I am both visible and invisible, relevant and irrelevant: I exist as flesh to be elbowed rudely aside, as an object to whom objects can be sold. This is not a comfortable state of affairs. I have caught glimpses of women peering out from grilles, I have seen a *fondouk* — a caravansary for Berbers and for animals — with two-tiered lacy wooden balconies projecting into a dirt courtyard, streets hung with skeins of colored wool. The mosque, its walls encrusted with shops and stalls, is the largest building in Fez, but elusive: one knows one is approaching one of its four main gates by the sweet smell of nougat, heaps of which are sold at every holy place. Above the mosque is a triptych of gold balls representing bread, water, and salt, the necessities of the desert, according to one explanation, talismanic protection against rats, scorpions, and serpents, according to another. Tattooed Berber women; girls in caftans wearing lipstick. Stalls selling junky rayon next to stalls selling jewelry of eighteen-karat gold. The soapy smell of cedar from the Atlas Mountains, the sharp smell of spices, and the hot masculine smell of copper welding shroud, almost but not quite, the sickening smell of the tanneries, which adheres to me. Walter Harris said Fez smelled of incense and dead cats.

"My nostrils were assailed by a stench so powerful and nauseating as almost to be possessed of beauty," one European wrote — what nonsense; and Bowles believed that blood and excrement and sex were indistinguishable one from the other: "I personally am content to see everything in the process of decay," he wrote. A nasty aesthetic.

Shadows fall in a haphazard way. From time to time I sustain the sense of moving through darkness into light, though my feet do not know the way. (It is not possible to distinguish between reality and dream.) The lights of the bazaar are turned on; I feel complicit in the sudden bath of light. It is enchanting here; and it is sinister. Old trees grow in simple mosques, whitewashed walls around an enclosure blazing with artificial light. Alleys dark as death radiate from these sacred enclosures. The commonplace — heaps of boiled eggs in straw baskets, glasses of fresh orange juice, a picture of Paul Newman — seems mysterious in this candid light on these narrow winding streets. All human activities seem both familiar and opaque.

If I spoke Arabic (or French) I would say, as Peter Mayne said to a guide: "I am a mad person who does not think it strange to be alone and to know nothing, and within a few minutes I shall be gone from here, and I am praying that where I am going I shall find a world where guides are born with the mark on them, so that they can be identified by their mamas and strangled."

Suddenly all the boys of the bazaar are running very fast, excitement speeding their way. My lack of comprehension gives Ismail pleasure. We are in the only new part of the bazaar, built in 1954 over the ruins of a fire that trapped and killed hundreds. The boys are running to a fire. Is it by accident that we are in that part of the maze where fire has killed before? It has the inevitability of a dream; and I wouldn't put it past Ismail to have staged it all.

He is clever; and I am capable of being seduced by that which I despise. I have mentally armed myself against being badgered, wheedled, or bullied into a shop to buy a rug. I do not want to buy a rug except when I want to buy a rug. By a series of maneuvers as tricky and twisty as the unmapped streets of the bazaar, Ismail has manipulated me into the shop where he will gain commission for any purchase of mine. Along the way, in tones as sweet as almond-milk and honey, he has asked, "You trust me, sweetheart madam?" to which there is no possible polite answer. I could have said no. We are — how exactly did this happen? — in a shop where I have no wish to be, surrounded by more rugs than are contained in all of Christendom. I buy a rug. I could have said no. How did this happen? He made me feel clever, as if I were choosing to stop here — in fact I actually begged him to stop in this shop. He contrived to have me do so. He made me feel clever,

clever man, before he made me feel like a fool. My embarrassment embarrasses me. After all, there are worse things than humiliation. Only it doesn't seem so when you're soiled with it. Ismail walks ahead of me, now, on the way back to my hotel, all pretense of being my friend forgotten. *El hammdullah:* Praise Allah! he says to one and all. Everyone in the bazaar knows everyone else — during the Nazi occupation of Fez, the Germans used guides as spies — and Ismail is sharing his delight at having found a sucker.

In Tripoli I bargained, too; but the bargaining was elegant, formal, choreographed for mutual pleasure and benefit, gentle. Every time I went to the *souk* I was greeted with generosity and smiles as genuine as the sun. I went alone, and I was safe and cool and pleasured by bands of sunlight on low white houses, dusty fig trees, the glamour of Bedouin carpets on sandy ground, blossoms in the dust. I loved it there. How good to remember that I loved it there. My closets are still full of the presents I got from the merchants of Tripoli for my birthday, for the birth of my son.

What Matisse found in Morocco was a kind of mystic vacancy, the peaceful presence of the sacred. I looked out from the balcony of my hotel room over the rooftops of the medina; and I felt nothing of the sort. (I had scrubbed and scrubbed to get the stink of the tanneries out of my hair, my pores; and I refused to look at my rug, which I could not remember having ever liked.) I asked for another room, one in the old wing of what used to be the palace of a nineteenth-century Fassi vizier, overlooking a garden.

A garden makes the difference. The Palais Jamai, admirably situated just within the ramparts of the medina, has a fine view of Old Fez; but that is not what I hungered for after my walk through the Old City. I wanted a refuge. And indeed the vizier who built the palace, true to the religion and culture of Islam — in which material things mirror the divine and have metaphysical significance — surrounded his palace with walled gardens, precisely so that the hurly-burly, the commerce, and even the public religion of the medina would be shut out, in favor of contemplative privacy: in the garden, there is *only* the garden — and Allah.

In the early morning, I sit on the porch that leads from my room; every leaf is articulated in the deceptively pale but dagger-like light. For a Moslem the world is full of tangible, palpable metaphysical symbols, each of which incarnates feminine and masculine principles. The garden is the reflection of the beauty of God. The porch is the transitional space between the temporal and the spiritual world between which the soul moves; the porch waits patiently to catch the light. It symbolizes the presence of the Divine Name, Nur — Light. The garden is quartered; the Koran depicts Paradise as four gardens — the Garden of the Soul, the Garden of the Heart, the Garden of the Spirit, and the Garden of Essence. The Garden of the Soul is the feminine principle; in order to enter it, one must cultivate the feminine quality of intuition. But as the soul travels toward God, danger lurks everywhere, even in the garden: "The soul is pulled away from the center by physical desires. The mystic is in a state of receptivity with a readiness to be satisfied; but if the soul is actually satisfied, the mystic is expelled from the garden much as Adam was expelled from Eden." Every garden must contain a fountain, flowing water, and the fruit of trees.

Mine did. I say *mine* because no one else ever seemed to walk through space enclosed by quartered hedges of bougainvillea and of thyme to enter a world of sultry roses, with fragrance so silken as to seem illicit, joined to banks of virginal daisies; spicy marigolds and weedy geraniums, date palms, apricot trees. I was never conscious of any division or dichotomy between body and soul in my gardens; I was full of good feeling toward my body at the same time as I had the distinct sensation I was floating above it.

The sky was bleached, white, when I awoke; sky and air were one; and it was breezy and cool, almost cold. By eleven it was hot. Under these sensual weather conditions, one is nicely conscious of the skin being an organ, which is played.

The birds were extraordinarily friendly, bold. Moslem mystics believe that birds understand higher states of being: "We have been taught the language of the birds, and all favors have been showered upon us." Though to the Western ear the music of the medina is apt to be perceived as a monotonous variation on three notes, rhythm is seen, in Islamic cosmology, as a way to achieve higher states of being. I don't know about that; but it seemed to me in the early light of dawn that I could distinguish between the song of the blue-headed sparrow, the bird sacred to Islam, and the cry of the hawk, and all the birds in between: it was remarkably like being high and listening to a jazz band — one learned (by dint of not trying to learn) what all the players were doing individually as well as collectively. The birds land on one another. They sit on ashtrays and fluff their feathers. Bees drink nectar from apricot jam. The burbling of pigeons mingles with the burbling of fountains. The garden and the fountain are one: "A garden enclosed is my spouse," wrote Solomon. "You are a garden enclosed, a fountain sealed. . . . Your shoots are a garden of pomegranates with the fruit of choice berries; henna with spikenard; spikenard and saffron, calamus and cinnamon, with all the woods of Lebanon: myrrh, aloes, with all the chief spices. A fountain of gardens, and a wall of living water from Lebanon."

These are universal symbols: the prophetic river in the Hebrew Scriptures is filled with water; the evangelical rivers in the Christian Scriptures are filled with spices. In different cultures the symbols are read in different ways. Traditional Moslems have taken the holy writings to mean that the veil is a kind of extension of the cloister, that the woman, seeing but unseen behind it, moves through teeming life as if sequestered in her own garden, and furthermore, that "if [women] go outside their houses without authorization from the men, the angels will insult them until they go back to their houses. . . . The Koran maintains that women have got two times to go out of their houses: the first time is when they get married and they want to go to the groom's house and the second time is when they die and the man takes her to the grave."

Once a young midwife in Tripoli, unable to turn a deaf ear to insistent pleas, agreed to leave her house at night to deliver a patient of her baby — without a woman accompanying her and without the explicit permission of her father. It was a ruse. Ten men took turns raping her for two weeks. It was generally agreed, in her community, that she was to blame. She had broken an elementary law, never mind that her compassionate nature had caused her to do so. Her father disowned her. The man to whom she was betrothed disowned her. The men who raped her received no punishment.

It is when I think of stories like this that I am compelled to say to P.L., "Look at that café. Not a woman there." There is never a woman in a café, save me. Naturally I bore P.L., who thinks I am speaking from abstract ideology.

Once in Libya the car I was riding in struck a young child who had dashed into the road. He seemed not to be hurt; but we wanted to take him to the hospital to make sure. No mother in the world could possibly refuse — it seemed to me then, and it seems to me now — to accompany her son to the hospital. She did refuse; and she refused on behalf of her son, too. I cannot bring myself to understand this.

But in my cloistered sweet garden, where swaying palms are home to many black birds, surrounded by monkey puzzle trees and lacy pink tamarisk trees and the voluptuous purple of jacaranda, I think, not of these sorrowful things, but of my garden in Libya behind a tall whitewashed wall on a sandy road, lined with prickly pears (which the Arabs call "Christian figs"), that led to the sea. There I planted sunflowers (and behind them — my grasp of gardening was rudimentary — petunias); and kind Mohammed watered them. Morning glories and grapevines made an arbor of my baby son's stone-flagged room; date palms, male and female — poor Mohammed, of tactful and delicate sensibilities, had a hard time explaining the gender of fecund date palms to me. And citrus trees and pomegranates, and poinsettia, blooming red and blooming white in hot sunny weather. There were caves in the back garden. I never went there. They had been built by the ruling Italians to serve as air-raid shelters. Bats lived in them.

At night I hear birds scratching, scudding, and sliding under the eaves of my hotel. (The amber patterned ceiling of my room looks like a pitched tent translated into wood.) They seem very near, and their night sounds have a touch of malice, or of insanity. What I like best is walking into my darkened room in the heat of day — the brass key is so hot it burns my hand — feeling the marble cool beneath my feet; white watered silk curtains sail on the garden's breeze; my eyes grow accustomed to the dark.

Moulay, our driver, takes me to the nearby imperial city of Meknès to visit the tomb of Sultan Moulay Ismael, the late seventeenth- and early eighteenth-century despot who made use of everything that came to hand — he immured the bodies of dead slaves in the walls of Meknès, their blood mixing with cement to form a kind of glue — and who killed for sport, "as a matter of personal and daily satisfaction like the pleasures of the table or of the harem. . . . With his own sword he would strike off the head of the slave who held his stirrup as he mounted his horse, or several heads of his own Black Guards as he rode down their ranks; he disemboweled the living and organized displays of torture for the titillation of his senses; there was, in fact, no imaginable atrocity of cruelty and bloodlust in which he did not indulge." He liked to wear yellow when he killed; he envisioned Meknès as an Oriental Versailles.

We drive through a triple-arched doorway in the bastioned and concise punctuation of the gateway of Bab el Mansour, to the tomb of the tyrant and his mosque — the only mosque Christians are permitted to enter. I sit near a seventeenth-century hexagonal fountain, and a guide — an old man — unties and removes my sneakers, a demeaning task that seems to take forever. The mosque and harem have connecting doors. The tomb is flanked by two seventeenth-century grandfather clocks, gifts from Louis XIV, substitutes for the hand of his daughter, marriage to whom the sultan had ardently sought.

Sultans were infatuated with things European: the palace of Sultan Moulay Aziz, who ruled from 1894 to 1908, became a veritable playroom, stuffed, Gavin Maxwell writes, with Victrolas, "toy railways, typewriters, musical stuffed birds, . . . clockwork toys," gold and silver cameras with jeweled buttons, fireworks, bicycles, "grand pianos and kitchen-ranges; automobiles and immense cases of corsets; wild animals in cages, and boxes of strange theatrical uniforms; barrel-organs and hansom-cabs; a passenger lift capable of rising to dizzying altitudes, destined for a one-storied palace; false hair. . . ." A German sold the young sovereign — who was nineteen when he ascended to the throne — a motorboat, which was never put out to sea; an American sold him a British bulldog with false teeth for $40,000.

If these grotesque purchases had not in themselves drained the coffers of imperial Morocco, the commissions on them did. There were and are so many middlemen in Morocco; it is believed that the sultan was obliged to pay 500 percent in commissions to them. His vizier got loans from Europe to cover the boy's extravagances — and these debts led directly to Morocco's becoming a "protectorate" of France.

Among Moulay Ismael's lesser sins was cannabalizing the ancient ruins of Volubilis to build his imperial city.

A ruined city on a windswept plain above a sea of grain

through which the wind soughs mournfully, Volubilis is plaintive, affecting not only because it encodes loss but because the monumentality and repetition of Moroccan Islamic architecture — calligraphy and diamond-shaped mosaics and stucco fretwork — create a desire for the representational iconography of the West, a longing for something less stern, less symmetrical.

What is left of Roman law and sensibility and vivacity here? All is gone. The colonnaded women's bath is populated now only with geraniums; the once luxurious rooms of the bordello are home for nettles and scorpions; the merest trickle of rusty water drips in the troughs where white and purple togas once were washed. The rocks are worn where clothes were beaten centuries ago — it is lovely in the sun to touch the smooth rocks, touch nourishing fantasy. Even lovelier are the faded mosaics — the Moslem interdiction against portraying animals, birds, humans, and flowers in art, taken seriously in Morocco, produces what often appears to be a sterile sameness in art, which breeds ennui. Here are dolphins sporting; a man riding a horse backward; a jolly squid; a witty prawn.

On a stone block there is a representation of an enormous phallus; Moulay points me toward it, then retreats, smirking.

Under an aborted triumphal arch a young woman faints from the heat; her guide prattles on.

I used to walk for hours alone in Libya's Leptis Magna, magnificent, coherent ruins by the sea; I gathered loose chunks of mosaics and amethyst and lapis lazuli as if they were wildflowers, and sat with them in a Roman house that looked as if it might have been deserted only yesterday, imagining what my life would have been like then, in that house, or in that amphitheater by the sea — which exercise was scarcely more difficult than imagining why I had chosen the life I lived in the country where the ocean tasted of tomatoes at harvest time and I swam through ruined underwater villas in the striated waters. The past yielded its meaning more readily than the present. It hurts my mind to think of Qaddafi and those ruins; perhaps the sand has covered them all.

"Nothing endures in Islam except what human inertia has left standing and its own solidity has preserved from the elements. Or rather, nothing remains intact, and nothing perishes, but the architecture, like all else, lingers on half-ruined and half-unchanged." — Edith Wharton

I felt so grudging, taking against Islamic art this way. In London I went to the Victoria and Albert to see ivories and enamels and rugs, ceramics, and textiles, glass, and pottery from Moslem Persia and Turkey and Syria and Egypt. Freed from the constraints of strict interpretation of aesthetic law, they achieved joyous spontaneity of form (freedom in an enclosed garden of thought): gazelles leapt; lions frolicked and cuddled with peacocks; tiles bloomed with flowers as well as flowery arabesques — and everywhere that intense blue, into which one could without a murmur sink; and on the sheaths of the swords of Damascus, an invocation of the holy name of God — just as it is tattooed on the mons veneris of Moroccan prostitutes.

From Volubulis one sees the city of Moulay Idriss, white and shining on a conical hill (giving the architects of Islam the last, radiant word). White birds escort our car to the holy white city.

Moulay Idriss, the great-grandson of the Prophet Mohammed, was the founder of the first Arab dynasty. NON-MUSSELMAN FORBIDDEN inside the holy man's tomb, however; a low cedar gate bars the way. In this spot Edith Wharton saw blood dripping down from the whirling caftans of dancers, "forming fresh pools among the stones . . . pools fed from great gashes which the dancers hacked in their own skulls and breasts with hatchets and sharpened stones." The dancers, howling, a brotherhood of mystics and martyrs, were baptized in their own blood. In 1953 black bulls were sacrificed and eaten here, a form of protest against the corruption of the French-designated sultan; and in the fifteenth century, it is said, live bulls were eaten here. It is pacific now, where frenzy on occasion reigns: boys with fingers interlaced lounge against rough walls, breathing their love at each other (the casualness of homoeroticism in Morocco takes one's breath away); a young boy wears a shirt stenciled with a picture of Madonna (proving to me that the whole world has gone to hell); a man with double-jointed crippled fingers brays like a donkey and collects alms; a tall, handsome, elegant old man in a blue djellabah smiles at me with blinding blue eyes and seems inclined to pat my head. (How I wish he would, I have never felt such an outsider as I do here.) Outside the holy place lollipops are sold, and beads, and nougat, of course; and in the town there is a multilevel market where I find the season's first apricots, white; and artichokes and lambs' heads and cows' feet and beans and peaches and plastic sunglasses and henna (powder and leaf), and the ubiquitous boiled eggs, and bulls' testicles, and an attenuated hippie, drunk, who Moulay — who is dreadfully stubborn — insists is a Berber. I am a hair away from being enraged at Moulay: he has patted a young girl's behind. Giving him the benefit of the doubt and for the moment attributing nothing more to him than tenderness, *Why don't you get married?* I say; he is thirty-eight. *Because the mothers I hate,* he says. What is troubling about his hatred of women is that it doesn't trouble him at all. I am tired of behaving well and protecting Moulay's pride; so I speak to the "Berber" . . . who is American, from Philadelphia (and high on *kif*). This doesn't bother Moulay at all — in some basic way he can never, where I am concerned, be wrong: I am a woman, he is a man.

It is the women's hour in a local communal bath, a *hammam.* In a large room logs and sugar burn to heat and sweeten water for the bath — they produce the smell of barbecued sausages. I am led by a crone down crooked stairs to a room so dark and hot I think I have found hell, an inferno of flesh, pinky beige. Women as unselfconscious as young animals wash their bodies with hot water and cold water from plastic buckets, pull at their nipples and their breasts, entirely self-bemused. They invite me to join them in what is less a matter of hygiene than a hypnotic social ritual; I do not. They are as alien to me as the moon; and as familiar. A door opens in the darkness and clouds of steam precede the entry of little girls, who giggle at my strangeness and stick their tongues out at me.

On the way back to Fez, Moulay plays Christmas carols: *And the snow lay round about. . . .*

My friend Biagio has asked P.L. to take a picture of an olive tree leaning against a saint's tomb. "You'll know it when you see it," he says, "you can't miss it." What can he have meant? There are hundreds of saint's tombs, white, and hundreds of olive trees, and to which his memory and his affection have attached singular value we can of course not guess.

We leave Fez for Erfoud and the deep South; a nine hours' drive, a jeweled blur. (Fez — in which the past and the present, elegance and incipient violence, formality and decay are braided — is working in me; I think of it with mingled revulsion and longing, I miss it.) P.L. and I are never quite sure where we are, assiduous considerations of maps and guidebooks and signposts notwithstanding. Moulay's command of English serves only to confound us. ("What's that, Moulay?" "King house." "Which king?" "Yes. King.") Palm trees yield to sycamore and cedar; then we are in the midst of apple trees and lilac bushes. We see storks in giant nests on pitched roofs in ski resorts. We know we must cross the Atlas Mountains — the Middle Atlas? the High Atlas? — to get to Erfoud. It would be nice if we could judge, which we cannot, when we have crossed the mountain pass. ("Moulay, is this the pass?" "Pass." "Have we passed the pass?" "No pass. This pass." "What?") Now the world is rocky rock, snow-covered mountains in the near distance. On top of rock, rock is piled — fetishistic piles of rocks, perhaps they are messages. Endless plains. Goldenrod. Miles of stone walls without mortar. This air is ambrosial, mountain sweet — does that mean we haven't crossed the pass? There is a porcupine on the side of the road. Only his feet and his quills. His meat has been eaten by a shepherd. (Rumi: "The soul is a porcupine, made strong by stick-beating.") Fresh animal ordure, a good smell. A lake of small white flowers. Fluorescent purple ice flowers. Now forbidding black mountains rear and then we are in a tunnel and exit into a land of kasbahs, *ksar* — pure, simple, robust cubist forms by the river Ziz, sand castles, water soluble — groves of palm trees, oleanders, almonds. We drive through arcaded garrison towns, town after town, yellowy arcade after yellowy arcade; animals' heads, hairy, unskinned, are cooked on open fires. We eat hot bread and ripe bananas that have a slightly bitter aftertaste. Inky hills, a slight underglaze of green. No sound in the world at all. Houses crouch on bare hills, there is no presumption in them. Fields of jagged upright stones no different from other stone till one sees the design in the apparent randomness: these are Arab cemeteries, the dead are an intimate part of the landscape. Berber women dressed in black with spangly colored ribbons and barbaric jewelry — unveiled, but beasts of burden nonetheless.

Twilight is the magic hour. We pass through white horseshoe gates with green enameled tiles and we are in a market square that might have been painted by Carpaccio or Bellini. We are in another and very old world, a world of incantatory charm and voluptuousness. The hallucinatory confusions of the past hours have been preparation for this moment; weariness and irritable exhaustion have been wayposts on the journey toward delicious languor. Now no question demands to be asked, no conflict resolved: we are in the South, the Sahara, in Erfoud. Where every thing and every body is self-possessed and necessary, and every object has unquestionable integrity. The bruised and excited uncertainties of the last twelve hours have led to this absolutely perfect moment at dusk; time is timeless here, endless and circular, as it is in arabesques. There is nothing one could possibly quarrel with, each thing being indisputably what it is and whole-unto-itself. White-turbaned men sit along palm-lined walls, their faces turned to the storyteller in the center of their rapt group. Lanterns light the way for cartloads of black-robed women heavily veiled — and even this seems right, even the single kohl-lined eye that peers out from each enveloping garment seems — as Wharton knew — poetically right: "All the mystery that awaits us looks out through the eye-slits in the grave-clothes muffling her. Where have they come from, where are they going, all these slow wayfarers of the unknown? . . . Interminable distances unroll behind them, they breathe of Timbuctoo and the farthest desert. . . . These wanderers have looked on at the building of cities that were dust when the Romans pushed their outposts across the Atlas." Blue men, tall handsome men wearing indigo turbans, and blue robes that stain their skin, ride on white camels, their faces veiled (black eyes flashing) to keep the sand from their beautiful dark faces.

In the morning the square has lost its magic, it is just a provincial square, tawdry, sober, penitential.

Next to my bed, ants have made a feast of a three-inch waterbug I killed; it is practically skeletal now. Hundreds of ants carry off bits of carrion waterbug flesh. The porter heaps DDT around the ants, on my shoes, and (why?) in the toilet. And on my bath towel, which he proceeds to flap in the faces of passing guests.

P.L. says flies are attacking his teeth.

M., who is Australian, looks like a spinster schoolmarm. She has lived here five years, selling her indifferent watercolors at the hotel where she sits from morning to night. One cannot imagine her life; she is plump, pleasant, a woman of few words — and, one imagines, a few compelling obsessions: "The light," she says.

There is a French/Italian/American movie company staying at the hotel; it is making a French Foreign Legion picture. Extras are dressed as blue men, ugly shoddy shoes peeking from beneath their indigo robes. It is hard to tell the real blue men from the fake blue men; and it is even harder to tell whether the "real" blue men are really real: Nomadic Tuaregs, the cultivated tribe from which the blue men come, famous for their poetry and intellect (though the Western mind finds it difficult to reconcile intellect with the willed wandering of tribals), live mostly in the western Sahara, southern Algeria, and southwest Libya (once I saw Tuaregs dance in the oasis of Gadames in Libya; their eyes and swords and teeth gleamed, their blue robes swirled, creating storms in the desert sand and in my imagination).

We drive south from Erfoud twenty kilometers to Rissani; there is a *souk* in the ruins of a seventeenth-century kasbah, and a *ksar*, too. (Properly speaking, a kasbah is a fortified castle, while a ksar is a fortified town; this is almost a distinction without a difference in the desert; both are made of mud mixed with fibers from palm trunks, a material called pisé; almost all have high, small windows and incised geometric carvings on their crenelated towers. They are designed to look inward, to courtyards and communal space, and they are defensive; they are grand; should a heavy rainstorm come — not unknown in the desert — they melt.)

I love the market in Rissani. Shopping in Morocco has become for me a transaction almost as personal as sex. And having Moulay around is like having a third person in bed; he insists on interceding and thrusting himself into my experience. (Somewhere on the long drive from Fez to Erfoud we passed stalls where crystal quartz and emerald quartz and amethyst quartz was sold; it was very beautiful. "I you no me like buy here," said Moulay (who has trouble with his pronouns, perhaps because he can think only of himself); "wait Marrakesh." Marrakesh, his home town, is where he is best able to collect commissions. At that time I was still trying to humor him — like many women I am afraid men will exercise retribution for slights from behind the wheel of a car — so I didn't buy the glittering stones. Naturally I never saw anything like them again.) In the animal *souk*, donkeys and sheep and goats are being sold — soon it will be time for the ritual sacrifice of an animal, an obligation for all Moslems, although, Allah being kind, even a chicken will do.

The tall gaunt countrymen who come to buy here have no

contract with us; their disinterested naturalness amounts to majesty. (I forgive them, even, for beating copulating donkeys with bamboo sticks, spoiling the animals' driven pleasure.) I am the only woman in this market; and it makes no difference to the men in turbans and wool caps, their business is not with me. I feel the returning happiness of being alone, unregarded, ignored, unessential to the world I move in. Wandering among pyramidical piles of sweet-smelling fodder, I see water carriers — men dressed flamboyantly in short red button-bedecked jackets, conical straw hats, and leggings, shining copper drinking vessels attached to their persons, water in goatskins with furry hides, taps attached by tube to the dead animals. There is nothing hostile in the din.

In another part of the market I make out the forms of babies hidden in the depths of black haiks — a life in the sun begun with a life in postwomb darkness (sunlight always makes a liar of Marx, who never was able to understand how weather and geography formed character).

A Berber woman with bright green eyes sells jewelry, Venetian beads, matched and mixed with old coral and dull silver; dried roses, and musk — the sexy smell of which threads its way through the less aphrodisiacal smells of the market (musk comes from the gland of a musk-deer or a gazelle, a fact my mind skitters away from but insists on returning to). From sludgy piles of waxy white *schmaltz*, animal fat, and pyramids of red salt mined in the salt caves of the Atlas, I move to a painter's paradise of spices, reds and oranges and gold of saffron and pimentos; and fragrant ambergris, which I bargain for. Moulay, who has left me alone with donkeys, is suddenly behind me, a one-man chorus of interjections and loud protests; I pretend he is invisible and inaudible, willing him not to spoil my pleasure.

In the pre-Islamic Libyan Saharan oasis of Gadames, bound in culture and mores to centuries past, I met a man — the village *caid* — who said: "I remember Josephine Baker." In his tribal oasis, women were not allowed above ground except at twilight, to draw water from a well. When he spoke of Josephine Baker, he cried. . . . It never does to suppose you can grasp the essence of a person's life by precise observation of what is obvious about a person's life. . . .

*

Dust to Dust. The kasbah of Rissani — three centuries old, built by the first king of the ruling dynasty of Morocco — is of the earth, earthy, a cave. We walk through cool underground streets, tunnels — tunnels in a womb. Pools of light from high windows illuminate great doors with great hinges. Women in black glide through distant arches; in this prenatal light they are all beautiful. Four beauties lean negligently against a low doorway. This is like our first home; and what we can imagine of our last. No wonder these men think women are dangerous — they are wombs within wombs, the beginning and the end. Outside, in the square — it hurts our eyes to see the sun — four little girls in pink play with a sardine can with a ribbon attached to it; they pull it as if it were a cart. Already they smell of musk.

Another kind of cave, a Berber tent formed of waterproof sheep's wool rugs, on a windswept plateau. Outside are two circular enclosures, one of wire and one of stone, for sheep and goats and sheepdogs. I hold a baby lamb, six days old, in my arms, and he licks my neck and chews on my hair and all of a sudden I miss my children. Moulay points to the lamb's sex, he is always doing this. It is clean and fragrant inside the tent; but there are flies. An old man rests in the corner, leaning, in striped robes, on his staff. (This is all, I can't help thinking, very MGM.) The tent is divided into kitchen — where on a brazier tea is prepared by a blue-eyed woman — and visitors' parlor, where, on many rugs, we drink the sweet tea (after a while the exotic becomes familiar, or you translate it into familiar terms, so as not to go mad). The tattooed woman competes with me for the attention of a cat. This has very little to do with the cat, and everything to do with the men I am with. Her hennaed hands flirt with the cat, with the men.

The Land Rover bounces over miles of greenish-black scrub, trackless desert, to get to the sand dunes of Merzouga. In this altogether lonely, dry, and stingy place, a solitary man at prayer is facing Mecca, his red motor scooter resting at his side: if you are a Moslem you are always oriented in the world Allah has made for you. Ahead of us light plays on sugary sand . . . purple, mustard, rose, green, pink light — all of these colors and none of them: the sun is setting in the desert, and a new palette has to be invented

for this. Saffron, ocher, violet, pink. Camels, silly, supercilious —
and remarkably dignified — stretch their necks on the ground like
lazy cats. Every fold and curve and hollow of every dune is maternal and alluring.

My quarrel — unspoken — with Moulay is coming to a head. He
is incensed because I have bought a pillow from the Berbers in the
tent (it doesn't help that I am feeling as guilty as if I had exercised
the false entitlement of a colonialist for having admired and asked
to buy a domestic household artifact to satisfy my greed for acquisition). I wish Moulay were a charming scoundrel, he would make
me laugh. He is a scoundrel plain and foolish. Somewhere along
the line Moulay, along with every other guide in Morocco, has
been told that, in the economy of the West, there is a factory, a
middleman/businessman, and, at the end of the chain, a hapless
tourist-who-buys. "No buy here, buy factory" is a sentence he can
manage. He says that there is a mineral "factory" outside of Erfoud, emerald quartz and crystals and amethysts.

In a large yard, men are sawing rocks, ordinary rocks, and
then (I *see* this) painting them with silver paint from a little can so
that they will resemble some mineral, perhaps manganese. *Moulay!* Yes, madam, he says blankly. *Look!* Why not like? he asks.
Because, damn it, they look like plantar warts with silver gunk on
them. Is emeralds, he says. And I am Queen Victoria. He takes me
into the "factory," down a flight of stairs — why I follow docilely I
do not know — and there, amongst the fake rocks, are hanging
two scarves of indigo blue. Just yesterday I had told P.L. I admired
them and wanted to buy them. When I tell this story to P.L. he
says: Oh, they know everything; if you want a scarf they know it
before you say it. When he hears me tell P.L. I saw them faking
silver stones, Moulay says: *Not happen.*

We are heading west to Ouarzazate at the junction of the Dades
and the Dr'aa River valley. Once again we pass through wilder-
nesses of rock; through canyons straight and sheer (and sterile and
smug, like impending doom in the form of a vise). This is the kind
of landscape that breeds fanatics (as, paradoxically, the sensual
South breeds ascetics). We drive over wrinkled fat mountains
that look like soft constructions in a cheap amusement park,

mountains that look like an illustration for the travail of creation, the dry torment of God, the dry despair of man. Once again we are subject to the lethargy induced by a surfeit of impressions (and once again we are never quite sure where we are). We are rescued from nervous irritability by the kasbahs, dense and dramatic, those defensive sand castles that look both barbaric and domestic, that line our path, and by the valley palmeries, the sea of palms, that gather by the rivers. Imagine! There are hollyhocks in these palmeries — hollyhocks from *Dick and Jane,* flowers straight from an American childhood . . . and cabbages and corn and pomegranates, figs. "This River Water is an orchard that fills your basket." — Rumi.

A Berber woman is picking roses. The roses grow near the high corn, which rustles like torn silk. They are pink. The intense orgasmic sweetness of roses on the dry desert air and the sweeter, more urgent cry of the muezzin calling the faithful to prayer persuaded romantic Victorian ladies that wild men would be good to them; women fall in love with a country and marry a man.

The car never smells neutrally of "car"; it smells of woodsmoke and of mint, of roses — what an extravagant country this is. When you think you have reached an apotheosis, more is added: Now, sweetness upon sweetness, it smells of moonflowers.

Men who want nothing in return stop to offer us small green apples.

Little boys, sad and reproachful, sell camels made of palm fronds by the roadside, and fat, eviscerated, sand-stuffed lizards.

I walk, blessedly alone, through a palmery: palm trees interlaced with olive trees; plots of tomato plants that are trained on bamboo poles in the ruins of a kasbah; snowy mountains in the distance; the intelligent sound of moving water.

These are the good things about our hotel in Ouarzazate: the green, vanilla smell of pink oleanders (which are poisonous); jasmine, white and yellow; roses, eight feet tall, that, miraculously, do not droop of their own weight; the fig jam we have for breakfast; the fun of regarding Arab ladies who lunch: silk caftans, Gucci bags, red toenails, modest head coverings. Their bodies are like battlefields of cultures in contention.

We have dinner in the Glaoui kasbah of Tiffoultoute, five

kilometers west of Ouarzazate. They were wild men from the south, the Glaouis. It is said of T'hami el-Glaoui, pasha of Marrakesh and staunch supporter of the French, that he never pardoned and he never forgave. He was a falconer. He had "talent scouts" everywhere in Morocco and in France, agents at railroad stations who pretended to be guides and procured for the pasha fine European women. He never forced his favors upon Europeans; he was barbaric, intelligent, ambitious, insatiable, and generous with jewels. Winston Churchill admired him. The kasbah that bears his name is best seen in the moonlight, when its deficiencies of style yield to its magnificence of size.

Nature goes on and on and it is completely indifferent. The countryside is dun, the ksour are dun. Immured in the car, watching everything through plate glass, I feel neurotically removed from everything I see; I want to walk in a ksour; what good is looking at a ksour if you can't walk in it? Moulay says: "There they you kill madame me not want trouble you." Of course they won't kill me, why should they. The walls of the ksour are very high; you have to be at least five feet tall before you see the mountains — the world — above the wall: children are always at a disadvantage. Old men and women and boys and girls gather around me, candid and friendly, their rough hands curious, their manner kind. In a long narrow room I sit on a rush mat and drink tea — mud still adheres to the roots and stems of the mint. An old man with a sweet disposition crushes almonds, still in their furry shells, with a rock; almonds and biscuits and sweet tea. A toddler looks on; three flies gather in the corner of his left eye. More babies are brought in, more children wander in — I am much taken by a seductive little boy called Mohammed — more tea is served. The room is washed an irritable blue (clothing hooks; pillows; a Koran; a calendar provided by a tire company; bellows; a soccer poster; a radio; a flashlight; a brazier). Palm fronds are brought in to ward off flies but the women and children don't trouble to use them. Fancy new glasses appear from a hidden cupboard and I drink fresh buttermilk into which I dip chunks of unleavened whole wheat bread — it is delicious. The tattooed woman of the house tells me I am happy; I am. She takes me to see the cow from which the buttermilk came, in a courtyard where squash and henna grow. How nice to be so close to the source of production. She takes me to another room where there is a baby six days old. The baby is beautiful, its eyes and brows kohled against flies; it is wrapped in swaddling clothes tied with striped wool yarn. It lies very still in my arms and I love its milky smell and do not want at all to leave it.

The sky in Zagora is white, metallic, huge, unfriendly. The sun is a paler shade of white, the sun of an Arctic winter. What makes one place brutish and another kind? We are at the same latitude as Erfoud; but we might almost be on a different planet. Our hotel has four swimming pools and two guests — P.L. and me. They call me "the woman." The wind is a djinn, knocking everything over, pool umbrellas, our dinner. It comes from nowhere and leaves in its wake an intense dry heat — the air is taut. The dining room smells of offal. Only in the pale fires of night is this dreadful town of tired gray and timid pink bearable. We go at night — led by a child who burns rags to light our way — to the house of one Hassan, who sells amber and coral. (There are no stars.) Hassan has curly ropes of hair, he is a handsome animal. He is a nomad from the Sait Tata tribe and he is on the road six months of the year, on the silk route, his white camel takes him to Mali and Mauretania; the rest of the time he is sedentary — he sleeps under the stars on his roof. He takes American Express. I don't believe a word he says — except for the part about American Express — though I almost like him for using the word *sedentary*, an ambitious word. He puts a string of amber beads around my neck and grinds his body into mine, a sexual gesture devoid of sensuality. He counts too much on his good looks; his eyes are cold; I want to kill him.

Dinner in an outdoor pavilion in a garden restores my good humor; but when we leave the lovely garden, Moulay is fighting with another guide over commission — commission from our lovely meal. The violence born of desperation and extreme ill-will scares me. (It is seared in my consciousness that women are dangerous, and, paranoia reaching great heights, I am sure the fight will have consequences affecting me, my person.) My hotel room opens into the courtyard, anyone could get in; I lock the picture windows and secure the door by means of a steel-door sheath; the air conditioning does not work, this is a tomb. It is too much to hope that the people who build kasbahs could build a hotel to suit a Western woman's mood.

"The sun's flame is a white hawk." The Sufi Brotherhoods court meaning in nothingness, affirmation in negation, they whirl to fulfillment in the emptiness of the desert, under a blank white meaningless sky.

But I am unhappy on the edge of the world. My head aches and my eyes hurt, my blistered lungs are stung by sand; I read *Murder at the Vicarage* and announce my intention to stay in the car until we reach the oasis of Taroudant.

Orange trees, their burden of fruit like Christmas decorations, screen the windows at the head of my bed; from the French doors to my terrace — where I have a breakfast of crepes with butter and honey and a steaming mug of strong white coffee — I see a wide lawn, watered in lazy arcs; I light the fire in my fireplace (the logs are eucalyptus, astringent and sweet — their fragrance mingles with the fragrance of roses resting on a small blue marble-topped table); everything pleases me. I eat a pale apricot, its flesh white.

I walk from my villa to the pool on a herringbone brick path, past lipstick-red pomegranate flowers, into gardens of controlled luxuriance: calla lilies and nasturtiums, hibiscus, and lotus and water lilies, and banks of papyrus and elephant palms. A gray-and-white cat stalks me on the way to the pool; he is bow-legged and his head is primly and permanently cocked to one side so that he looks continually imploring. He is a silly cat, one of several that stalk the great house — he never shows up in time for meals.

In the 1930s, Baron Jean Pellenc built the sophisticated hunting lodge which, with the addition of twenty bungalow villas, has become the fabulous Gazelle d'Or, the most luxurious hotel in Morocco — and all of this from two wells outside the red-walled, dusty, somnolent, amiable town of Taroudant. The long windowed halls of pale peach and blue, the circular rooms covered with antique silk Berber embroideries and floored in onyx marble (and stylized astrological symbols: Moroccan Deco) are full of fabulous stuff massed in stylish abundance: Aladdin meets Erté.

The swimming pool is polar cold. After a while cold feels like a different kind of warmth, hypothermal hypnosis, a fugue state, sweet.

When the sun goes down and light leaches from the sky, jacaranda blossoms form a haze of bluey purple and provide the color the sunset did not. In this deceptive light palm fronds look like velvet and caress the white-blue-gray-yellow sheltering sky.

Outside the Gazelle d'Or beautiful boys lounge in groves of olive trees, motorbikes at the ready, to follow tourists to the *souk*, where they will offer their services as guides. They are prepared to offer services of another kind; they are singularly unthreatening; they look like a Grecian frieze.

In the market sheer white nightgowns are fingered by women in heavy white veils.

A date merchant offers me a meal of dates — dates of every grade (this is like wine-tasting, sugary), dates for sheep and dates for sultans.

From the humble flower of the fennel, dried, come Berber toothpicks; the milk of fennel solidifies into sticky black resin — it is valued for its scent, and it attracts bees.

I love this market, the courtesy and gravity of its artisans: I learn how to mix henna with lemon juice to stain my palms; I buy stencils used to apply henna to hands and feet (the stencils look like Matisse's 1953 *Decoration, Flowers, and Fruit,* paper cut-outs and gouache. A silversmith invites me to watch him make crude silver bracelets; he is proud of his mud mold and his crucible. He is more interested in explaining his craft than in making a sale, which I call nice.

I sit in the pink square, utterly at ease and seduced by the pulse and rhythms of life, of this life in particular, which seems to me to encompass, in a little space, all that life can hold.

A Magic Man walks through the square swinging a censer, incense waving the Devil away. (Am I the Devil?) Shoeshine boys ask me for "chewngumbonbons." Chanting the Koran, young men link arms and then unfurl a bright green flag — the occasion is both religious and ardently nationalistic, the adoration of a holy man. There is always a fine edge of danger in Morocco, often implicitly homoerotic; that is what some people find to like in it. I love Taroudant in spite of it.

Mama! In a white-tiled room an apple-cheeked girl who might be from Russia or Vermont anoints me with hot water from a brass bowl. I am in a *hammam* and she is bathing me. In clouds of steam she soaps me and scrubs me with an abrasive mitt. Beads of dead dirty skin form a mosaic on my undefended body. I lose track of time. She scrubs like Mama did. I am a child again; and surrender and vulnerability are — I know with a child's lost trust — good, and will be rewarded. She applies mud the color of burnt coriander to my body, no part of which is untouched. Her fingers are practical, assertive, not inquiring, not lewd. This is innocent sensuality, sensuality without sex. First you got dirty, then Mama washed you, usually angrily. The rosy girl reverses the order: first she makes me clean, then she applies mud, and then she washes me again. Buckets and buckets of water (*I baptize you in the name of the Father . . .*). She washes all my tiredness and all my anxiety and all my guilt away; every crevice is cleansed. Not a word is spoken between us. I can no longer tell one part of my body from another — it's all flesh, one organ. Sweat rolls into my eyes and I don't care. The girl tucks my foot in between her thighs. This is strange but not alarming. Did the harem include these pleasures? She covers me with silken cream, rose petals and spices, musk. I am wrapped in herbal towels in an anteroom where diffuse light enters by a skylight and I hear birds sing. A spider on an invisible thread swings like a pendulum from my throat to my ankles.

I walk home along a path of roses.

My spirit swings like a pendulum between tension and delight.

Cat Stevens spends his summers in Essaouira (*Morning has broken, like the first morning / Blackbird has spoken, like the first bird / Praise for the singing, praise for the morning / Praise for them springing fresh from the Word*); it is an agreeable seashore town, white and blue, of lost minor glories, its fortified walls and neutered-baroque toylike ramparts and its straight-as-an-arrow medina designed by an eighteenth-century sultan's captive French engineer. At dusk, along the sea walls, women in peach and rose caftans and black and white haiks take their ease pacifically in the pale light of streetlamps and glide tantalizingly through the medina — twilight is Morocco's finest hour — pausing under arches theatrically stagelit by naked bulbs. (This is Morocco's Bath; who is Morocco's Jane Austen?)

At noon gaily colored fishing boats bring great bloody white fish and serpentine fish, conger eels and jellyfish and baby stingrays and sardines into the busy little working port that was once a pirates' haunt; they are sold under reed awnings amid fish-kabob stalls with umbrellas of primary colors.

Parallel to and behind this world of apparent simplicity is another world, a world of omens and portents and poisons and spells and sorcery, packaged magic: *tseuheur,* a paste of antimony, pubic hair, and menstrual blood is sold for use by women with recalcitrant lovers. In the "herbal store" one buys a white stone, *pierre d'alun,* that staunches blood; roots and leaves to cure rheumatism, toothache, bleeding gums, gas, diarrhea, and infidelity; *kif* — hashish; opium; "secret incantations" to make one thin and to make one fat; ground animals' horns to promote desire and ground bones to reduce one's enemies to impotence. One of the stated reasons men fear women — the older the woman the more dangerous — is that women are the geniuses of spells and poisons.

The herb man has pictures of Devonshire thatched cottages in his stall, and pictures of twenty actresses who vied for the role of Scarlett in *Gone With the Wind.*

Sun and sea purify, scour away filth. But into the mellah of Essaouira the sun never comes. *Mellah* is the word for salt. To Jews, who came to Morocco from Spain to escape the Inquisition, was relegated the task of salting and preserving the severed heads of the sultans' enemies (so that they could be exhibited on walls as trophies of battle); and the area to which Jews (who paid a special tax for "protection") were consigned was called the mellah. The mellah is no longer the exclusive domain of Jews; it belongs to all the poor. Its buildings, tenement buildings, tall and narrow, lean against one another, blocking out light — the sea is an absent presence. Sewage runs in the dark and stinking streets. (Moulay, who has followed me everywhere, does not follow me here.) A child fondles a rooster, his pet (and his dinner). An old lady — perhaps she is my age — bounces from wall to wall, stoned on *kif.* A man in a starched blue caftan, smiling, carries a plastic bag of tomatoes; he is clean, and he breaks my heart. I slip on a fish head. A rat, pink, hairless, and repulsive, runs over my foot. Two dead rats lie, backs up, in a gutter. Whores laugh at me — their made-up faces are naked. When I get back to my hotel, I throw my sneakers away, having fetishistically projected all my fear and loathing onto them; animism is making inroads in my soul.

The names of Allah and of the king are carved high on the bare hills above Essaouira.

*

In Essaouira we dined on the roe of sea urchins; baby prawns boiled in seawater in their shells; fried calamari; grilled mussels, grilled stingray and grilled sea bass; haricots with garlic and lemon; and creme caramel — to the music of the Bee Gees.

In the Glaoui kasbah of Tifoultoute we had Moroccan salads — chopped carrots and chopped beets, artichokes, squash, and eggplants with tomato; leaning against magnificent Berber rugs in this land of proclaimed abstinence we drank whiskey and rosé wine; we had beef slowly stewed with apricots and quince and saffron in an earthenware vessel — a *tagine*. And we had a chicken *pastilla*, layers of pastry dough filled with chicken, almonds, and eggs and dusted with sugar and cinnamon, reminiscent of the elaborate pies Florentines confected — meat and birds and fruit and sweets and eggs — to avoid the strictures of the sumptuary laws (*four and twenty blackbirds baked into a pie*).

In Meknès we ate a tagine of chicken cooked with olives and lemons and saffron, while we watched a listless belly dancer go through the motions of her dance; and *harira*, a thick soup made with mutton broth and mutton chunks and chickpea mash flavored with tomato and lemon and tarragon — we ate this with dates instead of bread, a romantic food that is served every morning of Ramadan to break the fast. I never tired of it.

I never tired of roadside food — kabobs; and simple salads of onions, olives, tomatoes, and parsley flavored with coriander and cumin; rough bread; mineral water.

In Fez we had couscous (boring grains of semolina) with seven vegetables; and lamb braised in cumin, lemon, and cinnamon, so tender it fell off the bone; and crisp layers of fried dough filled with a hard sugar icing; and an almond-honey pastry called horns of gazelle, the nicest thing about which is its name.

In Marrakesh, in the medina late at night we were escorted to the palace of a nineteenth-century Moroccan Jew; we walked on rose leaves and in candlelight near a hexagonal tiled fountain ate pigeon pie. In the French restaurant of the Mamounia Hotel, we were served a brain the size of a walnut, fried in batter; whose brain it was remained a matter of concern to me through the chocolates and the framboises; and still does.

(In 1953, Gavin Maxwell tells us, at a time of rabid antisultan and anti-French feeling, a restaurant in Casablanca served "savoury stews composed of nothing but human flesh . . . an obvious and profitable way of disposing of a continuous burden of embarrassing corpses. . . . Only the extreme carelessness of the cooks . . . led to discovery. A medical student . . . found himself holding on the end of his fork the distal end of a human penis.")

"The world is in intense motion, ascending . . . to meet the descent of the Absolute in manifested forms. . . . The flow occurs in such an orderly, successive manner, according to definite patterns, that we are unaware of it, and the world appears to us to stay the same." — Teilhard de Chardin, *The Divine Milieu*

The enlightened soul is said to comprehend that just as permanence is contained within flux, change is contained within repetition. I began to fear that I was spiritually infantile, for I grew weary of the repetition, the unchanging geometrical mosaics, the stucco fretwork and endless scalloped arches, the predictable admixture of cedar/marble/tile and calligraphic arabesques of Moroccan architecture; I was tired, too, of vast incoherent crumbling ruins — for it is true, as Wharton remarks, that "in Morocco, as a rule, only mosques and the tombs of saints are preserved — none too carefully." Even Fez, which in the end brought me home to redemptive affection for a disowned part of my past, began to seem like a bastard hybrid of formality and decay. Grilles were only grilles — I failed to see in them "the appearance of the Absolute as uncontaminated unity, multiplicity disappearing into darkness" (particularly as they were mass-produced, ugly, and ubiquitous). And once one accepted the principle that the gate represents the beginning of the soul's journey to the Absolute, the gate — however handsome — remained a gate. The "harmonic rhythms" of arabesques endlessly repeated left me cold.

It wasn't the pattern in the randomness I was looking for, it was the randomness — the surprising wonder and aesthetic jolt — in the pattern. Perhaps I would find it in Marrakesh, the Red City, the marketplace of southern riches, the common ground and pleasure ground of all the tribes.

Everything glorious — everything purple and red and apricot and gold — that is found in Morocco is found in superabundance in Marrakesh, a city on a plain surrounded by the horseshoe of the High Atlas; everything tunneled and spacious and tendriled and muted and blazing and mysterious and gay is found in Marrakesh. . . . I went to see The Sights.

In the nineteenth-century palace of the vizier of Sultan Mouley el-Hassan, "the loveliest and most fantastic of Moroccan palaces," the fountains no longer play; if it were not for the niche — which orients the devout to Mecca — in the jumble of faded and moldy and unloved rooms, one couldn't distinguish the mosque from the harem, once a "lovely prison" where wives and concubines spent day after patterned day in the company of eunuchs with names like Musk and Amber and Thyme, Camphor and Essence of Roses. Vulgar stained glass (which Edith Wharton, a Victorian decorator at heart, admired) remained — "Catholic glass," Moulay called it — but no attempt had been made to preserve a tapestry of velvet claret and cinnamon and saffron that had all the subtlety and nuance the omnipresent green and red and black mosaics lacked. A mangy cat regarded himself in a dull mirror of no distinction. Only in the garden — among very unpashalike geraniums — could some remnant of the marvels of juxtaposition (arches and doors and sudden, intimate vistas) be seen; the garden was growing rank. Grilles. Doors within horseshoe arches.

Once the doors of the harem closed behind a new acquisition she knew that she would never again leave the women's quarters of her master until she was carried out to the cemetery. From then on she was a woman of the harem, her life bounded by its jealousies and rivalries and petty squabbles and household breakages that were judged and punished by the Glaoui himself; her conversation limited to the endless sexual gossip of her fellow concubines; her sexual life limited to her necessarily infrequent turn in her master's bed and the sometimes passionate solace of her own sex. She would never again see any other man than T'hami face to face.

Through a discreet palace door and into a rectangular garden came, in their perfumed winding sheets, the Saadian dead. Servants were buried anonymously, members of the royal family under a carpet of green and red and black diamond-shaped tiles, in pavilions with scalloped arches and honeycombed faience, and identified with calligraphic arabesques.

Marble, stucco worked as if it were filigree, . . . that sort of thing was so much better done elsewhere, in India, Italy. Here it is like it would inevitably be if some Victorian crafts-man had re-invented the style. . . . Airy grace [is] foreign to the Moroccan genius. The Moors need simplicity, space, and bigness to show their quality. The Saadian tombs . . . beside the Diwan-i-Khas in the Old Fort of Delhi would seem like store suits beside a Paris couturier's models. — Gavin Max-well, *Lords of the Atlas*

All over the city, but particularly in the vicinity of the huge square water tanks of the twelfth-century Aguedal and Menara Gardens (which, for people of the desert, must seem like wonders of the world, all the waters of the world, but which have little intrinsic beauty or charm), students, man and woman, boy and girl, walked and stood, books in hand (and hand in hand), learn-ing by repetition and rote; they rocked their bodies as they read in the meager shadows of trees, almost as if they were davening.

I didn't see the blue walls of the Atlas rising over the red walls of the city, a sight that has moved men to tears; they were shrouded in heat-pollution haze (though I guiltily persist in believ-ing that it was my weariness that obscured them); I saw, from almost every place, the venerated Koutoubia mosque, its minaret surmounted by three golden balls and a tear, and, five times a day, by a white flag raised on a rough wooden scaffolding, to herald the hours of prayer.

I fancied that if I had been permitted to enter a mosque the architecture — and so much more — might have been made clear to me. I peered into a mosque, feeling like a thing unclean; I saw, through a metal grille backed by a wooden grille covered with chicken wire, a cool forest of columns, a cool male world; my heart beat fast.

I saw the blue mountains at last, in the light of a sinking orange sun; I was in the Jemaa el-Fna, the great dusty square of Morocco, a perpetual nighttime carnival from which the *souks* radiate — Vanity Fair, Bedlam. My first impression, as I walked through circles of human onlookers surrounding circles of acrobats and witch doctors, snake charmers and letter writers, was that Hell was better organized than this. Birds of carrion flew overhead. Dentists sat at wooden trestles with heaps of loose teeth and ready-to-wear dentures and pliers. Lice-pickers sat next to hair-cutters. A Punch and Judy show incarnate: a little boy is beaten with a bamboo stick (this is a charade) to force him to perform; I watch for ten minutes; he is still being beaten, the crowd is still laughing (with a marked lack of merriment). The foreplay goes on too long and I leave without knowing what acrobatic wonders the little boy performs. A man does a lewd approximation of a belly dance. Another wears rubber flip-flops on his ears the better to mimic a donkey. A three-piece band — flute, drums, a kind of guitar — punctuates the storytelling of a Berber. A snake is draped around the shoulders of a protesting tourist. Cobras and monkeys compete for the attention of men who take onanistic pleasure in fishing with red plastic doughnut-shaped hooks for liter bottles of Coca-Cola. Crowds collect at numbered food stalls: fish in caldrons of fat, yellow cumin-stained grease rising to the surface; eggs in vats; chicken tripe with chickpeas; lamb sausage; pots of harira; fried offal; foul-smelling gray meat from deep pots of boiling liquid grasped and pulled apart by hands. Electric light bulbs compete with the fires of the braziers, burning pale against a pale sky.

I leave the hurly-burly for the terrace of the Café France, above the mandala of circles, the crowds. And suddenly, while I'm not looking, the pale hour turns into night — the night lights no longer compete with day — and it becomes possible to believe anything . . . that people feast in the anticipation and conscious-ness of satiety; that the stories they hear are true; even that they are happy. I am. Everything rises and converges: incense, smoke, voices, flutes; and the enduring, punctual call of the muezzin threads its way through this tapestry of sound which amounts to a kind of silence that encompasses singing, drums, wailing, ululat-ing. Voices curl in the smoke, all part of the intricate pattern, a sensory flash frozen, stasis and movement: a unity. My friend Biagio has told me to see Morocco from the corner of my eyes; I didn't understand him. Perhaps he meant that everything hap-pens when you are not looking.

*O*nce the former governor of a large Southern state came up to me at a country club, where I was the guest of a man with an impeccable Wasp pedigree (he went to sleep with the *Social Register, The Book of Common Prayer,* and a gun on his bedside table); and the governor, without preamble, asked me: "Are you Mediterranean on *both* sides?" Yes, I said. "How . . . *marvelous*," he said, and, apparently stunned, turned on his heel and walked away. I don't think he'd ever met anyone who was "Mediterranean on both sides" — certainly not at his country club.

We live in a tribal world.

Fifty years ago I was a flower girl at the wedding of my uncle Pat to my Sicilian aunt Mary, about which, with Verona-like doom, my Abruzzese family said: "It will never last." Two years ago, when she was seventy-three, Aunt Mary left Uncle Pat; when she was asked why, she said: "Enough's enough."

Italians can sum up a lifetime in two words. When, on the set of *Godfather III,* she was explaining to me why she no longer managed the business affairs of her husband, Carmine, Italia Coppola (Francis Coppola's mother, aged seventy-eight) said: "Enough's enough." . . . *Basta.*

Very often I find myself thinking, lovingly, that Italians are perverse; in fact, in Italy and in Italians, the baroque and the minimalist, the mannered and the succinct, passion and pragmatism are combined.

I can never get enough of Italy.

Once, in a small Tuscan town, in the company of a friend, I consulted a street map. I asked passersby for directions. My friend scolded me for not deferring to his superior understanding of urban geography. I was having a lovely time being shown the wrong (and long) way round by Tuscan peasants. A fight ensued. I said, "Damn it, I'd rather be happy than right." He said, "I'd rather be right than happy." My friend was not Italian.

I had a lovely time in Sicily watching *Godfather III* being filmed. I thought that I was watching a work of art in the making. I was not. Everyone on that set — with the possible exception of Francis Coppola — believed he or she was involved in a work of art. We were all wrong. *Godfather I* and *II* are works of genius, *Godfather III* is not. Something peculiar happens on a film set — a kind of alchemy that fuses energy to hope and clouds one's critical judgments. . . .

But without a measure of hope that takes the form of determination nothing at all could get done. Films couldn't get made, and peace couldn't get made, and love couldn't get made, and poetry couldn't get made. The best work is a fusion of love and praise.

To say that he was unhappy isn't quite the point: when I interviewed Gore Vidal in Rome, he seemed to me to have lost any capacity or inclination he had ever had to praise. And he certainly eschewed the exercise of hope. It's one thing to live without illusions (though belief in the absence of illusions is itself an illusion); it's another to take pleasure in seeing one's prophecies of doom vindicated in the event. . . . I know this, too, from having been raised in an apocalyptic sect: to greet disaster with the smugness of having been right about it is an affront to life. . . . On a sunny day in Rome, to say that neither goodness nor hope counts for much is a kind of sin; like suicide, it's contagious.

The Hill Towns of Tuscany:
In Search of Shrines and Castles,
Gardens and Walled Cities (1989)

✦ ✦ ✦

THE APENNINES — green, gold, and in the distance blue — curl around Tuscany like the bejeweled arm of a benevolent giant. The sun makes a great business of setting behind these friendly mountains, as if it were in perpetual and conscious competition with Renaissance painters . . . or as if to extend an invitation to enter the Renaissance painting, walk into the frame, and bathe in the glories of art where art — this art that is so profound a part of our received understanding of the world — was born.

Walt Whitman called the American landscape "the large *unconscious* scenery of my native land." Here, in the sophisticated countryside of Tuscany — where the earth, once covered with dense forests, and blessed with what in the first century B.C. Varro called "fat soil," has been cultivated since the time of the Etruscans, eight centuries before Christ — nature possesses a unique intelligence: when a soft gray cloud slips behind a velvet hill in the luminous light of dusk, it seems to do so with will and volition. Nature allows us to think it has a conscious will of its own. But this humanized land of undulating hills and anointing light has been formed and shaped by man.

It is civilized, it is old; and nothing here — trellised slopes of vineyards, waving fields of young green wheat, nodding fields of sunflowers gold as the gold of Midas's dreams, silver-gray olive trees, the bitter yellow broom that grows in solitary places, decorative exclamatory cypresses (like spiraling black fire) — is arbitrary. The patchwork and the cross-stitching of crops and flowers and trees that go every which way are orderly and logical, although it takes some time inside the picture frame to perceive this. No lines converge capriciously. The earth yields its bounty cyclically; man is bound to the procession of the seasons — and the astonishing (and calming) irregularity of the Tuscan landscape is a result of an ancient understanding of the needs of the land, its cycles, tides, and latent offerings. Man has imposed his will on nature here; but he has done so with nature's complicity and guidance. The joy of Tuscany is that — paintings, towns, land, and man — it is one continuous fabric: civilization.

If only we had a swimming pool, everything would be perfect. Even the fat bees are listless in the long grass and the purple clover. Lightning, a concentration and an incarnation of the summer heat, is stored waiting in rosy clouds.

We have rented a country villa — more properly speaking, a *contadinesco* (peasant) house, refurbished with sufficient grace — near the road that runs from Florence to Arezzo in the Valley of the Casentino, where the Arno rises. It is my sentimental conceit that the Arno is born in the tangled bushes behind our house. There several brown streams mingle; they look turgid and sluggish, but they are slappily and splashily (disproportionately) murmurous. They fill the simple house with music. And although the weather is beastly hot, at night I sleep under two blankets, as icy blasts come from the shallow river. At sunset, when fragrance is intensified, the smell of river water is married to the fragrance of peaches ripening on the kitchen table, and roses insinuate their sweet and cinnamony fragrance into this heady bouquet, and the green-soapy smell of pine, and, in August, the patchouli smell of newly mown hay.

(In Florence, at the fifteenth-century Pharmacy of Santa Maria Novella, I will try to capture this fragrance — I will buy a bottle of *fieno* (hay) cologne, and one of rosewater; but it will evaporate immediately on my browning skin; and I will grow pale again.)

One night I awaken to a sky filled with milky radiance. The sky itself is blossoming; stretched above me is a tapestry of white and black flowers. Only gradually do my intoxicated senses understand that the elms and acacias outside my bedroom windows are patterning the moon-flooded sky. Thereafter the moon tugs at my senses every night and I awake and think: *White nights;* and fall simply asleep.

One of the nice things about nature in Tuscany is that it has houses in it — farmhouses, and castles, too.

All walled cities are not alike. Some seem to wish to hold you in and others to keep you out. Perched, as Henry James said of Montepulciano, "brown and queer and crooked" on their hills, looking, from a distance, like "some big, battered, blistered, over-laden, overmasted ship, swimming in a violet sea," the approach to them is often more serendipitous than, in the event, are the cities themselves. From a distance they look harmonious, complete (walls *resolve*); they offer the extravagant promise of safety, a free-dom within fixed boundaries, snug protection from the alarming and contradictory demands of everyday life; they appear to offer the architectural equivalent of that psychic unity that is our ideal. . . . They don't always deliver.

I tried hard to like Arezzo, the walled city nearest to us; in the end I conceded the last, laconic word to Aldous Huxley: "a boring sort of town," he called it, almost self-consciously devoid of effu-sion or prettiness.

"If I have any good in my brain," Michelangelo, born in nearby Caprese, said to Vasari, his fellow artist and chronicler of artists' lives, "it comes from being born in the pure air of your country of Arezzo." I can only think he was talking about the country*side* and not the commercial, wealthy city itself (its wealth deriving in large part from the design and manufacture of gold jewelry), an intimidatingly symmetrical city both frenetic and se-vere.

Arezzo, which has an enviable position on a promontory where three fertile valleys — the Valdarno, the Casentino, and the Val di Chiana — meet, makes it almost impossible for a tourist to find his way within its gates. Italians are not famous for giving directions: *tutte le direzione* — "all directions" — reads a road sign frequently encountered, which, as it defies linear logic, may go some way to explain why, when Italians say "right" (*a destra*) they invariably point to the left (*a sinestra*), and vice versa. In Arezzo, as the usually good-natured Kate Simon points out, no matter how diligently one labors up hills following the signs pointing to Arezzo's main square, Piazza Grande, one invariably finds oneself instead in the Passeggio del Prato, a big, tailored park wherein the Fascists, with their usual barbaric disdain for scale, saw fit to place a huge white memorial statue to the poet Petrarch, who was born in the old city. This medieval/Renaissance city Hawthorne called "modern" (he meant it was cold) and not "picturesque" (he meant it was withdrawn). Indeed, once I'd arrived at the Piazza Grande, I didn't quite understand I was there (nor did I especially, in this stony stoniness, care).

Gray rain turned the broody yellow houses and battlements and palaces a monochromatic gray: the city resembled nothing so much as a dignified prison. (It is said that flowers bloom, hidden from public view, in courtyards behind walls; I call that ungenerous.) Dante called the natives of Arezzo "snarling dogs," and I did sometimes wonder if the Aretines took positive pleasure in confounding foreigners. One long table at the monthly antiques fair was covered with a tarpaulin, and when I asked to see what was underneath, I was rewarded with a lascivious leer and a view of gynecological instruments old and new — it took me several moments to understand what they were, after which my stomach took a nasty turn.

Never mind. Arezzo has one great and abiding glory (one does not as a consequence love sober Arezzo, but one forgives it all): in the barnlike Church of San Francesco are the fifteenth-century Piero della Francesca frescoes, *The Legend of the True Cross*, than which the Renaissance has nothing more sublime to offer. When one is in Piero's thrall, when one enters scene after scene of what H. V. Morton called "a brilliant, dignified world," one is tempted to believe that his is the gospel of the Renaissance, all other works a gloss upon it. We owe much of our understanding of perspective to Piero — but to say that is to utter a dry commonplace. There is nothing soppy, no fake emotion in Piero's paintings, no manipulative piety, and absolutely no sentimentality; there is only nobility and lucidity. In this dispassion and matter-of-factness there resides mystery. In this simplicity is not idealism but the ideal. This detachment is a form of magnanimity; one wonders if this — the thing being simply what the thing is — is the way God sees.

These soft-hued paintings are architectural — they prefigure cubism. And — although it is always a mistake to confuse the work with the worker — they must surely have been the product of an integrated soul; they incline one to the aesthetic appreciation that color and form are not two separate elements of a work of art but one and the same. Keats said Euclid alone gazed upon beauty bare; not so — Piero did and showed us how. The folk legend of the True Cross, a naïve tale, is told gravely and with unchallengeable authority. *And this is how it is,* we think; *it could be no other way.* Looking at this radiant work we are at the still center of the moving world. How beautifully Piero understood the magic of ordinariness, the holiness of everyday life.

"The sunshine had the density of gold-leaf; we seemed to be driving through the landscape of a missal." — Edith Wharton, *Italian Backgrounds.*

Piero's birthplace is the sleepy arcaded town of Sansepolcro near the border between Tuscany and Umbria, the main street of which smells of perfume, owing not to any innate sweetness but to the presence of a large Helena Rubinstein shop. In the modest little Civic Museum of Sansepolcro is the painting Huxley called "the greatest picture in the world" — Piero's *Resurrection,* a 6.5-by-7-foot fresco in a marble frame. (Sometimes extravagant praise turns one against a painting, as one feels one may not be up to it — in which regard it is helpful to remember that Piero della Francesca, fifty years ago, was rendered no homage at all.)

The Jesus of this *Resurrection* — risen from the sepulcher while soldiers sleep in physical and emotional abandon — is God. There is no other way to apprehend his watchful majesty and solidity. He is of heaven and of earth. In this unforgettable picture — which swam before my eyes each day at dawn, a cherished afterimage — the article of faith that instructs us to believe in a God who became man and shared the human condition is vivified; it is superb visual propaganda, an insistent, supremely quiet call to belief.

In this same room is Piero's polyptych, *La Madonna della Misericordia* — the Madonna of Pity — a Mary very lovable, towering, and also sweet. Against a solid gold background the Mediatrix stands, holding open her mantle, beneath which kneel sinners and saints. Crowned queen of heaven, she is a simple girl; she looks very much like her son — but then Piero's people, with their downturned lips and oval faces, all bear a family resemblance . . . one sees their counterparts in Sansepolcro.

We make a pilgrimage (I have come to regard each journey to see a Piero as a pilgrimage), driving past fields of poppies and cornflowers and verbena, through an avenue of pines, to the pretty cemetery of the medieval town of Monterchi. (Italian cemeteries are invariably pretty, their dead in rows of drawers like filing cabinets, floral offerings in silver vases and beet jars.) Here, where life and death mingle as naturally as fragrance and light mingle in the spun air, is a small chapel standing all alone, in which is a sensual, inward-looking and weary Mary, one eyelid drooping, arrested in a moment of intense privacy almost terrifying (voyeuristic) to witness: one hand is on her hip, the other fingers her belly. She is guarded by twin angels, mirror images of each other (as Mary is the mirror image of every pregnant woman), who pull back the flaps of a tent to reveal her to us — a woman in the ninth month of her pregnancy, not an icon, but yearning, straining flesh. This is Piero's *Madonna del Parto*, before which village girls light wicks in olive oil and pray for a safe delivery. This fully pregnant Mary — pregnant to bursting — is both theater and protagonist of the greatest story ever told. One doesn't have to believe the story to believe the painting.

A young Asian man stands in the small chapel copying the Madonna.

Piero loved and honored women.

He died on the day Christopher Columbus landed in America.

Tuscany, honey-sweet and mystical and honeycombed with caves, has for centuries been the home of hermits. Until the thirteenth-century, Sansepolcro belonged to the monks of Camoldoli, whose hermitage is in the heart of the Casentino fir forest, three thousand feet above meadows where Chiana cows and white oxen graze under acacia trees. It's a funny kind of place, composed of sanctity and of kitsch: twenty identical detached cottages, or cells, each with its private chapel and walled kitchen garden, house monks who live in voluntary silent isolation, meeting one another only rarely, for Mass, and, in fraternal tenderness, on feast days. Visitors are not allowed into the hermitage proper. (I entered the iron gates for a few moments to find myself in what looked remarkably like a Catskill Mountains resort crossed with a prototype for a utopia.) Holiday campers and hikers with heavy boots and hairy legs surround the settlement and lots of people visit the ancient Camoldoli pharmacy with its odd assortment of goods: "Tears of the Abbot," an after-dinner *digestivo;* eucalyptus and acacia honey; chestnut, prune, strawberry, and blackberry jam; creams and unguents to enhance the beauty of the women the monks will never in their lifetime see; tisanes for insomnia, nerves, and liver — the liver, or *fegato,* being as important to Italians as neuroses and fitness are to us.

In the Camoldoli library there are dusty Oxfam posters, pictures of bloated brown babies (who'd buy them? who'd display them?), repro Deco jewelry, and New Age books on sale to support Catholic missionaries. Lots of noise and lots of nuns and lots of junk, and sugared fruit on sale at stands. . . . It all seems rather pagan and it is certainly incoherent; and with this noisy commerce and traffic outside, the cloistered hermitage seems like a theme park gone awry.

And yet: the vegetarian monks, ecologically minded, plant five thousand new trees each year. . . . "Their relationship to the earth — their ancient mysterious mother — must have been the most intimate as well as the most interesting part of their lives," Edith Wharton wrote; what must they make of the doings outside their gates?

Inside the pharmacy there is a skeleton with this legend: *I am the true mirror, every other mirror distorts, in me you see what you truly are.*

La Verna is the most sacred of Tuscan shrines. Here, in these tortured outcroppings of rock, St. Francis — to whom, in his mystical union with the physical world, the swallow became a sister, the wolf a brother, and clods of earth "lovers and lamps" — received the stigmata, the first person ever to receive in his body the visible wounds of the cross.

La Verna is romantic: a long white picture gallery, like a parenthesis, culminates with a window that looks off to a quintessentially Tuscan view: blue hills folding into blue hills; a numinous haze (gold dust) — the world is endless, sweet, and blue. In the Chapel of the Stigmata is a giant terra-cotta by Andrea della Robbia of the Crucifixion in a frame of lemons (blue, yellow, bone white, sherbert green). The work of the fifteenth-century artist whose best ceramics are at La Verna cannot be called beautiful, but transcendentally pretty. Della Robbia was a virtuoso, which is not the same as a genius.

Romance yields to stronger stuff: here St. Francis saw a rock rent in two while meditating on the Crucifixion. It is damp and cold in the silent, unpeopled cave, an icy womb. One experiences viscerally the mixed pleasure and pain of penetration (entry) and the anguish of birth (exit). One apprehends both the terror and the appeal of a hermit's meditative life, the thrill and the anguish of living on mortification and on air. One feels a reflexive urge to *kiss* something: the iron bed on which St. Francis slept, the rough-hewn cross at which he worshiped. For, whatever happened here, *something* happened here. (I have felt this certainty twice before — once in the *scavi*, the underground necropolis of St. Peter's in Rome, where Peter is thought to be buried, and once in a temple in India, where I felt the presence of a god and heard the music of a flute.)

Si non credi, ammira! si sei sciocco, scrivi il tuo nome sul muro. "If you do not believe, admire! If you are crazy, write your name on the wall." . . . So reads a sign in the long white picture gallery. . . . And of course someone *was* crazy and did write: MARIO WAS HERE, he scribbled.

> We stood on a bare, windswept upland, with the whole of the Val d'Orcia at our feet.
> It is a wide valley, but in those days it offered no green welcome, no promise of fertile fields. The shapeless rambling river-bed held only a trickle of water. . . . Long ridges of low, bare clay hills — the crete senesi — ran down towards the valley, dividing the landscape into a number of steep, dried-up little water-sheds. Treeless and shrubless but for some tufts of broom, these corrugated ridges formed a lunar landscape, pale and inhuman; . . . it had the bleakness of the desert, and its fascination. — Iris Origo, Images and Shadows.

Something happened at La Verna, and something happened in the Val d'Orcia, at Castelluccio and at La Foce, too. Driving back from a visit to the thermal spa of Chianciano Terme (CHIANCIANO

FOR A HAPPY LIVER, the signs say), we came upon the secular shrine of Castelluccio Bifolchi fortuitously, feeling the premonitory thrill of discovery before we saw, engraved in the courtyard of the castle the sign: *"You who pass and see the peace of this valley pause and remember our deaths."* . . . *This castle is the gift of Marques Origo.* In this castle, and at her nearby villa, La Foce, Iris Origo spent a memorable part of her graceful, instructive life.

If she had written only two books — *The Merchant of Prato* and *San Bernardino of Siena,* classics that are indispensable to an understanding of medieval and Renaissance Tuscany — the reputation of this exquisitely modest woman would be secure. Her legacy to us is as enduring and as prodigal as Italy itself. As a girl, well born of American and Anglo-Irish parents, she lived in the Villa Medici in Fiesole, a center of cultural life in Florence. In 1924 she married into an Italian noble family; she and her husband, Antonio, bought La Foce and its land:

> Besides the villa itself and the central farm-buildings around it, there were twenty-five outlying farms, some very inaccessible and all in a state of great disrepair. . . . The olive-trees were ill-pruned, the fields ill-ploughed or fallow, the cattle underfed. . . . In the half-ruined farms the roofs leaked, the stairs were worn away, many windows were boarded up or stuffed with rags, and the poverty-stricken families (often consisting of more than twenty souls) were huddled together in dark, airless little rooms. In one of these, . . . we found, in the same bed, an old man dying and a woman giving birth to a child.

The Origos set themselves the heroic task of arresting the centuries-old soil erosion of thirty-five hundred acres of the Val d'Orcia, turning bare clay into wheat fields, rebuilding farms and bringing prosperity back to their inhabitants, restoring the greenness of mutilated woods.

In this beautiful aim, in the interval between the world wars, the Origos largely succeeded. But then Mussolini, and then civil war, came to the Val d'Orcia. During this terrible time, Iris Origo, at grave risk to her own life, concealed and sheltered partisans, escaped allied prisoners of war, Italian deserters, and Jews, and provided for her tenant farmers and for orphans of the storm, foxed the Fascists and the Germans, housed and schooled and gave medical attention to scores of refugee children — all (in the words she uses to explain the motives of a partisan) "from the simplest of all ties between one man and another; the tie that arises from the man who asks for what he needs, and the man who comes to his aid the best he can with no unnecessary emotion or pose." All over Italy, she wrote, this miracle was being performed: "For a short time all men returned to the most primitive tradition of ungrudging hospitality, uncalculated brotherhood."

During this time, when she and her husband were faced with the destruction of all they had created from clay, she kept a diary, limpid, sincere, "no unnecessary emotion or pose." One entry read: "Arrived in Rome, for the birth of my baby." Four days later, the new mother and her baby were in an air raid shelter, "the old dungeons . . . where Lucrezia Borgia was imprisoned — very deep and very damp"; and she made no ado of it. Toward the end of the war, she found herself very nearly without possessions; and this woman, from whose character had been scoured any hint of a sense of entitlement, wrote: "It is a very odd feeling to be entirely possessionless, but it seems curiously natural. One feels that one is, at last, sharing the common lot." That is not a consummation most people of her class would devoutly desire. She had gone through the eye of the needle.

In the Middle Ages it was believed that, God being light, sin made us opaque; if, according to this theology of light, man would eschew sin, his body would become radiant with light. I think of Iris Origo as being radiant with light. She gives us a new way to think of feudal overlords, in whose tradition she was acting. It is difficult for us to think of the Middle Ages as in any way benign (when I went to school, history was this: there were the Dark Ages, then a long tunnel, then the Renaissance), but it may be useful.

One night I went to the Castelluccio to hear a town-sponsored concert — Mozart, Boccherini, Dvořák — and I thought of the days when Iris Origo played with crying babies, making a game of disaster as bombs fell outside the courtyard. After the concert dinner was served in the garden that had belonged to Iris and Antonio Origo; from the long green lawns, one could see the volcano of Mount Amiata, soft green fields between. Machine guns had once stood on these parapets, tanks rolled up and down these avenues of cypress trees, mines were planted, and partisans and the farmers who helped them were killed where now there are hollyhocks.

Brazen torches and soft candlelight illuminated the faces, the pretty dresses, the jewels of perfumed women. I thought of Iris Origo to whom, not fifty years ago, a radio and a hairnet (the only lost possession she allowed herself to complain of) were so precious.

Thereafter, in southern Tuscany, I thought of her and of her goodness whenever my path took me where hers, in such terrible and ennobling circumstances, took her.

Pienza: Little boys, happy and bold, are sitting on the decorative Renaissance well of the main square of little Pienza; maintaining perfect separation of the spheres, men sit in cafés earnestly discussing the news of the day while women, enjoying a more domestic communion, sit in the lanes knitting, crocheting, returning strangers' greetings with unguarded smiles and guileless curiosity. This square, Piazza Pio II, has been called "a perfect, minuscule core of Renaissance order and urbanity." Fifty kilometers south of Siena, Pienza lacks the monumental symmetry of later Renaissance towns, for which (bearing Arezzo in mind) we can be grateful. The serene square, whose grace lies not in niggling exactitude but in the harmony of its proportions, was commissioned by Pius II, whose birthplace Pienza was. "You did well, Bernardo," he said to his architect, Bernardo Rossellino, "in lying to us about the expense involved in the work. If you had told the truth we wouldn't have parted with the money."

Blessing the fact that no town in Italy, however planned and honored, is a museum of dead artifacts, I take pleasure in the sign I see in the cloisters of a deconsecrated church: NO MOTORCYCLES ALLOWED. Boys play badminton here, where once monks enjoyed the hanging gardens. I take pleasure in the long street, Corso Rossellino, which leads to the perfect square, which is lined with food boutiques selling herbs and honeys; paté of radicchio; an artichoke sauce for pasta; red-pepper pesto; and the fresh and aged pecorino cheese for which Pienza is famous. Delicious-smelling shops sell fragrant "natural" creams and unguents. Trendy (but I don't care), Pienza has been "discovered"; it is pleasantly touristed, not overrun; it is after all too small, its appeal too reticent, a perfect miniature, but a miniature nonetheless.

Iris Origo — who, called by events to action, was by inclination a scholar — loved this town, "the creation of that worldly, caustic man of letters, Aeneas Silvius Piccolomini, Pope Pius II, the first of man of taste in Italy," she wrote, "to enjoy with equal discrimination the works of art and those of nature, who would summon, in the summer heat, his Cardinals to confer with him in the chestnut woods of Monte Amiata, 'under one tree or another, by the sweet murmur of the stream.'"

Pienza, and much of the Val d'Orcia, was deserted by farmers after World War II. The cities called; they must certainly have seemed more hospitable than this battered land. The farmers made the choice between what they perceived to be stagnation and the promise of mobility; their relationship to the land had been ruptured by bombs and mines and killings — it was blood-drenched and too well known. They chose the future. But the hills are green again here — the Origos' work was not in vain. Now not Tuscans but Sardinians shepherd their flocks on this land (and come to town with wheelbarrows, selling cheap watches and trinkets made in Taiwan).

The land is green; but the struggle for good must always be renewed. Now there are political posters and signs in Pienza, calling for action and deploring the "unauthorized excavations" and light industry that encroach upon the sylvan beauty of these hills (smokestacks among the mulberry and ash trees, the beeches, chestnuts, and elms). The world is always in need of saints.

A swallow lies wounded in the Corso. Everyone in town makes the bird his business. The boys with their ices look for sticks to make a splint for the swallow's broken wing.

Montepulciano: John Addington Symonds called Montepulciano "the lordliest of Tuscan hill towns." I did not like it at all. Two thousand feet above the sea, it has spectacular views of both Tuscany and Umbria; but I felt as Henry James — who went to see it "for the beauty of its name" — did: Once I got there, I had no idea what I was doing there or what I was expected to do. Montepulciano seems to require a lot of one — one is supposed to love it because one has been told to love it; but I think it is loved by people only because they were, to their very great surprise, successful in getting to it and therefore feel entitled to enchantment. From the distance it is seductive, it swoons violet over a sea of blue and green hills. The road to the heart of the walled city, the Piazza Grande, is practically vertical.

No one among us wants to toil up these hills. The only driver among us is afraid, with reason, to drive. Everyone is cranky. We make our vertiginous way, finally, to the top of the town outside the city walls — a way not quite so terrifyingly vertical as the roads within the walls — following the car of an Italian driver who knows no fear. He is roaring with laughter at these strange Americans, gesticulating like mad in the rearview mirror. Our own driver cries.

In the early spring of 1944, Iris Origo walked with all her refugee children to Montepulciano from Castelluccio. They slept in trenches on the way. Bombs fell. The fields were mined. The Val d'Orcia was no longer safe from the Germans. She walked over a mountain range. "If only it would stop raining," she said, and that was the extent of her complaining.

Montepulciano is famous for its wine, Vino Nobile di Montepulciano. I was too much out of sorts to drink it.

Just outside of Montepulciano in Montefollonico, I had one of the best meals I have ever had in my life, in a restaurant called La Chiusa. I had zucchini flan, presented in the form of a tiny flower pot from which grew a squash flower; *crostini* of veal spleen seasoned with thyme and embellished with an herbed pecorino sauce; ravioli with sage and butter; and goose neck stuffed with veal and pistachio nuts; a sorbet of apricot; a salad of dandelions, basil, and valerian (from which Valium was originally compounded); caramel gelato on vanilla lace with chocolate sauce. The proprietor of La Chiusa wakes at six A.M. to collect herbs from his garden, and rises again at midnight (I do not know what farmers' lore governs this behavior) to pick vegetables with the aid of a flashlight (he knows only that his father and his grandfather before him did this). He has inherited over a thousand recipes, he says, sixty of which are currently in use. His menu is poetry.

In the summer of 1944, after the liberation of Italy, the Origos were carried triumphantly up the nearly vertical roads of Montepulciano to the Piazza Grande on the shoulders of partisans. Had all feudal overlords been like the Origos the world today would be organized very differently.

Butterflies and buttercups. In the lavender light of dawn a will-o'-the-wisp swims up to my window to greet me — in Tuscany one finds oneself attributing volition even to dandelion fuzz, which Tuscans call "little Father Christmases." No other place could have given birth to St. Francis.

We shop in the country village of Subbiano, whose history goes back to ancient Rome (subbiano = *sub Jano*). In the Monday morning market on the Avenue of the Martyrs of Liberation we buy everything from swordfish to hand-knit sweaters, suckling pig to Alessi glass-and-metal ware. The fishmonger, a pleasant man, gives us an extra ration of ice in which to preserve our *pesce spada;* he also cheats us. When, without animus, we call his attention to this, he says, smiling and unperturbed, "Of course. Italians have initiative." Then he gives us an extra half pound of swordfish.

In the café at Subbiano — which is exclusively a male domain except on market days — a little girl cries because her crayon has broken. Her mother says: "She is crying because of them," meaning us, "the foreigners." The mother speaks as if we were dumb and made of stone. She cannot imagine what we are doing here. The little girl offers us a part of her cookie to eat.

Our house is struck by lightning. Lightning cascades down the chimney, spilling into the fireplace. My southern Italian aunts used, whenever there was a thunderstorm in New York, to go around the house disconnecting all the electrical appliances. I thought they were spinsterishly mad. Now I disconnect all the lights. Not that it matters: every time there is a storm all the power goes out — *crack.* One day when the power is out, an ectoplasmic white sheet of lightning enters the living room. There is a *hisssss,* then a zigzag streak, and then another of lightning-fire, orange, blue, red, issuing from the chandelier. I cannot curl up in my bed to escape my fear because my bedroom is in the path where lightning struck (I think it is alive and hiding, waiting to gouge my heels) and because my bedstead is metal and I am convinced it will attract the next bolt. . . . Life has not taught me that lightning does not strike twice.

We go to see Marino, the *contadino* who — by what Byzantine arrangement with our absent landlords we cannot ascertain — sometimes mysteriously appears to perform mysterious tasks around our house. We tell him of the lightning, the disgusting smell of burned wires, our fear. He responds enigmatically: "Solar panels." More to the point — his point — Marino's son died long ago in a thunderstorm. Marino tells us this in mime, jumping up and down and making comic-book zigzags in the air with his weathered hand; he mimes because he cannot believe we understand Italian; as he does not understand English it is not in the nature of things for us to understand his tongue. Marino's wife, he gives us to understand (somewhat in desperation, he amplifies gestures with speech), had "her insides cleaned out — *whoosh* — women's things," as a result of her son's death (which, in spite of myself, I am beginning to regard in the light of farce as Marino rises to greater and greater heights of mimicry). His wife cries. I am with a friend who, not trusting her Italian, carries a Berlitz dictionary. She looks up the word for *sad: "triste."* She says she is *triste.* In fact she is crying in commiseration with Marino's wife although she does not know the word for *sad.* "What solar panels?" I say; "what about them?" Marino shrugs.

Near a tennis court in Subbiano there is a café where old men play cards and young men play cards, and often they exchange roles — the young are mentors to the old, the old are mentors to the young. The young are watchful of the old, but not condescending; old people here are not redundant. The old are tolerant of the young, and if they are envious of their blooded youth their envy finds no overt expression. This café is near a hospital. The old men playing cards are young compared to the very old men and women who come here with their families, and with their nurse, a beautiful, vivacious girl (the leaven of the world). They play. They sprinkle one another with water. There is no scorn or fear of old flesh; if the young see their future written in these ravaged old bodies, they are not repelled by it. The very old people are spoon-fed gelato — and nobody loses dignity in the process. A baby coos and there is integration between those at the beginning of life and those at the end of life; and we are accepted too. In America, very old people often appear to have no identifiable gender. In Italy, men are men and women are women to the brink of the grave, and, one supposes, beyond it.

From afar, the hill towns do look alike: cubist and abstract, compact and humane, fortuitously arrested — or so in fancy it seems — in the moment of tumbling; this is architecture without architects, ordained . . . growing out of practical needs and constraints.

We drive through healing light. Time and green space and healing light for all: the world here looks enduring, less imperiled than the world at home; dreams of apocalypse are lost baggage.

There are crosses on the road, and sometimes shrines, to mark the place where occupants of cars met fatal accidents. The charioteer-drivers of Italy's *superstrade* disregard their moral.

How can such agreeable people, men and women, become such maniacs on the road? Their necks permanently tilted, looking for the advantage, they jockey for position at 140 kilometers an hour. Speed holds no terror for them. And yet I am less afraid here than I am in New York traffic. Whatever guides their behavior, it is not a careless hatred.

Old men and old women on bicycles, pensioners, are dressed as neatly as for church; every button on the men's shirts is buttoned almost to a stranglehold (my father dressed like this: propriety was honored always . . . sometimes to a stranglehold). We pass these signs:

LADY GOD IVA CLUB

LADIE SHAREDRESSER

BODY SPORT FIGNESS CLUB

Italians do not appear to have grasped entirely the principle of billboards. Signs flash by. They bear no relation to the proximity, vicinity, or direction of the shop or factory they are rather halfheartedly advertising. The nearer one gets to that which is advertised, the fewer the billboards. This phenomenon — which is as difficult to explain as to experience — has led to frustrated drivers going miles out of their way. Native drivers pay absolutely no attention to the billboards or, indeed, to almost any road instruction at all.

ZOO FAUNA EUROPEA: Billboards advertising this xenophobic zoo — which claims the dubious distinction of being the only zoo in Europe that has no African, Asian, or American animals — are all over southern Tuscany; the zoo is in Poppi, a diminutive arcaded town both dour and picturesque, surly because of its claustrophobically small scale, which makes foreigners feel gawkish and unrelated. Above the narrow ancient porticoed lanes is the perfectly preserved medieval castle of the Guidi counts, with whom Dante allied himself in battle: on the plain which this toylike castle overlooks in apparent benevolence, the war between the Guelphs and the Ghibellines exhausted itself. Set in a garden of old-fashioned flowers, the Gothic castle is anomalously cozy, friendly, its courtyard busy with a multiplicity of forms and intersecting lines (like a Piranesi drawing), and coats of arms — so many heraldic emblems it looks like an illustration for *Boys' Comics*. Birds congregate around the merloned tower. The palace looks as if it ought to be in the window of F. A. O. Schwarz. . . . And in its frescoed chapel I got goosed. I managed to convince myself that the offender — blond, tall, blue-eyed, feral — was a barbarian from another land; but it spoiled the castle for me. . . .

In Poppi I got goosed and in lovely Cortona I fell in love and went to the hospital, but not in that order.

The palaces and houses of Cortona's main piazza are arranged in a random, haphazard manner, asymmetrically; the square should as a result look untidy, but it wears instead the air of inevitability which is the result of the combination of logic and intuition we call harmony. It is charming — both princely and villagy, like an illustration of a happy fiefdom from the Brothers Grimm. Off this piazza, Piazza della Repubblica, crooked lanes lead in all directions (just as they might in a fairy tale), some to grand views of the Val di Chiana, which the walled city of Cortona floats above, and some to darkness so dense and spooky H.V. Morton was moved to call Cortona "a nice place for an assassination." A steady buzz of English and American voices fills the square, Cortona being a center of language and art studies, and many students having returned or remained — to learn, one supposes, how to live. At the hour of *passaggiata* Italians reclaim their town, and in this leisured, ritualized processional, from which no one of any class, station, or age excludes himself or is excluded, and in which no coupling or grouping is untoward, no face or body mass-produced, the rhythm of the day swings to its completion — an echo of the liturgy of the seasons, a satisfying cosmic full stop.

I thought I was dying. "My knees are weak and I am dizzy and I feel nauseous and as if someone were ironing my back," I said to the admitting physician, with whom I fell in love. "But why do you have iron in your back?" he asked, my Italian being imperfect. Syntax at last unsnarled, he took me to Cardiology, where again, and with another doctor, I fell in love. (Italian doctors, as amiable and caring as Italian hospitals are badly organized, try to circumvent red tape and bureaucracy, which is one reason they are lovable — the other being that they are handsome, and have intelligent hands.) My heart and my lungs having been pronounced reasonably fit, a consulting physician, with whom I also fell in love, offered a tentative diagnosis: *fuoco di S. Antonio* — fire of Saint Anthony — which sounded so romantic I decided to have it whatever it was. Alas, it was not to be. My memory jogged by all these handsome doctors, I remembered that I had that morning groggily taken not one but two prescription pills. "Too bad you don't have *fuoco*," said one of the honeybunch doctors; "so easy to cure." "But I have nothing at all," I said, "and that should be easier to cure." "You have life," he said, "and that is very grave."

All this — the talking, the consulting, the examinations, the falling in love — took three hours. Then I went to the administrative office, where, in an effort to determine how much I had to pay for my x-rays, I spent two hours. They didn't know what to do with me, I had no private doctor, no national health plan, *no papers*. The nice lady in charge called Arezzo, Florence, Milan for advice. "But surely, signora," I said, "the calls must cost more than the x-rays do." "*Non importa*," said she good-humoredly; "I am the director of the x-rays, not the director of the telephone calls; and what the director of the telephone calls must do to arrange her budget is not a matter for our concern." This is Italian logic at its most demented and most endearing. (The x-rays cost five dollars.)

In Cetona I saw Etruscan bones.

Little is known about the Etruscans — where they came from, where they went; their language, derived from the Greek, has not been deciphered (incised writing on sarcophagi and cinerary urns looks like that of dyslexic children). They were an oligarchical people who dominated fifteen thousand square miles of what is now Italy — from the Po Valley to the Gulf of Naples — before the Romans did. One knows them from their enduring art, from which D. H. Lawrence was able to extrapolate that they were "sensitive, diffident, craving really for symbols and mysteries, able to be delighted with true delight over small things, violent in spasms, and altogether without sternness or natural will-to-power." To which I would add that they had a wry sense of humor — their way of managing the world and, in particular, death, the ultimate reality.

I'd seen Etruscan artifacts in the Archeological Museum of Chiusi. The Etruscan tombs on country roads outside of Chiusi, to which a museum custodian brings you, are a bust: I'm convinced that any farmer with a hoe and a pick would take any credulous tourist to any hole in the ground and convince him it was an Etruscan tomb, so unrevealing are these burial places. But the museum is dandy: plastic sculpture, terra-cotta and stone forms, funerary and cinerary urns, on one of which lunatic griffins shriek, while a monster-man extends Silly-Putty arms, the Etruscans being unwilling, apparently, to give death the last laugh, or the last grimace, either. On their urns are vivid mythological figures, ardently dancing. The Etruscans liked to miniaturize (another way of making the world manageable); the museum is full of little cooking implements, braziers and pots which probably accompanied the dead on their journey but which look as if they ought to be in a dollhouse (a perfectly manageable world).

Perhaps because the Etruscans are so mysterious, some fanciful Italians like to claim they are descended from them. . . . The contessa di Cetona — an honorific accorded to her because she lives in its impressive castle — believes she is the reincarnation of an Etruscan.

We are sitting in the garden of the twelfth-century castle, having toiled uphill for what seems like miles. Beyond electronically controlled gates are elliptical, crescent-moon-shaped brick steps, sunk in moss, which lead, through a walled tunnel, to the spicy garden, the castle, the crenelated tower. The walls of the tunnel are lined with rectangular funerary urns in niches. In bas-relief women carry vases, men play cards. Our host and hostess are on familiar terms with the dead.

The garden is on a platform overlooking the town, the hills, the immediate world. Six-hundred-year-old cypresses punctuate formal rosemary hedges, a maze, that give the garden the top notes of its fragrance. Bees apply themselves to Passion of Christ — delicate flowers with three tiers of purple, white, and butter-yellow petals (they resemble a fountain and symbolize the Trinity); their scent, piercingly sweet, provides the undertones of the enveloping fragrance. (The honey that comes from them is highly prized.) Bits and pieces of the ancient world are here and there cunningly and casually deposed: stone balls, found on Etruscan funerary urns (the size of the sphere is thought to have represented the measure or class-position of the dead); Roman stone pineapples; a swimming pool lined with stones from an ancient Roman bridge. Water spouts from the mouth of a grotesque stone mask. Cicadas hum.

Bats swoop. We sit under espaliered peach and pear and apple trees. Anna, "the contessa," brings us several shoeboxes, Gucci, Ferragamo, in one of which there is a skull. Her long fingers play over it. This is what she says: Her gardener found, in this garden, the skeletons of four Etruscans — a woman on whose white bones was a "barbarous necklace," a man, and two small children, and also two skeletons presumed ("their foreheads were so low") to have been "brutes of a kind, undeveloped, animals, perhaps." The light is fading and none of this sounds strange. Anna, fondling the skull, applying her fingertips to the smooth edges of its orifices, says: "Do I not look like her? Is she not I?" It is this Etruscan — whose skull, in the failing light, does indeed look like an x-ray of Anna's aristocratic face — that Anna believes she is a reincarnation of. From the piazza below comes the sound of singing. Anna puts her skull in the Gucci shoebox. We are served dinner on a slab of granite resting on aborted Roman columns. There is much wine, made by Anna's silent husband, Aldo. Inspired by the wine, perhaps, my Roman friend Sheila, who has run up to the tower, calls down to us, Rapunzel-like: "There is an Etruscan effigy here — come, look! It is I!" Sheila, not given to flights of fancy, has now invented an Etruscan ancestor for herself.

The memory of Anna's mother, ninety-five, resides, not with the Etruscans, but in World War II. She takes me by the hand — her own hand, parchment white, has the bones of a sparrow — to the drawing room of the castle to show me her Piranesi prints and her Chippendale chinoiserie: "Look in this mirror," she commands. I do. "Look at the frame. Do you see? It is pornographic, of course; we hid it from the Germans, buried it — do you see?" I see a boy and sheep, and what they are doing does not need to be deciphered. Anna's mother, ninety-five, winks.

Aldo drives us, in his Mercedes, down the brick stairs. By this means we are jounced back to reality.

It's all very well, but where shall we swim?

In heavenly Lucignano, bathed in a delicious bath of medievalism.

Lucignano is built of five concentric circles and has the most interesting aesthetic of any town in southern Tuscany. As one walks the ancient cobblestone streets — no curbs, no barrier between pedestrians and houses — one feels as one always hoped to feel in Tuscany, girdled, sheltered, embraced. From the inside of the houses it is a different but complementary story: from back windows one sees gardens and the world of hills beyond. This town has the personality one wishes for all one's friends — a blend of extroversion and introversion that results in happiness; one burrows in, one reaches out. It can be no accident that Lucignano, flower-bedecked, blessed with five intimate and overlapping piazzas and a simple, friendly main street with simple, friendly cafés, is a town of happy people. When the sun shines in Lucignano, one forgets Freud and Marx.

In this town — the very sweetest of all hill towns, I think — there is a restaurant called Da Totó. Here we eat and here we swim.

We are served in the garden by the children of the courtly proprietor. The solemn children ask, "Shall we make you the meal?" by which they mean, "Shall we choose what you are to eat?" to which the expected answer is yes. This nicely removes from us the burden of choice. The garden is like the garden of my dead grandfather (for whom, in sunny Lucignano, I yearn): basil and tomatoes and oregano grow next to gladioli, hot green peppers next to dahlias, a tangle like the tangle that is memory, as unchallengeable as memory, exactly right. Dandelions are as respected as mimosa. This is the way the garden of memory grows — it is not hierarchic, everything that grows in it belongs in it.

Jugs are tied to the branches of the pear trees underneath which we sit: When the pears are ripe they will fall into them, and will eventually form the basis for grappa. This is a sunnier, less convoluted mystery than ships in bottles.

The children bring us bean soup with a dollop of raw olive oil; noodles with a sweet *ragù* of wild boar and wine; penne with a sauce of fennel, tomato, and cream; linguini with sardines; roast chicken; roast pork — the pigs are fed on olive husks; Vin Santo (homemade; Tuscany's dessert wine) and apple cake; grappa.

It is a wonder we can stand.

I float. The courteous, smiling children — in gay bikinis, now, their work done — frolic at a respectful distance; this is a private, family pool; they like us at Da Totó, they encourage us to swim here and turn other importuning diners away, I don't know why. I float for hours. Around me are bell towers and roses. The children splash. I have no need of further adventures. Rapture consists of resting absolutely still on the welcoming waters, afloat in children's laughter, the silken fragrance of roses, the chimes of church bells, the delectable and buoyant air. Larks sing.

Pure Gore (1990)

✦ ✦ ✦

IT IS DECEMBER, and the air is a wash of silky light, astringently cool and yet sunny enough to allow one to bathe in multiple sensations of warmth. Under white canvas umbrellas the beautiful ladies of Rome in their beautiful furs cross narrow ankles; old men read their papers and sigh for remembered pleasures.

On this gorgeous day the restorers' scaffolding that has obscured the pillars of the Pantheon for a year is removed; the building that is both prototype (cave) and culmination (temple) of all the buildings on earth is revealed in its amazing beauty. Gorbachev is in Rome talking to the Pope. All of Rome — Catholic, Communist, everyone young and old — is wreathed in smiles. Perfection of weather and of hopes. The Berlin Wall is down. Old shibboleths crumble. There is a spirited will to joy. It is easier than usual to breathe.

"So are you rejoicing?" I ask Gore Vidal.

"Whatever for?" he asks. "Surely rejoicing is somewhat premature," he says.

Gore Vidal has lived down the street from the Pantheon, in the historical center of Rome, since the midsixties; he lives in a penthouse with a wraparound terrace in the Palazzo Origo — one of the more resonant addresses in Rome: It belonged to the noble family-by-marriage of writer Iris Origo; unselfseeking and modest, her life distinguished by more than graceful prose, she had what Vidal calls a "good war." . . . Vidal knew Iris Origo and her Anglo-Irish/American family, of course. He knows, as they say, Every-

113

one. One would think that to be in the proximity of this kind of nobility — not of rank but of heart — would make one contagiously happy. And, as a gloss upon one's happiness, one would, if one lived in the Palazzo Origo, have merely to cross the street to Delfino's, where the Italian version of take-out is purveyed: tender Roman artichokes in satiny olive oil, chicken *alla diavolo* grilled to golden succulence.

"Does Rome still thrill you?" I ask Gore Vidal.

"I still look at it," he says.

In London, from which city I have just come, copies of his new novel, *Hollywood*, are heaped in the windows of all the bookshops.

"I have no cause to say Hosannah," he says.

"A cat can't be in heat only three weeks after she gave birth, can she?" A slim milky white cat with pale green eyes insinuates herself among our limbs, uttering a mournful cry of dumb lust. The elegant kittenish creature, which pleases Vidal because, motherhood notwithstanding, she doesn't (a Lolita in heat) look the least like an adult animal, gave birth to a poor thing with a deviated septum; the offspring died in an attempt to suckle, drowned in its own mucus. This week Vidal, sixty-seven, is being operated on for a deviated septum (which makes his face slightly asymmetrical and his voice nasal); he is apparently not a superstitious man.

His drawing room is cold, the coldness of marble — colder than the outdoor café at which I take my midmorning coffee — and dark, very dark, though the sun shines brightly on the terrace, and the great chandelier in the dining room is blazing. The only source of heat — the sun seems not to reach this room — are two bouquets of roses, yellow and orange, tightly curled.

We stand on the terrace, with its fresh view of Borromini's San Ivo alla Sapienza, its white corkscrew steeple joyously boring into the sky; the dome (from which wildflowers grow) of the baroque San Andrea della Valle; the Roman Synagogue (which Vidal has never been inside); and two hills, the Janiculum and the Aventine. It is a shock to go from the sunny terrace to the dark living room, like coming out of a movie theater into bright sunlight, only in reverse.

Tapestries, ancestral portraits, a fanciful mirror — kitschy and also rather lovely — from the Royal Pavilion at Brighton, leather, bibelots. I am pleased to sit on a chair frequently occupied, until his death, by Italo Calvino, of whom Vidal has written with affection and esteem. On the table in front of me are walnuts and sundried figs on wooden skewers, from Vidal's house in Ravello, on the Amalfi Coast. On the table next to me are a photograph of Paul Newman — faded almost to sepia — with a floppy dead fish in his hand and a bewildered expression on his young face; an unframed colored snapshot of Vidal, a still from *Gore Vidal's Billy the Kid*, in which he played a bit part; and, partially obscured by the colored snapshot, a framed picture of a 1940s kind of woman's face — arched and stenciled eyebrows, dark glossy lips, shoulders emerging from some heavy shiny stuff. A dusky male servant pads quietly, making unobtrusive arrangements here and there.

Vidal launched Calvino in America; in 1973, he reviewed all of the Italian novelist's books in the *New York Review of Books*, the principal outlet for Vidal's essays since 1964. It was an act of writerly love. (Calvino returned the compliment by calling Vidal — incomprehensibly to me, I am afraid — "a master of that new form taking shape in the world of literature, which we may call the hyper-novel or the novel elevated to the square of the cube.")

"So is there another contemporary writer you love?"

"That was about it," he answers.

"That was it? Just Calvino?"

"Well, I mean I like certain books, but there are no writers that really excite me. . . . As you are Catholic, I suppose you believe you'll meet him some day."

"Calvino? I allow for that possibility. . . . And you?"

"Christianity — your idea of a suffering God who became man — is just ludicrous. Before Christianity came along we were doing very well. We had philosophy for the most advanced, plain old superstition for the superstitious, and mystery cults for those who were worried about the afterlife. Something for everyone. . . . Calvino is in my brain."

"So he's alive."

"Till the brain goes."

"Anybody else? Updike?"

"A very charming and very skillful writer," Vidal says. "But not very intelligent. They wanted a right-winger and they got one. He should have been a preacher. 'Reverend Updike' sounds exactly right to me."

"Baldwin?"

"Love him? No, I didn't; I respected him. He was so hostile to Mailer and to me and to other young writers of the time, it was very hard to be around him. . . . He wrote only one really good book — the one with 'Beale Street' in the title — a kind of a perfect novel, a small novel, you can make a small one come out properly, and he does. It's the least piss-elegant. His problem was that he was on the one hand this eloquent black preacher with an extraordinary gift for a phrase, and on the other hand Bette Davis, writing books about show biz. . . ."

Perhaps I am being unfair to him, I think; I broaden the question: "Whom are the writers you admire?"

"My favorite writers when I was reading a lot were Apuleius and Petronius, and my roots are in them — much more than in Hawthorne or Melville, whom I don't care for. When your spiritual home is classical, romantic woolly American writing is just very distasteful. *Moby-Dick* is my idea of an irrelevant work. Most of Melville's admirers haven't read it. . . . George Eliot is good — you have to be forty and know the world to know how good she is. . . . Let me think. I like the novels of Carson McCullers; I like the short stories of Paul Bowles; I loved Waugh when I was a kid, I thought *Scoop* was the funniest book I'd ever read, I don't think I could reread him; I enjoy Graham Greene, but he tends to be 'the mixture as before.' I like some young fellow — Ellis? something like that, I can't think — who wrote a book called *States of Desire*, I think. . . ."

He is elliptical in his praise, as one might be who believes effusion is vulgar . . . or as one might be who places himself under constraint not to use the word *love*, believing that if he does, he will be held sternly to account for it. He has been generous in print; in stylish and moving essays he salutes writers as diverse as Saul Bellows and Tennessee Williams, about whom no one has written more lovingly, or with a clearer eye. When he speaks, he is inclined to become reflexively jejune. His chilly drawl is the exact counterpart of the openness and generosity of Italian. It is almost with reluctance that he says, about his friend Williams:

"When the romantic does it well he gives you heart and liver. He did. It was great art."

And yet, in spite of the sense he conveys that nothing — including generosity — counts for very much, stories about his own financial and emotional generosity, his no-strings-attached giving of money and time, abound. Writers speak of his willingness to bear their burdens when they endured terrible personal crises; at least one artist owes her villa in Umbria to his having come through with a personal loan at a crucial moment; a child in Ravello, of which village he is an honorary citizen, is said to owe her eyesight to his efforts to get her medical attention. (It is also perceived to be true that he brooks little criticism; he has apparently abandoned friendships for reasons "tantamount," one ex-friend says, "to your saying you think he's perfect except for one dreadful shirt.")

The Vidal-on-display is the Vidal who, in a series of noisy debates in 1968, traded venomous insults with William F. Buckley, Jr. (he called Buckley a "crypto-Nazi"; Buckley called him a "queer" and threatened to sock him); the Vidal who sued Truman Capote for libel when the playwright wrote that Bobby Kennedy kicked him out of the White House for drunkenly daring to place a hand on Jacqueline Kennedy's bare shoulder. (Jacqueline Onassis and Vidal are by way of being related: Both their mothers were at one time married to Hugh D. Auchincloss. For a while, according to Vidal, Jackie claimed him as a brother.)

The Vidal-first-met is Vidal-the-cynic (he calls himself a realist — "an unbearable thing to be") who performs his iconoclastic but not wildly original liberal-left act on the Johnny Carson show (Carson and his then wife Joanna stayed at Vidal's villa in Ravello with him when their marriage was in bad trouble — this is one act of kindness he can't not mention, perhaps because names of the very famous are delicious in his mouth); the Vidal who exchanged deadly quips with Norman Mailer on the Dick Cavett show. Vidal-the-Brahmin is a somewhat weary and attenuated version thereof. He is tired. He is dully mischievous. He is sad.

On Cavett's show, in the early seventies, Vidal mentioned, rather in passing, the fact that Mailer had stabbed his first wife, Adele, "in the back." A bellicose Mailer replied that he'd stabbed Adele, not in the back, but in the front — and that Vidal was too obtuse to recognize "the existential difference." (Janet Flanner instructed them both to behave themselves.) Soon thereafter, according to Vidal, Mailer threw a glass at him at a party given by Lally Weymouth. . . .

One gets the feeling that although Vidal elevates (or demeans, depending on one's point of view) his personal life to the level of abstract political principles, he is unable not to rehearse his pugilistic encounters with Mailer, perhaps because both have been called "our greatest living man of letters." This is a war for turf, boys' games for high stakes.

An armistice has been declared. The two writer/performers have patched it up — no more public feuding; they both attended the 1986 Moscow conference on nuclear disarmament at the invitation of Gorbachev; and Vidal, citing "the T. S. Eliot theory that to be a far-out poet you'd better look like a bank clerk," says — with just a hint of pomposity — "We ought not to be acting out private dramas in public to give our detractors purchase. . . . Norman and I are now quite friendly, I see him when I'm in New York. His wife is wonderful, astonishing. Very beautiful. Wonderful red hair. Very lucky man."

Surely the word *lucky* must often have been applied to him . . . not by himself.

He, taking the dim view, believes that we are all brought up in cages and are doomed to know the world only from the particular set of bars we find ourselves behind. His cage was golden, the cage reserved for those born to privilege. "How did you get out of your cage?" I ask. "Ah," he says; "that's what everyone would like to know." And that is what he is disinclined to speculate about . . . at least out loud.

("Are wicked mothers invariably beautiful?" I ask, pursuing demons of my own. "Mine was," he says. "Do you want to talk about your mother?" "No.")

Parts of his childhood sound made-to-order by Hollywood and the other capital of make-believe, Washington. His grandfather, Thomas Gore, was a blind Bible Belt United States senator whom a barefooted seven-year-old Vidal escorted to his Senate seat. His father, Eugene Vidal, was an aviation pioneer and a member of Franklin D. Roosevelt's cabinet. Vidal was the first child to cross the Atlantic by plane; he was four years old; he was piloted by Charles Lindbergh.

He graduated from Phillips Exeter Academy in 1943 — he was seventeen, and he never went to college. He enlisted in the army. When he was nineteen, stationed in the Aleutian Islands, he wrote his first novel, *Williwaw;* it was a critical success. In his third novel, *The City and the Pillar,* published in 1948, he wrote matter-of-factly about a homosexual relationship between two young men. The book was not advertised in the *New York Times* (*The Kinsey Report* wasn't either), and he complains of the fact that his next five novels were not reviewed in the daily *Times,* or in *Time* or *Newsweek.*

One can understand how this must have hurt. He wears his scars proudly, almost as if he wouldn't know himself without the stigmata: in 1976 he was elected to the National Institute of Arts and Letters — "the American Academy and two hundred immortals and so on; they sent me a very pompous telegram congratulating me, and I sent them a little short telegram congratulating them on having elected me. And then I said: I cannot accept this election as I already belong to the Diners' Club. John Cheever told me it was the rudest telegram he'd ever seen. He said: Couldn't you at least have said Carte Blanche? I don't want anything to do with the bureaucracy of literature in the United States."

He once wrote that "very early, the idea of fame — eternal fame — afflicted our race."

If generosity consists of being able to take as well as to give, it is fair to say that Vidal is lacking in generosity; surely his wounds have had time to heal? They suppurate. *Burr; Lincoln; 1876; Empire;* and *Washington, D.C.,* his series of historical novels — which he prefers to call "novels in history" — have been best-sellers. His books have been translated into twenty languages and have sold an estimated 30 million copies. He has written successful scripts for television, and box-office successes for Hollywood (*Suddenly Last Summer,* for example); his plays (*Visit to a Small Planet,* for example) have been produced on and off Broadway.

He has been a golden boy with perpetual promise perpetually renewed. He has not, on the evidence, fared badly. Unless, of course, he wishes also to be regarded as prescient, as political and sexual guru, undisputed king of the literary and political mountains. . . . Or president of the United States. . . . Can anyone want so much?

"In 1984 I won the Pulitzer Prize for *Lincoln,*" he says. (In fact he did not.) "There were three judges, as always, and two voted for me; the third — a lady, some sort of novelist, I think — said she would go public if this prize were given to such a bad writer. . . . I have never been able to get her name right. Look it up. . . . How many Americans can tell good writing from bad? I'm sure that little lady couldn't. They gave it to a very minor novel by a very good writer, Alison Lurie. And that was my Pulitzer.

"Of course the little lady didn't mean I was a bad writer, she meant I was a bad person — they always say bad writer when they mean bad person."

For his political beliefs, Vidal says, "they" — the literary establishment, the defense establishment, and "all of journalism . . . the media are in place to make it impossible for anyone who is serious to be serious" — are against him: "I must always be discredited because nothing I say is true — because I'm evil and an expatriate, and I hate America. They just go on, they drip torture. . . .

"When I chose to go back to being a novelist in the early 1960s, I needed a classical library, and the best two are the American Academy here and the Academy in Athens, and Greece is altogether too ghastly a place. In London the company and the conversation are too good, one would never get anything done. In Paris one would eat and drink oneself to death. Rome was pleasantest."

Outside his bathroom hangs a framed list of sixty-four signatures, those of residents of a small town in Maine who sent him birthday greetings on the occasion of his sixty-fourth birthday. "Will Philip Roth receive that on *his* sixty-fourth birthday?" he asks.

When he left the army, he went to Antigua, Guatemala, to write — it doesn't seem possible for him to write a novel on American soil.

"All that stuff they make about me being an expatriate, you see, it's the easiest way to discredit me. 'How can he write about America when he doesn't live here?' I *didn't* leave America. I've always had a house in America — in Los Angeles — and one in Europe. *Many* people have two houses. . . . Drip torture. . . .

"I hate possessions but I have to have houses because I have to have books. I buy houses to put the books in. That's how it starts. I once had a house on the Hudson, a Greek temple built in 1820. I finally sold it and got rid of everything in auction and I found that I owned forty-two sofas. Just think of that. I do not have sofas now."

He has been sitting sprawled on the sofa, his arms flung out, his pudgy fingers splayed, his smallish feet neat in shiny polished black moccasins. The green pullover he wears over a shirt untidily open at the waist to reveal a furry stomach wars with the warring colors of his face — flushed red over gray, the unhealthy complexion of a man with high blood pressure. He rises slowly and shuffles, this man, once regarded as devastatingly handsome, to the door.

He feels "marginalized, demonized, trivialized." Why are "they" persecuting him?

"I am just too dangerous to have around. I have the number of the country. I have their number. I know how they'll behave, I know how they *have* to behave. . . . Forget the politicians," he says. "They're the cosmetic government. The real government are the very rich, something like a dozen families who always pretend they don't have anything to do with it, but of course they do, they control it. It's like going to Rockefeller's house and saying, Well, he isn't in charge, he didn't cook the lunch. They hire the cooks, they hire the presidents, and they hire the Congress. And now their kids — those who don't play polo — are taking Senate seats because it's a sort of glamorous thing to do.

"The only enemy the United States has on this earth is the American government. . . ."

In 1960, Vidal ran for office in upstate New York's 29th District, and, although he lost, got almost twice as many votes as the head of the Democratic ticket, his friend John F. Kennedy. From 1970 to 1972 he was co-chairman, with Dr. Benjamin Spock ("a funny guy — looks like a mortician and knows nothing about politics") of the People's party. In 1982, he ran in the California primary, campaigning for a year and a half. He came in second in a field of nine, with nearly a half million votes; he'd spent the least of the top four candidates — about $50,000. Jerry Brown ("poor innocent mouse") spent, he says, a couple of million.

"I wouldn't be able to keep myself in the Senate — you need something like twenty million dollars; and I can't ask people for money. I'd lose a Senate race anyway, because the Republican party and the defense industry would have spent a hundred million to keep me out and to keep that seat. . . ."

He said then, as he says now, that the American government is a government "of the rich, for the rich, and by the rich — socialism for the rich and free enterprise for the poor." He believes in the legalization of drugs. He believes that the government, or "a rogue element in the CIA, the DEA, or whatever, introduced drugs to gain total control over the lives of everybody in America so that they can rip it off and make money. Now they are talking about taking over the army camps for drug takers. Mandatory blood tests, urinalysis, lie-detector tests. . . . They have set up the infrastructure of a police state and they're not going to give that up. And it isn't done because they're worried about our health. They know that sooner or later somebody's going to try to overthrow this government." Vidal says he is "almost always right" — and that he is almost always resented for having been right.

"I cannot give print interviews and win. You are the invention of the writer. The *Washington Times* demonizes me, they have a big cartoon of me that looks like the Devil, and the *Washington Post* trivializes me in the Style Section and it's all very giggly, just terribly giggly stuff." As for the *New York Times* (which reviewed *Empire* on the first page of the Book Review), "I'm high on their enemies list and they're high on mine."

"Well, it's no more than I expected," he says, consulting a glass of scotch. "I don't want prizes, I don't want jobs in universities, I don't want to give readings. They can't understand that I'm not like them.

"Am I sad?" The air, so cold, is thick with sadness. "My blood pressure must be a sign that something is irritated by them; it's much more likely it's reading the *New York Times* and not my own misadventures that sends my blood pressure up."

It is difficult for me to understand — unless the answer resides in his temperament — exactly why he seems to be stricken with a terminal inability to entertain joy, or to praise. He says: "What people do with me most often — it's a very daring trick but it almost always works — is what I call 'the reverse.'" He gives in evidence an appearance on "The Morning Show" hosted by Tom Brokaw. "Brokaw said, You've written a great deal about bisexuality. And I said, Well, actually I haven't — my new book, *Creation*, is about the fifth century B.C. Well, he wouldn't stop. And I said, Look, Tom, this is very early in the morning, bisexuality is a late-night subject, you can't get people in the morning who want to talk about it. When Brokaw started for the third time, I said, Now I'm going to talk about politics, we won't talk about me, we won't talk about your favorite subject — bisexuality — we'll talk about Jimmy Carter.

"A year later there's a cover story in *Time* about the three boys — Rather, Brokaw, and Jennings — and Brokaw said, 'There are some really tough moments in the business; for instance, when I was doing "The Morning Show," I had Gore Vidal on, and I wanted to talk politics, and he wanted to talk bisexuality.' That's what I call 'the reverse.' I ran into Brokaw at a party and asked him why he'd lied. He pretended he couldn't remember. They do it to me all the time."

He inhabits no gulag. He is denied no worldly success. *Hollywood* has been selected by the Book of the Month Club. He has just made a movie in Italy with Jim Belushi; already Hollywood is talking about making *Hollywood* into a miniseries.

"If I spoke from a loser's stance," he says, "nobody would pay any attention to me." The reason "they" hate him is that he's a winner . . . a winner, however, who doesn't feel like a winner, a man to whom success appears to be indistinguishable from failure.

The white cat mews and we mew back.

We drink scotch, we talk about phobias — his, mine. He has a friend who is so afraid of Fifth Avenue that he cannot even be driven down it in a limousine. I am afraid of lots of things. The next day Vidal's greeting to me, as I come out of the creaky lift (which he never takes), will be: "Did the streets get you?" Two of the characters in *Hollywood* are so afraid of the dark that they cannot sleep alone; men, they sleep with other men — for comfort, not for sex.

"What is the joy of writing a novel? Finishing it."

Vidal calls *Hollywood* a "contemporary novel." It takes the reader through the administrations of President Harding and President Wilson, and parallels matters of state with the silent-movie world of the twenties, moving back and forth between Washington and Los Angeles to make a circle of corruption:

> Films fed the people involved; people involved fed the films. L. B. Mayer reinvented America and the world. The world of Andy Hardy became *echt*-America, as did Norman Rockwell; and not only did America fall for it, the world fell for it. And eventually they give us Ronald Reagan because he's a reminder of the great glory days, standing tall — city on a hill — a visible reminder of something that was imaginary to begin with. But it's soothing; and these are troubling times, so it was inspired to have him there — it was a disaster for the country, but it was an inspired kind of art work.

After his more personal books did not receive universal accolades — perhaps nothing short of being compared to Henry James would have satisfied him — he might have thought (though surely his intelligence would have advised him otherwise) there was refuge and safety to be found in writing "historical" novels, less danger of exposure and failure if he set himself the task of explaining and chronicling American history through the seeing consciousness of remote fictional characters. He might have thought that putting history on parade would make him less vulnerable than putting what were perceived to be his own feelings on parade. Such hopes, if hopes they were, proved illusory. And criticism from historians was more than he'd anticipated.

Whether or not it is legitimate to mix real characters with invented ones as Vidal did became a question much vexed.

"I make it very clear: people who were figures in history I don't play around with; they do and say what they did and said — as much as we can tell. After all, what is history? If you think history is reading all the *New York Times's* statements about a president you're not going to get anywhere near it.

"What I have done is to take the narrative back to its origins — right back to Homer. To Dante. To Shakespeare. To Tolstoy. I'm writing about the rulers, the victimizers, the kings, the gods, the heroes. I am the chronicler of the American republic — which ought to be described in terms other than the godawful history books that kids are supposed to read and wisely don't."

Vidal has been attacked by academics — "scholar-squirrels"

or "hagiographers" to him — for "fictionalizing actual political figures. I also fuss about this," he's said; the academics have fallen prey to the naïve delusion that there is "a final Truth revealed only to the tenured few in their footnote mazes.

"Look what I've gone through just with Lincoln's syphilis! Lincoln told his law partner that he had syphilis, he gave the name of the town and the name of the girl, and the name of the doctor he went to in Cincinnati. There was no cure. It was epidemic. *And he had it*.

"You know, when I seem not to have gotten it right or the thing contradicts itself — every time I've made a whopper, and I've made a few — it's always been from following 'authority.' I've always gotten it from *the* biography — and the biography's wrong. Well, it's coming to an end. I can't get the energy anymore for it." *Hollywood* — the history of a war he is inclined to believe was fought to preserve the banking interests of J. P. Morgan — will be followed, he says, by a final one "from my point of view, in the present, looking back on forty-five to fifty years."

His critics say that all his "historical" novels have been written from his point of view — which, it may be argued, is the only point of view available to him.

His friend Tennessee Williams was unable to understand his life without writing about it. Vidal says: "You can say about me that I don't possess my own mind till I've written about it. I never know what I think until I write and sometimes I don't know even then."

Caroline Sanford, the heroine of *Hollywood*, insofar as *Hollywood* has a heroine, says that the word "faithfulness" in marriage has absolutely no application and makes no sense unless one has religious faith. Vidal concurs: "Faith is a Christian word, *fideles*. It's not a word that would ever grab her" — or him. Vidal believes that "there is no such thing as a heterosexual person or a homosexual person, there are only heterosexual or homosexual acts. There is also no such thing as a heterosexual or a homosexual 'sensibility.' . . . What did Lyndon Johnson and Bertrand Russell have in common other than pussy? And what on earth does Eleanor Roosevelt have in common with Roy Cohn? One was a saint and the other a beast.

"What is wrong with other-sex even if you're married? What

is wrong with same-sex even if you're married? It's no big deal. One would rather not be the occasion of someone else's pain but we all are sometimes and that's part of being alive, it goes with the turf.

"Genetically there's monogamy built into woman — they need nine months for that egg, and a long time to make a commitment — and none at all built into men. For a man the sexual act is quite enough, it doesn't have to lead to a relationship; sometimes it's far more kinetically exciting knowing that it does not. . . . Boys hate kissing, girls start that stuff, you love that stuff. 'Just hold me,' that's all a woman wants. Boys aren't like that."

Vidal has been with his companion, Howard Austen, for forty years: "Well, there you are," he says. "Fidelity is such a large word. Human relationships change all the time. There you are. . . .

"The Italians have sex right. They just do it."

Howard's voice sounds from his bedroom. Howard's bedroom is papered in antique floral Roman wallpaper, muted reds and purples and hints of old gold — Pompeian colors. Striped drapes and a striped bed canopy; chinoiserie. Curled on the bed, drinking excellent coffee from eggshell china (a gold spoon), I watch a documentary of Vidal's campaign in California. He looks young and fit.

It has grown darker and colder. In the drawing room Gore Vidal pulls the velvet drapes, lights the lights.

He likes to dish. . . .

Margaret Thatcher: "She became all boy to become all prime minister."

Nancy Reagan: "Poor Nancy, just in over her head."

Barbara Bush: "One knows that the beloved Barbara doesn't like anybody . . . except 'our kind.'"

The duke and duchess of Windsor: "I liked her, she was very funny . . . it was all in her tone. . . . A 1920s flapper, a wise-cracker. Awfully shrewd. *He* was, I think, the stupidest man I have ever met — and there was not much charm with it. He was so thick, no matter what you were talking about he never grasped it. We were once talking about coronations and I said that at the high point of the coronation of the Roman emperor two masons with trowel and mortar appeared and said: We are here for your tomb, lord of the world. And the duke said, Oh yes, I'm a Mason too, you know. . . . She never quite came out and said it, but she implied that she'd like to have been a royal mistress — which would be a lot more fun than going to open flower shows. . . . She was never imperious with me, no, no. I knew too much of her family in Baltimore, it was a small world in the thirties. . . ."

Jane Fonda and Tom Hayden: "She is a shit. He's just a standard conservative politician, a little more liberal than most. He's given opportunism a bad name."

Charlie Chaplin: "Paulette Goddard told me he was circumcised. She couldn't think of the word. She said, You know, he has one of those *things*. I'd asked her if he was Jewish or not because there'd been something about it in the paper. Oh, she said, With Charlie who ever knows, he lies all the time, who will ever know? But you know, she said, he has one of those *things*."

Arthur Schlesinger, Jr.: "A hired hand of the ruling clan, and specifically the Kennedy clan. He's awfully bright but he's told too many lies. . . . I the novelist am more objective and realistic, with hardly any ax to grind, than he, the official historian."

Jacqueline Onassis: "Quite intelligent. She got everything she wanted. Specifically, money. I'll tell you a story: We were up in Hyannisport . . . this is the first summer of their presidency . . . after dinner I was playing backgammon with Himself, it was just Jackie and me and the president. And he was laughing away at some interview I'd given to *Look* magazine about what it was like growing up in Merrywood when my mother was the reigning Mrs. Auchincloss. It was a very unreal world, you didn't know there was a Depression on when you were there — there were five white servants in the house, a great, great social distinction in Washington, where domestic help was usually black. It was very grand. Well, I became a private in the infantry when I was seventeen, so I was not much affected by all that. Girls are different; if you're brought up in an unreal world, you stay in one. [Jacqueline Kennedy Onassis lived at Merrywood, the Auchincloss estate across the Potomac from Washington in Virginia, when her mother married Hugh D. Auchincloss.]

"I was saying how sort of enchanted, how out of time and place Merrywood was, outside of the real world. . . . The president said, 'What's all this golden-season crap you've been peddling about Merrywood? It was *The Little Foxes*.' He said, 'How do you explain how all eight of you, whatever — all Hugh D.'s children and stepchildren — are all such disasters?' Now it had become very irritating to me, and I think also to Jackie, the worship of the Kennedy family as the greatest family that ever lived, as if all the rest of us were inferior. Well, the president went down through the whole lot of us, saying why this one was a failure and that one was a failure. He skipped Jackie and me. And Jackie and I looked at each other over the backgammon board and then we looked at Jack and she said, 'Go on.' Jack got a little embarrassed. Jackie didn't say anything. I said, 'Well, naturally we can't be like *your* family' — intimating that such perfection was not given to mere mortals — 'but if you do feel that we are individually flawed by being the children or stepchildren of Hugh Dudley Auchincloss, Jr., I would put it down to one reason: each of us had a mother he knew married only for money.'

"Jack was quite shocked. He said, 'Oh, well you . . . you . . . you mean *security*.' I said, 'No, I mean money, big money.' And Jackie said: '*Yes*.'"

Gary Hart and Barney Frank: "If you can't answer them politically — if Gary Hart's going to win the nomination — you say he fucks call girls and try to catch him with one; you don't answer what he's going to do with the Pentagon budget, which is all that matters. . . . Do you think it mattered that he lied? I don't. Not about that. I'd have said, Yes, and so what? Why don't you pay attention to what I'm saying politically and stop all this?

"If you do care about that sort of thing — cheating on his wife — then I think you shouldn't vote, because it's not politics.

"I was startled to see that *Newsweek* put Barney Frank on the cover — an act of absolute viciousness, antifag and antiliberal, what's a more beautiful combination to sell newspapers?

"All we hear is private lives. 'Isn't he a nice man? . . . Is she really a wonderful woman or is she putting it on? . . . Is that her hair?' When a magician is going to pick your pocket he's doing something with his right hand and you're staring at that while your wallet is being taken."

Rep. Barney Frank lived for a time with a male prostitute, for whom, it has been alleged, he secured favors, and who, according to his own testimony, ran a prostitution ring from the basement of the congressman's home.

"You really think that bad judgment in one's personal life is going to affect one's political judgment? I don't see how they're analogous. You take a Christian point of view, I'm pre-Christian. He certainly made a mess. But what does that have to do with legislation? You should know better. You've been brainwashed. Work it out."

Eleanor Roosevelt: "I saw a lot of Eleanor in the last ten years of her life. She was so down on sex. One couldn't imagine her in bed. But when I read her published letters, I was convinced that her love [for a woman journalist] was one hundred percent physical. She told me that after Roosevelt died she found evidence that he had broken his contract with her and continued to have an affair with Lucy Mercer."

If that was reprehensible, it was "not because of marriage vows, but because he'd broken the agreement that she'd work her ass off as a presidential wife and he'd stay away from Lucy Mercer. FDR might have thought it was fun to take Lucy away from Eleanor, she was her girlfriend first. Eleanor went to her husband's funeral like Medea. . . ."

Jimmy Carter: "He was Rockefeller's creature. And Coca-Cola's before that. You think he was a good man? What's that to do with it? What you want in a president is not someone nice, but someone who has an interest in the people at large — not the people who gave him the money to get there."

I wish he hadn't said that goodness had nothing to do with it.

The newsstands in Rome can't keep their customers supplied: Everyone wants to read about the events in Eastern Europe.

"There are two things going on in the world," Vidal says; "one is a centrifugal force to save the planet — a bringing together of all the economies in order to preserve the air, water, and soil. I'm not saying that it is going to succeed, I'm saying this is one of the forces in the world. Then there's another force at work, which is that everybody is sick of the nation-state, everybody hates it, it's a very artificial contraption. So under the aegis of — let's say first the Western world — there will be some sort of confederation which will allow freedom to the people within: Scotland will no longer have to think about Westminster, Wales will be off on its own, so will the Basque country; all of the ethnic disturbances that are going on within the Soviet Union will be resolved. If these things balance out, it will be ideal for the human race: you would have a world state which could preserve the planet and stabilize the economy, and simultaneously you would give individual groups, tribes, and factions a chance to be themselves within that world state.

"It's far more likely that the bad guys will take over the world government, they'll forget to save the planet and we'll all be slaves.

"History is nothing but a record of the migration of tribes. The white race has had a very good millennium and has made very many enemies out of everybody and misbehaved very badly. So now we're forced to make new alliances." This is how he perceives *glasnost*.

"The Japanese hate us, and, which is worse, are contemptuous of us. They think we're just totally incompetent, less intelligent than they, lazy. They come in every quarter and buy treasury bonds that keep the government going. All they'd have to do is not come in one quarter. There's no way of keeping up this famous empire.

"America has not created a civilization. We've started, every now and then, but the waves of immigration meant we had to start all over again — to absorb people who had to learn the language, people who brought certain things of value but slowed down other things. Now we're taking in such huge waves, particularly from south of the border, who apparently do not intend to learn English or take our culture seriously at all — a whole new ball game.

"We did create the movies, which is the only thing we'll be remembered for.

"I repeat myself. I do this so well and so terminally. I'm paying a toll. I don't mind, I don't really mind at all. On the other hand, my blood pressure is very high, and I have to take a beta-blocker for hypertension."

A strange side effect of the medication Vidal takes for his blood pressure is that he is no longer able to cry. His eyes will not produce tears.

"We — Howard and I — go to Southeast Asia for at least one month in the winter." (I have asked him, so wintery in the evening sun, what he does to refresh and renew himself. Scenery was not what I had in mind.) "Thailand. I have many Buddhist friends and I've started to learn meditation for my blood pressure. To remain tranquil and serene — which can only be done by not wanting anything. And that's the trick. Not wanting anything, you are on your way to enlightenment, on your way out of a world of pain, a world that is painful because of desire. I am nowhere near being a candidate for that. I'm doing kindergarten exercises — you empty your head, all you think about is breathing, in and out, in and out — quite hard work, but it brings my pressure down. I know what true solace is but I don't turn to it. I'm too much a Westerner and I'm too shaped in the jungles of Washington to be anything but a carnivore.

"What is true solace? Not to be what I am. Stop thinking of yourself, stop thinking of what you desire. 'I find that when I do not think of myself I do not think at all.'"

"Are you afraid of death?"

"The Italians decide when you're going to be dead sometime before you are put away in the ground. You can see it in Ravello. You can see old people becoming nonpeople. I'm sure everybody's nice to grandfather at home; but in the square there comes a moment when no one listens to him, he is shut out. Nothing harsh about it. They're baby-mad, child-mad, and they're mad about themselves in middle age, but there comes a moment, a shadow line, when a person ceases to be a person to the town. Of course there's a sort of theatrical grief at the funeral. . . . Haven't you seen it in Ravello? In the square? The very old sitting in a line in front of the post office? And then one day the line thins out. . . .

"There are plenty more where we came from," he says.

"At my age," he says, "nobody is afraid of death. I think what you're afraid of is the passage to it. I think I might take a short cut."

I protest. Suicide sets a bad example, I say; and it is contagious. "There are plenty more where we came from," he says. "I don't think anybody has ever felt totally at home in human society."

Just down the street his servant is buying tangerines. The shop is brightly lit. The warm air is threaded with cold. In the piazza of the Pantheon everyone looks at home in his skin. The thin music of a flute comes from a wandering musician. Lovers hold hands.

The Godfather (1990)

✦ ✦ ✦

TAORMINA, SICILY. There is no sound in the courtyard of the Castle of the Slaves except for the insistent, thin, papery rustle of palm trees and the subdued swoosh of traffic outside guarded stone walls. Set among Mediterranean lemon trees and hot-pink bougainvillea, the miniature castle, silly and sinister, like a building in a fairy tale, looks as if it were dying from fungoid rot and mold. What those incised hooded eyes and curly ears on its aborted turrets symbolize no one, in this land of abundant symbols and fetishistic charms, knows; nor does there appear to be any architectural reason for the colonnaded pavilion that sits incongruously atop the mournful edifice the Sicilian sun refuses to brighten or to mellow — except, perhaps, to provide a vantage point and resting place for the sad ghosts of accumulated centuries.

Al Pacino's dog, Lucky, is digging up the garden.

Though I have never been here before I have been here before.

For all its otherworldly loopiness (it might have been designed by a quietly deranged child), the eighteenth-century villa is familiar, as familiar as archetypal objects in dreams are familiar. I experience the mingled dread and anticipation of revisiting the scene of a blood crime that belongs not to the real events of the real world but to the world of real dreams.

This is the place where, in *Godfather I*, the beautiful young wife of Michael Corleone (Al Pacino) was blown up in a car rigged, by a rival Mafia family, to kill Michael, the exiled son of Don Vito Corleone (Marlon Brando).

Godfather I and *II* — I feel this viscerally — are part of *my* history, *my* unconscious, lucid and gorgeous vehicles for primary themes of good and evil (and family) and sin and redemption (and family) and communion and alienation (and family), power and honor — and family. . . .

Francis Coppola, the movies' director, is here filming scenes for *Godfather III.* "It's only a movie," he says, "after all."

The set is hushed when Coppola, big, bearded, sloppy, walks on. He is followed by a pale old man who is chewing his cud ruminatively, a shuffling old man whose feet look tired in their old-man's shoes. The old man's layered cardigans are hitched up in the back. . . . I remember my father looking like this before he died, his sweaters riding up over his age-rounded shoulders. Poor old man on a cane, head bowed, fedora dusty. *Shouldn't somebody get that guy off the set?* a still photographer whispers; and suddenly there is a communal intake of breath: the old man is Al Pacino.

He dies. For the first of several takes he enters death gently. His old hands peel an orange, his heavy head nods, and he dies.

Would the Angel of Death claim Michael Corleone — this man in whom family feeling and evil are so intimately braided — so softly?

On the next take Pacino slumps in his chair, loses his precarious balance and falls, face hitting and scraping the gravel. Heedless puppies frolic over Michael Corleone's inanimate body. We are all motionless in the brilliant sunlight. And then Diane Keaton, Al Pacino's real-life girlfriend and Michael Corleone's ex-wife in the movie, swings her arms in a wide arc and applauds, breaking the spell, disrupting the magic. ("It's only a movie, after all.")

The next day, on the Corso in Taormina, a young antiques dealer remembers me from the set to which he has enterprisingly gained entrance: "He doesn't really die, does he?" he asks me; he pleads: "It's a joke, isn't it? He doesn't die?"

I tell Al Pacino, who says: "Did he mean me? Or did he mean Michael Corleone?"

"I don't think he could tell the difference," I say.

"Well, I can't tell the difference either," says Al Pacino.

And, in fact, reality and fiction intersect weirdly, tantalizingly, and electrically on the set of *Godfather III,* with its cast of thousands (and practically every member of Coppola's family involved or in attendance). The result is the kind of wild tension born of exhilaration and creative despair, which, if it doesn't kill art, nourishes and resolves. The organizer of the inner and outer chaos — the artist — is Francis Coppola. The crucible from which his art springs is that which his art broodingly and lyrically explores. From what Sicilian novelist Leonard Sciascia calls "the agonizing religion of family" come the *Godfathers*, the story of a Mafia Family told by a man obsessed with family.

"You want a scoop?" Coppola asks. "I'll give you a scoop. I'm not all that interested in *The Godfather*. I hate gangster movies. I hate violence. This is not the real world. There's nothing romantic about this," he says, and then, reversing himself, "brigands are always romantic," he says. Weary and irascible after 106 days of shooting, the man who perversely disavows the fruit of his unconscious soliloquizes disjointedly: "I don't hang out with those guys, with mafiosi. *Godfather* isn't my life," he says, a disclaimer meant as insurance, perhaps, against failure as spectacular as his previous *Godfather* successes. "Mickey Mouse was just a rodent."

I am hearing from Coppola the residue of restless conversations and quarrels he has endlessly with himself. He takes some decoding.

His wife, Ellie, who for twenty-seven difficult years has been his constant and most talented decoder, says, about Coppola's *Apocalypse Now*, "he could have made any film, a film about Mickey Mouse, and it would have turned out the same. It would have become a personal journey into himself."

When he is on target, as he was in the *Godfather* movies of 1972 and 1974, he carries us with him on the journey; his work mirrors our preoccupations, our agonizing journeys into family history and family mythology.

The feeling on the set — fraught with a monitored delirium — is that he is very much on target with *Godfather III*. The word *masterpiece* is on everyone's lips; so is the word *Shakespeare*. The crew and the actors are enlivened with the great expectations Coppola cannot quite disguise; he suggests that the themes of *Godfather III* are the themes of *King Lear*.

When he does not know he is being observed, Pacino, an introverted man, dark and beautiful, claws at the sky, his mouth open in a soundless howl of rage — this is mighty Lear brought low, screaming at the heavens, betrayed and rejected by those he best loves and trusts, stripped of all that gave life and power and riches meaning, suffering the unnatural grief of a man whose child dies before he does; and this is Michael Corleone, betrayed and rejected, embodying the principle that no man is destroyed except by his own actions.

"Do you love Michael Corleone?" I ask Coppola. "I am — I identify with him," Coppola says.

Godfather III is apparently a story of the pathology of violence and the pathology of finance, the story of Michael Corleone's starved and desperate desire for economic legitimacy.

An aging and diabetic Michael chooses the Vatican as the agency of his secular redemption; through venal Vatican bankers he wrests control of an Italian bank.

In 1982, the Vatican played a murky part in the billion-dollar collapse of the Banco Ambrosiana, and this provided the vehicle for Coppola's family story — this, and the revival of Europe as an economic power. *Godfather III* is as much like a cowboy movie as like a gangster movie — it is about frontiers: Michael's hopes reside in Europe.

How much more legitimate than the Mafia is Wall Street? How much more attractive? "In my time we earned our money with our courage and we paid for our failures in the harsh currency of death," says one of the Mafia dons. (A don much more closely resembles both the hero and the villain of a western than he does a thug. He is governed by a rigid code — *omertà*; a "man of honor," he would rather die than be dishonored. He is a man of virile silence — who is also, of course, a killer.) "These new ones drain all of it with a stroke of the pen. I defy and defend my tiny world against them."

This is good stuff. But at a deeper level *Godfather III* is not only a story about a Mafia Family, it is a story about families; it is about loyalty and love and betrayal, about the pain of seeking legitimacy within the family and for the family, and a story of the emotional violence in men's hearts. It is about the family as icon and reality, the family as the source of joy, sorrow, deformity, and redemption.

There is nothing that is not contained in the family, the institution to which, even if we are not pledged, we are bound. *Godfather III* is the story of Michael's needs, of Coppola's needs, and of our needs, into which Coppola has so brilliantly tapped. In the process he reflects and vivifies our divided views of the awesome power of the Church. He goes beyond an exploration of the materialism of religion; he taps into our experience of sin and our violently divided feelings about sin — its deliciousness, and our simultaneous need for absolution. He gives us the world, the flesh, the Devil, and God — all in the context of the family.

And he gives us a dazzling hero/villain, Michael Corleone (with whom he "identifies").

The Corleones are dangerous men to love. In our dreams is a simple formula of a simpler world: the men of a family want (and have) power, and the women of a family want (and need) protection. *Godfather* slyly offers the illusion that this contract is capable of fulfillment; and it just as slyly withdraws the offer. In Michael Corleone both our sentimentality and our cynicism find justification: When dangerous men become helpless, they become terribly appealing; and women, the caretakers and caregivers of the world, come with hearts full of love to the rescue. They welcome an opportunity to exercise pity and to extend mercy to the powerful who are powerful no longer.

In Coppola's films, women mediate between men and the world, between men and their own worst instincts and fates.

"Every family has bad memories," Michael says to his son, Tony, who rejects his father's ways. "The father is a drunk, the mother is a whore. A son takes to drugs, somebody dies young of cancer, a child gets hit by a truck. They live in poverty, they get divorced. Somebody becomes insane. Every family has bad memories."

The Coppolas have bad memories, too.

It is the fifty-sixth wedding anniversary of Francis's mother and father, Italia and Carmine Coppola; coincidentally, Francis Coppola is filming a wedding scene in an exquisite little baroque piazza high above the sea. Carmine's leonine head lolls and he drops off to sleep as his son, in heavily accented Italian, directs Italian extras and bit players. Carmine snores. Italia prods him awake: his snores exasperate her because they "bring shame to him." He opens an eye long enough to tell her they don't embarrass *him*. It's hard to know where their real tenderness begins and their mock irritation leaves off. Italia is wearing tight black pants, a not-altogether-clean fuchsia silk blouse, a reversible Chinese jacket with a Mandarin collar, men's brown polyester socks, and sling-back patent-leather spike heels. She has lipstick on her teeth and she is wearing bright green eyeshadow. She is seventy-eight.

While his mother and father play at quarreling, Francis directs Keaton and Pacino, who have joined the wedding party and are dancing together — it's the kind of scene he does so brilliantly, the encapsulation of the intimate within the spectacular. When the scene is over, Keaton, very much "on," greets Italia and Carmine and says, rather too brightly: "Fifty-six years! How *did* you *do* it?"

Carmine: "I survived."

Italia: "Can you advise me what to do with this man?"

Carmine: "That's why men die younger, they work."

Francis: "What does that mean, Pa? She scrubbed the floors and washed and waxed and cleaned and cooked. . . ."

Italia: "And I survived because I said Yes to everything — and kept the checkbook."

"I grew up very Italian-American, not like De Niro, who grew up American," Coppola has told me; he has been hearing these conversational feints and jabs all his life. He grew up watching domestic guerrilla theater, Italian-American style.

"I keep the books," Italia says; she is as talkative as Francis now is taciturn. "My Carmine lost all his money on Wall Street — if it was up to him we'd be living on potatoes and onions. I keep the checkbooks. I'm seven thousand away from a million dollars."

(Carmine Coppola invested five thousand dollars in the company that produced the futuristic Tucker car; Tucker's business collapsed. Years later Francis Coppola made a movie about Tucker; he has a passion for the beautiful cars . . . and what he and his family suffer is grist for his artist's mill. In the economy of an artist, nothing ever goes to waste.)

"Who are these people who ignore me, can you advise me?" Italia has taken a pointed dislike to one of Francis's assistants, who pays her little attention. Italia keeps score of slights; she is the caretaker of family grudges and animosities — for example, she is vocally indignant about relatives who "came out of the woodwork" when "Francie" achieved fame, even though "Francie" is eager to accommodate them:

"What am I, shit? Francie wouldn't be here if I didn't have him in my stomach. . . .

"I'll tell you a story. One of Carmine's brothers was in love with me too. He died. His mother said, Good. *Good?* Is that a way for a mother to talk? She said it would bring dishonor to the family if two men loved the same woman. She shouldn't have worried. I wouldn't have married him.

"Do you think Carmine should dye his hair? Can you advise me?

"I used to manage that man, Carmine, I was his business manager. I gave it up. Enough's enough. I made it work. I made everything work. I was his legal secretary and I made everything work. Enough's enough.

"I was born in Brooklyn, at 525 Grand Street, above the old Empire Theatre, you know that place? My brother was a trumpet player at Radio City Music Hall when Carmine played in the orchestra there, that's how we met.

"You know, he wanted to marry a beautiful blonde. But he hung around me. He got jealous when I danced with someone else. So I said, Dance with your beautiful blonde, Carmine. . . .

"They think the genius comes from Carmine's side. If Francie hadn't been in my belly, where would he be?

"My father gave Paramount Pictures its name, did you know that? You didn't know that. He brought American films to Italy. He wrote Neapolitan songs. Yeah, they sang one in *The God-father*.

"What do men know. I love that Ellie, she's a saint. I wouldn't put up with it. Even when Francie was with That Other Woman, he loved Ellie. And when That Other Woman wanted him to leave Ellie he wouldn't. Ellie — she stayed and she gained."

"Ma!" Francis's sister, Talia Shire, no longer the supplicant she played in *Godfather II*, plays an impressive matriarch this time around, dignified, honored. She seeks to stem the tide of her mother's confidences. (Francis Coppola is watching his mother from across the piazza; he looks exasperated . . . amused . . . alarmed . . . resigned.) Talia, pretty, practiced in small talk, casually friendly, talks about her three children, about diets. She tries to drive the conversation into neutral. Italia is undeterred:

"You know what we gave Francie for his birthday? We gave him twenty thousand dollars. I gave him ten thousand and that Carmine, he gave him ten thousand. Why not?"

Why not. Francis Coppola celebrated his fifty-first birthday in Sicily. His Zoetrope Studios are bankrupt, and he is faced with paying millions in disputed loans. He is also, as Ellie Coppola writes, in spite of the exuberance his physical amplitude suggests — a lap commodious enough to have accommodated any number of perching protégées and starlets and rumored to have done so — and despite his family, "lonely."

"Twenty thousand can't hurt," Italia says. She is full of sweetness for her son.

"Francie's brother Augustino has been writing a novel for twenty years, what do you think of that? He's better looking than Francie, six two." So Francie said he'd show him. He showed him. . . ."

Carmine Coppola's father was an immigrant, a tool-and-die maker, in fact a gun repairer. One day he passed the opera house in Rimini — Carmine tells me this story — and heard the flutes singing in the mad scene from *Lucia di Lammermoor*. He swore to himself that if he ever had a son, his son would be a flutist. Carmine Coppola studied flute and composition and won a scholarship to Juilliard. He was musical arranger for André Kostelanetz, and he played with Toscanini, whose protégé, he says, he was. "I was out to grab everything," Carmine says. When he won an Academy Award for composing the theme for *The Godfather* he thanked Francis for allowing him to write the music — "but if it wasn't for me Francis wouldn't be here," he said.

Long trestle tables in the Piazza SS. Trinità groan with peasant food — salamis and cheeses and olives and rough bread and wine — set on fine old embroidery. Food is important to Coppola, important in his life and in his movies. The actor Joe Mantegna, who is of Southern Italian descent, Sicilian and Barese, plays the part of Michael's enemy Joey Zasa; he says that when he was a kid in Oklahoma he saw *Godfather* scenes of Mafia guys cooking gravy in the kitchen — gravy being the tomato sauce used for Sunday dinners and for family gatherings of a grave or festive nature — "and I felt right at home, I belonged." In a food-phobic society *Godfather* appeals to the part of our natures that naturally celebrates abundance and excess; and it appeals to every fantasy or image we have of hearth as sanctuary, a place of undefilable sanctity and warmth.

The cloister of the pretty little church of SS. Trinità is overgrown with weeds, forlorn; among its scraggly pine trees the wardrobe department sets up shop. Jackie De La Fontaine, an assistant in the costume department, looks wonderfully out of place in her cowboy boots and hat, and wonderfully at home with Italia and with Carmine. She is the mother of Gia (Gian-Carla), Francis Coppola's three-year-old granddaughter, who is home, now, with Ellie. Gia is the daughter of Francis's older son, Gio (Gian-Carlo). Gio was killed in a motorboat accident on Memorial Day of 1986; he was twenty-two years old. Griffin O'Neal, the son of actor Ryan O'Neal, was operating the boat when it ran into a tow rope that decapitated Coppola's son and changed Coppola's universe.

Jackie De La Fontaine was bearing Gio's baby when he died. *Every family has bad memories.* Jackie has been taken into the family.

A Sicilian band plays sweet, haunting music. Coppola is using the Figli d'Arte Cuticchio, a family of Sicilian puppeteers, in his wedding scene. Wedding guests dressed in dove gray and black and moss green and grape and olive watch while the splendid puppets, as large almost as life, and more brazen, perform.

The Sicilian *teatro dei pupi* derives from the Norman code of chivalry, which for centuries Sicilians, harshly and unjustly ruled, observed. Puppets idealize the Crusades and celebrate the feats of Orlando, Charlemagne, King Arthur and the Knights of the Round Table. Whatever form the story takes, the moral is always the same: a man's most sacred possession is his honor. To safeguard their honor, and their property — including their families — Sicilian landowners hired armed men, governed by loyalty, austerity, and secrecy; they conducted their affairs violently, and in due time armies created in the name of family and honor became the societies called the Mafia.

"Observe and learn how a great man rules his world," says a Mafia don of Michael Corleone. Michael Corleone calls himself "old-fashioned." He is governed by ancient ideals of chivalry. There is in him a stillness, a civility, and a courtliness that is lost in the modern world. Brando, Don Vito Corleone, had it, and we responded with admiration and a kind of love; his courtliness allowed us to think of him as good. But the chivalry led to explosions of violence, to blood and death and devastation. The silence was shattered by murder.

In the story that the puppeteers are acting out now, the

knightly puppets tell of a father who kills his daughter because she has fallen in forbidden love with a cousin.

"Don't you think it scares me that my life is just a movie I'm making?" Coppola once asked.

When actress Winona Ryder left the Sicilian set of *Godfather III* because of "nervous exhaustion," Coppola had a brainstorm as predictable as it was unwelcome to the other actors on the set: in spite of the fact that Madonna had offered herself for the part, he cast his eighteen-year-old daughter Sofia as Mary, an Ivy League–educated young woman who handles Michael's philanthropic affairs, a volatile woman who falls in doomed love with her cousin Vinnie, the fiery bastard child of Michael's murdered brother Sonny.

Sofia is not beautiful. Francis thinks she is.

It seems now inevitable that Sofia was cast to play the part of Michael's daughter. Coppola is always making the movie of his life: Whom else would he cast as Michael's child?

Sofia Coppola and Talia Shire — two family members are part of the cast; three if you count a couple of lines spoken by Coppola's mother, Italia, in a group scene — for which, when last I saw her on the set, she was vociferously demanding union scale.

When he was ten years old, Coppola contracted polio and suffered temporary paralysis of his left side. To while away the painful hours between treatments, he played with toy soldiers and a Charlie McCarthy doll. Then he went to a military academy. He is at his best with children. He carries wind-up toys and junk jewelry and candy for them in his pockets. He is like the Pied Piper. He is sweet.

On the corner of Elizabeth and Prince Streets in New York's Little Italy a bullet-shaped aluminum-skinned van is parked. On it are written words that would appear runic if you didn't know they were the names of Coppola's Zoetrope films: *Rumblefish, One from the Heart, Gardens of Stone.* Francis calls this vehicle his "Silverfish"; it is equipped with a kitchen, a Jacuzzi, and masses of advanced electronic equipment that allow Coppola to edit film as he goes along. Sometimes, long distance, he directs his actors from it, like a puppeteer. He has it shipped across oceans.

"Come here," natty Carmine says, "this is the power corner, we're the bookies. Sit with us." He is sitting with director Martin Scorsese's father, they look like two old men in a village in Sicily discussing the affairs of the great world.

"What's that Scorsese bringing his whole family here for?" Italia mutters, protective, as always, of Francie. "Do you know," she says to Carmine, "she takes Pitman?" She means me. She likes me because I take Pitman shorthand; she is a woman who knows the value of practical skills.

"Do you know Mr. Applebaum?" Italia and I have discovered that we lived, at separate times, three houses away from each other on Seventy-fifth Street in Bensonhurst. And we both went to New Utrecht High School.

"Who's Mr. Applebaum?" I ask.

"A teacher at New Utrecht High School," Italia says impatiently, "did you know him?"

"No." As Italia is seventy-eight it is unlikely that we should have known the same teacher.

"Are you sure you went to New Utrecht High School?"

In a neo-Gothic church on Mulberry Street, the choir from St. Patrick's Cathedral sings, in golden light, as Michael Corleone, old and tired and ill, is knighted with the Papal Order of Saint Sebastian. (It is Saint Sebastian we see in Renaissance paintings, pierced by arrows; he is the patron saint of soldiers.) There is a wonderful moment when a handsomely dressed gangster walks down the aisle, prepares to genuflect — and then turns first to hand his hat to his bodyguard. Even before God, the Mafia preserves distinctions of rank (this is the kind of detail only a director of Coppola's background and genius would know to include).

Beat me, insult me, I still love and forgive you, sings Santuzza, the young girl in *Cavalleria Rusticana,* the theme of which is doomed love, treachery, and revenge.

Coppola's sister, Talia Shire, I was told, was badly beaten in *Godfather I.* The actor who played her abusive husband got "carried away" (for reasons I am requested to keep to myself).

The orchestra was conducted by Coppola's uncle, Anton.

The Coppolas' history is entwined with that of the Corleones.

Sofia, whose voice is small and whose handshake is unconvincing, says that she was the baby baptized in *Godfather I* — in that dazzling scene where Michael Corleone stands before God to reject, on behalf of his godchild, the world, the flesh, and the Devil, and in which, in a shocking cinematic juxtaposition, his minions mow members of a rival Family down with machine guns. Images of blood and water.

It was in this very church in which Francis Coppola's alter ego is being knighted that Sofia was (in "real life," which becomes more and more indistinguishable from film life) actually baptized.

"Did I tell you Mary gets killed?" Italia says. "I'm not supposed to tell you that."

Carmine Coppola and the father of director Martin Scorsese are discussing food. Fava beans: Do you peel them or not peel them? (Two Italians discussing food are like two Italians discussing politics; these matters matter.) Sheep's head with brains — "the sweetest meat is on the jawbone." Carmine has a friend who eats the eyes. Blood pudding — pig's blood — made with raisins, blood pudding made from the blood of kosher chickens. Gnocchi. Snails impaled on straight pins. A Neapolitan cheese crawling with white worms, a delicacy eaten with bread and wine. Sounds awful, I say. No, says Carmine, they're so strong the worms and cheese cancel each other out.

Like you and Ma, Francis says; You cancel each other out. He walks away before anyone can ask him what he means.

*I*nterviewing Mario Cuomo is not exactly like interviewing Suzanne Somers. I couldn't help thinking, when I undertook to write about the governor of New York, that I might be writing about someone who could conceivably change the course of our history. You tell yourself — or are told by friends and editors — that your obligations are to the truth: to the facts, and the truth of your observations. Then (the idea is) you go blithely on — as if the subject were Suzanne Somers. Well, it doesn't work that way. Not for me. I liked Mario Cuomo immensely; and I wanted him to run for the presidency. But — I am writing these prefatory remarks in the first week of December — the governor has not declared (yet . . . I think he will, which may be a function of my hoping he will); I wrote the original piece in June. He is a very hard man to keep up with, and I am reconciled to the fact that this piece may, in some aspects, be hopelessly out of date when he does (or does not) run; his character, however, remains unchanged, as characters do.

Mario Cuomo (June 1991)

◆ ◆ ◆

THE MAN many people regard as the last best hope of the Democratic Party is thinking aloud about Sophia Loren. The governor of
New York — in whom pragmatism and a passion for justice, as-
ceticism and love of the sensible world, ceremoniousness and sar-
casm, are nicely wedded — is sitting behind his desk in the state
capitol in Albany, the spatulate fingers of his enormous, well-
groomed, baseball player's hands splayed out on the desk that
used to belong to Franklin Delano Roosevelt. He is putting a
problem to a visiting photographer: Why is it, Mario Cuomo wants
to know (having met Ms. Loren at a public function, in the company, he is at pains to point out, of his sweetly pretty wife,
Matilda), that a woman whose features are almost disfiguringly
large — "her nose is too big, her mouth is too big, she has a man's
hands" — looks perfect in photographs, and is in fact so beautiful.
Taken separately, her features don't work; together they add up to
something remarkable.

He could almost be holding the mirror to himself. His gestures
are large and his nose is large and his mouth is large and his deep-
set large dark baggy eyes are dramatically hooded, and the defining lines of his fleshy fifty-nine-year-old face are so deeply etched
one feels one could read him like Braille. . . . He thinks he looks
like a frog. He owns a whole lot of oversized character and personality traits that ought to cancel one another out, but that, alchem-
ized together in him, are something remarkable.

He is the most formidable and the most glamorous man I have
ever met.

It would almost certainly surprise him to be described in this way. (He says women like his face "because I'm safe. I was the perfect guy to marry. Yessir. I look like somebody's uncle.")

It surprises *me* to be describing an elected official in this way. I am not alone in finding it impossible to be in Mario Cuomo's company without actively desiring his approval; he inspires a desire to know him and to be known by him — which may be one of the reasons members of the press act personally aggrieved when the governor is less than forthcoming. "The single best rule for the intelligent conduct of life and society is 'love,'" he once wrote; and the conviction that this politician actually believes and lives by this dictum is irresistible — you can't help wanting a piece of it.

Spending relaxed time with him is both cozy and stimulating; he is alternately comforting and prodding, soothing and scathing, half nurse, half inquisitor.

He is a dance of contradictions: sentimental and nostalgic, analytical and sardonic: He is adamant that the Gulf War achieved none of its objectives, but he speaks of General Norman Schwarz-kopf with affection and admiration: "He's a classy guy. Charis-matic. I can see why women think he's sexy — Matilda does. . . . Fairer and younger in person — blue eyes . . . much more posi-tive-looking when he's not giving a briefing on destruction. . . . He was a choir boy at West Point."

When I talk to him about Bensonhurst, where I grew up, he says, with the nostalgia all of us have for the landscape of our youth, "Bensonhurst. Still beautiful. What street? Seventy-fifth Street? Still the same. They still have the same *sfigliatele*" — Italian cheese pastries — "they still have *butchers!*"

And they have racially motivated killing — Bensonhurst is the place where a gang of white youths clubbed a black kid, sixteen-year-old Yusuf Hawkins, to death. "Yeah," he says, "they got some meaner kids than they used to have. Things have got meaner since we were young, more violent. I think about that a lot." He believes in the power of good men and women to motivate and to lead; he believes in what he calls "achievability." And he shares our confusions and alarms.

"We had the world war when we were kids, but in a sick way it was kind of a virtuous thing — the other side was evil and we were good. Good guys and bad guys, it was absolutely clear. . . . That's what Bush successfully did with Saddam Hussein — making him Dracula and Satan and Adolf Hitler. . . . We had that very comfortably with Mussolini and Hitler — you had a war that made you feel clean. Then we grew up into Korea. Korea was at the very best a mess. Then we had Vietnam. God, what a disaster that was! Then Watergate! . . . A period of disillusionment and ugliness — the U-2, the Bay of Pigs. . . . 'Gee, Kennedy lied to us? *Why?* He's so handsome, so nice.' We grew up out of our naïveté into a harsh recognition that government could fight stupid wars, government could lie to us, the CIA killed people . . . and then we had a president we had to depose . . . and all this while, for whatever insane reasons, we were getting better and better at destruction. Probably the most significant event was the atom bomb. We *used* it — and nobody even gave it a second thought. As a nation we felt unbothered by introducing into the world this incredible, impossible-to-control power. . . . It trickles down. Of course it doesn't justify violence — any more than your having been abused by your father justifies your becoming an abuser — but there is that emulating instinct in people. . . . And I think television had a lot do do with this: a lot of this was going on and we didn't know it when we were young. Now they're able to put all the ugliness on television every night — My Lai, whatever it is — they're able to show it to you immediately. Listen, I don't know all the reasons, but there's no question things are meaner now. . . . I have a guess that there's a lot more incest and child abuse going on now. Even if you assume that there was a lot of it in 1950, you didn't *know* there was a lot of it in 1950. Once you know, I think, it proliferates. It's contagious: 'Well, this is natural, all right, so I'll do a little abusing.' . . . I think it lets some barriers down. . . ."

He is, as a writer, admirably precise, and his public speeches, both lofty and colloquial, are models of lucidity and immediacy that speak to the heart and the viscera as well as the cultivated mind — as the world and the galvanized Democratic Party discovered when he gave the keynote address at the 1984 Democratic convention in San Francisco, inspiring hope that he would make a run for the presidency in 1988. (His published diaries are used as textbooks in college urban-affairs classes; he wrote his own television commercials during the gubernatorial campaign.) But he is singularly easy to misquote, because his words owe everything to context and because he often talks in semantic arabesques — if you don't actually *see* the commas and the quotation marks that indicate he's set up an inner dialogue with an imaginary Other for your edification, it's easy to distort his meaning, or to hang him with his own words. His voice, a beautiful expressive instrument, often contradicts his words — as an actor's will, to make a point. This can be confounding if you're not paying close attention. His razzle-dazzle speaking style and his verbal ellipses are jam for the press; but his eloquence has led many people to feel a betrayal that is a perverse form of love — he never promised us the Rose Garden, but the search for meaning beyond apparent meaning in his words goes on and on.

He retreats, when you least expect it, into sudden reticence; an iron curtain of introversion shuts down over his extraverted personality; like a lot of people who talk a lot, he is less accessible than his manner suggests. A very private public man, he is contemplative and meditative, as often high on silence as he is on gab.

He is prudent in action, judicious; he is also combative, and — his detractors say — prickly and impatient. He is clothed in power; and yet he says he is and has always been an outsider, a man who "take[s] power too seriously to be totally comfortable with it, . . . always out of place . . . just a little incongruous: baseball player, professor, campaigner, politician, father, husband — always a little too round for a square opening . . . or a little too square." He once said, "I don't enjoy waving at strangers — I feel as though I'm presuming on them." Try to imagine another politician saying that.

He is immensely charming.

And tantalizing. When he says, about the presidency, "I have no plans to run and no plans to make plans," everybody overanalyzes the data: He'd make a fabulous president but a lousy campaigner, say some, citing his irascibility. When he was playing minor league ball in Florida for the Pittsburgh Pirates he punched a catcher in the face — the catcher was wearing his mask at the time. Cuomo hasn't punched anybody lately, but he doesn't suffer fools gladly — although (another contradiction) he pays as much lively attention to a blue-collar guy who is urging the death penalty on him as he might to a head of state. At a meeting in a church basement he answers with kindness untainted by condescension the rambling question of a drunk who wanders in from the Bowery — everybody else is trying to shut the drunk up, even the pastor. Some people, desperate, perhaps, to solve the riddle of what they consider his enigmatic, if not coy, behavior, say that the governor has been reluctant to run because of a constantly painful bad back that requires serious medication — a difficult charge to credit if you've followed in his churning wake for a day or so, or watched him play a game of killer basketball with men years younger than he, including his twenty-two-year-old son, Christopher. Others — on no more evidence than that his name and the maiden name of his wife end with a vowel — say he's afraid of Mafia connections being unearthed. (The governor has a nightmare: "I'm in Brooklyn, and some clown says, 'Hey, Mario, lemme take a picture.' I say 'Sure,' and there's John Gotti standing next to me.") It's been suggested that he will run because challenge, more specifically the scent of failure, is an intoxicant to him (which wouldn't explain why he did not place himself in the running in 1988). For everybody who says that, there is someone to say that he has a morbid fear of failure (which wouldn't explain why he ran for governor — and won — when pollsters gave him no chance to win against New York City Mayor Ed Koch).

When Mario Cuomo lost the New York City mayoralty contest of 1977, his son Andrew, the governor's trusted advisor, hugged Matilda, and he cried. "I swear Pop will never lose another race," he said.

The task assigned to us is to climb towards the light. . . . The soul can only rejoin God after having traversed a specific path. . . . Each one of us has his Jacob's ladder, whose rungs are formed of a series of objects. . . . The heart of God is boundless. . . . And yet in all that immensity there is only one possible place for each one of us at any given moment, the one we are led to by unflagging fidelity to the natural and supernatural duties of life.

Those are the words of Mario Cuomo's spiritual mentor, Teilhard de Chardin, a paleontologist who was also a priest, a Jesuit who loved the world. It is quite possible to interpret the career of Mario Cuomo as a climb toward the light, as he sees the light. Perhaps the reasons for his reluctance to run are pure and simple: a dutiful man, he needs to be sure he is on the right rung of the spiritual ladder at the right time, on the specific path that will lead him to God, balancing the state of the Union, and his ability to enhance it, with his husbandly obligations to Matilda, whom he has vowed to cherish.

It makes Americans nervous when their elected officials act as if their actions might be governed by their relationship with the Almighty; presidents are supposed to go decorously to church once a week and invoke God's name in times of war or natural disasters; a lot of people were less than thrilled when Mario Cuomo's friend Jimmy Carter allowed as how he was "born again."

There is nothing pale-pious or ecclesiastical in Mario Cuomo's manner. . . .

Da-da-da-da, Da-da-dum-dum. . . . He hums a jingle. "What's that?" he says. "'Mary Noble, Backstage Wife' or 'Helen Trent'? *Dida-ling-ding-ding ding.* Who was that? 'Just Plain Bill' or 'Lorenzo Jones and His Wife Belle'? 'Who knows what evil lurks in the hearts of men? The Shadow knows.' Who drove the car for the Shadow? Who was his girlfriend? Margo. Lamont Cranston and Margo. I'm an expert on the radio soaps. *'Jack Armstrong . . . Jack Armstrong . . . JACK ARMSTRONG . . . The Aaaall-American Boy.'* . . . 'Have you tried Wheaties?'" As a kid in Queens, he was listening to the Shadow when he heard that Pearl Harbor had been bombed. . . .

"Madonna? What do I think of Madonna? She's nice if you like Madonna. Me, I like Merle Oberon. . . . Robert Mapple-thorpe, who's Mapplethorpe, what am I supposed to think of him? *That's what I think.*" He shrugs and scratches the underside of his chin and extends his palm in an Italian gesture both economic and symphonic, usually accompanied by a sound that is half grunt, half sigh: "*Eeehh.*" This is untranslatable, but it means, roughly, "So what, do I care?" "People think I'm cursing when I do that. 'Ooooh, I saw you on television, you did that to curse someone.'"

"What does this mean?" He makes a gesture, forefinger and little finger extended, that I think signifies the Evil Eye. "No. No. *Cornuto.* Now you're gonna learn something, now you're gonna thank me. After all this is over, you're gonna say, 'One thing this guy did for me, he taught me something I never knew and I should have known because I was from Bensonhurst.' This is *cornuto* — horns: 'You are the horned one, you are the goat, you are the cuckolded one, you have been made a fool of.' . . .

"The men's movement, what's that? There's a men's movement? As in male/female? What the hell is a men's movement?" I tell him about the latest human-encounter therapy from California — men imitating primitive rites, sitting in sweat lodges and holding walking sticks and trying to get-in-touch-with-their-feelings. "Ask me another question. How the hell did I miss the men's movement?" He looks pleased as punch to have missed it. And he looks as if he's eaten an unripe persimmon.

"What century would I like to have lived in? The nineteenth. Why? Because it's the only one I know. You wanna hang around and play nice games? I'll play games, I'll talk about the eighteenth century: 'That seemed great to me, I'll go back there.' Forget about it. How would you brush your teeth? 'The Renaissance period seems perfect to me.' You kidding? No bathrooms. . . . I'm not a great historian, but I've lived half a hundred years now, and I've read a whole lot. I don't think times are terribly different. I think the basic things in life don't change a lot. The insecurity is always there, the little bits of joy are always there, the confusion is always there, the tendency to despair is always there and always will be there. When we grow ailerons and superintelligences, we may diminish some of these aspects, but until we leave the category *human* — which is what Teilhard says is what is meant to happen when we all become perfect and the whole universe grows up into heaven — until then we're gonna be what we are, what we've always been. . . . People are always the same. . . . What's an aileron? I don't know." The governor puts a closed fist on either side of his forehead and wriggles both forefingers to ape the "flying green creatures" that have ailerons.

"Christopher, now. He likes the fifties, the fifties were great, the suits, the music, nice, a gentler time. I liked it. But I like this time, too. What do you like more about the fifties? That you were young? Oh, well, that's different. You have to give some things up, too, you know. 'Too soon old and too late smart.' What did you know when you were young? You wasted all those years."

Well, he doesn't seem prickly to me. But I am suddenly aware of the fact that the man with whom I am joshing, the man who indulges me when I play games, this volatile leader who is in an unusually relaxed mood, may someday change the course of human affairs. ("Volatile? Me? No. *Mercurial.* Volatile could explode. Not me. I'm easy. Mercurial, you move all the time, you're tough to pick up, fast, you go through changes and phases. . . . Volatile is Sicilian — like Matilda. Volatile is Calabrese — like your people. Me, I'm Neapolitan. That's where the music comes from. All those songs you hear in all the cantinas of the world — Neapolitan. *W'e Marie / quanda sono che pensa per te . . . Vicin' u Mare . . ."* he sings. In dialect, he sings.) I apologize for playing games: "You don't really like playing games, do you?" I say.

But he is expansive: "Not necessarily. Remember spin the bottle? Do you remember spin the bottle, Tom? Did they have that game when you were a kid? . . . The Irish, they'll lie to you, you know, they're not like us."

Us. Tom, his press aide, is Irish. Like the governor (whose line of chat is reassuringly secular), I'm Italian. It will be suggested that he manipulated me, making much of my Italian-ness, his Italian-ness. I don't think so; I think his charm is intuitive, not calculated. I don't *feel* manipulated. After all, it's a nice human instinct to meet a person on grounds where you think you stand the greatest chance of connecting. He touches you at that point where you will feel individually acknowledged and enriched.

The governor is a religious man; religion provides the under-pinning for his thoughts and his agenda. But he's not a prosely-tizer: he respects goodness and achievability where, and in what-ever form — secular or religious — he finds it. In a speech to the American Stock Exchange he said: "Forget about love and compas-sion. That's too complicated for civics. Let's just talk about what you need to have an economy in this country. . . . The poor are in trouble. . . . The poor are getting poorer. That's true. They're *our* poor. They're our family. Even if you don't feel that as a religious matter, a spiritual matter, it is true as a practical matter. We cannot do without them. We cannot afford to set them loose and watch them drift away. It's not like that. You will drift with them."

To me — because I ask him if he still believes that it is possible "to make gentle the soul of man" — he says: "God meant for us to finish the work of creation. The Teilhardian idea is that He got it started and He places it now in our hands to advance it in the next stages. We are supposed to work with the miracle of creation; we are supposed to fulfill creation; we are supposed to improve the universe. We're not doing that too well now."

Bigotry, which Governor Cuomo rightly equates with stupid-ity, is far from dead, and a lot of people are scared of the prospect of a Catholic in the White House; but the rabid Know-Nothing anti-Catholicism of the last half of the nineteenth century has "virtually died. Kennedy had something to do with it. But I'll tell you what had a lot: the abortion argument in recent days . . . because it's clear now that you can be a Catholic and not feel compelled to do everything that every bishop would instruct you to do. . . . The ultimate norm of right conduct is living in conformity with a well-prepared conscience."

The governor has evoked the ire of New York's Cardinal O'Connor for his stand on abortion, and the wrath of proponents of the death penalty for his opposition to capital punishment. Some of his critics have seen an inconsistency in his supporting *Roe v. Wade* while at the same time opposing the death penalty. I had trouble understanding why he cited "lack of consensus and absence of a plurality of opinion" as factors contributing to his not opposing abortion. After all, I said, there is evidently no plurality of opinion against the death penalty either. He doesn't see it that way. His arguments are lawyerly: "I do not say that for a Catholic it would be wrong to kill. . . . In self-defense — to protect Matilda — I probably, under exactly the right circumstances, would feel justified in killing to protect another life. You might even make the case that you were *required* to defend your own life, which really belongs to God, even to the extent of killing someone, if that's the only way to prevent them from killing you.

"But I believe the death penalty as a civic response to murder is demeaning, debasing, degenerate, unavailing. It probably makes things worse instead of better, does not deter but rather encourages further violence, because it is an instruction in violence; it's the whole government saying, 'This is the best we can do when confronted with the ultimate violence — respond with the ultimate violence.' It is unfair because in our particular kind of democracy it almost always will be applied to madmen and madwomen who volunteer for it, or to people who can't afford the best lawyers. It is used to eclipse more intelligent responses to crime, and I am passionately against it.

"The Catholic Church teaches that abortion is wrong. The Catholic Church teaches — now — that life begins at conception; I pause to remind you that this has not always been the teaching. But I accept it to be a Catholic now, because I'm living now.

"When we had children, we lived by that rule. That's fine. But that's nobody's business. That's my business, Matilda's business, maybe my confessor's business. I happen to share it with you now, and I shared it with the public in a speech at Notre Dame.

"Now comes an entirely different question: What is and should be the law for this pluralist democratic society? The democracy has created a law, through the Supreme Court, that says a woman under certain circumstances will have the right to abortion. Are you permitted to live by the law if you are the governor? Are you permitted to say, 'I will protect your rights under *Roe v. Wade*'? Of course you are. As a matter of fact, you are obliged to do that as governor. . . . The oath you take as governor is to support the constitutional law. Does the Church allow you to do that? The answer is yes. . . . The Church has always said that you must act prudentially, on the civic side, as your conscience instructs you.

"Take birth control, a better example than abortion because it's clearer. Are you telling me that all the cardinals and the bishops who vote for politicians who are ardently in favor of birth control are committing sins? Are you telling me that all the cardinals and bishops and monsignori who are ignoring the chance in their pulpits on Sunday to condemn birth control are doing something wrong? What is it that allows the Church to acquiesce in your use of birth control — notwithstanding the fact that teaching it is a violation of the natural law? It is called prudential judgment. . . . Allowing people to live by their consciences and by the law in a democratic society — that doesn't violate anything I believe as a Catholic.

"In this country there is no law that says abortion is wrong. If it becomes the law, then you have to live by *that* law; and if the law says it's murder, it is murder by the civic law."

The governor's values were honed in the bosom of his family. So were his anecdotes:

"Talking like this is your idea of working? Forget it. This is an Italian's idea. . . . The Milanese comes down from the north — hardworking, sixty, sixty-five years old — comes down to Napoli. And there, middle of the afternoon, is a guy sitting by the water — young man, maybe twenty-one, twenty-two — and he's fishing. The Milanese says, 'Hey, what're you doing there?' 'I'm fishing.' Milanese says, 'Eeeehhh, you gotta work, you gotta work hard, you gotta get yourself a job and then you gotta get the money and save the money, then you retire, nice, you move around, maybe you go fishing.' The young man says, 'Nice, but that's what I'm doin' now!' Italians have an expression: If you get the overwhelming desire to work, sit down, be quiet, it will pass."

This is not advice he has taken to heart. He's almost defensive — he's funny — when he insists that he does, really does, know how to relax: "I can sleep a lot," he says, as if it were something remarkable, "when there's nothing to do. I mean I'll lie down watching the ball game and I'll fall asleep. . . . I like getting out of bed in the morning when I know there's something to do. But if I know there's gonna be nothing to do, I can take it easy." He says this as if a nap were a feat worthy of inclusion in the *Guinness Book of World Records.* He has been known to ask his aides, "What do you *do* at the beach?" He doesn't get it. His idea of a vacation is to drive to another town and have dinner alone with Matilda — which is the way they celebrated their last anniversary. He comes by this naturally:

His father, Andrea — whose name, which he pronounces André, he loves to hold in his mouth — came to America from a small town near Naples; his mother, Immacolata (Macu) lived in a four-hundred-year-old mountain building that was once a monastery, a house with a dirt floor, no electricity, and no indoor plumbing until after World War II. It was destroyed in the great earthquake of 1980. Jimmy Carter sent Cuomo to Italy on *Air Force One* as part of a relief task force. And he saw a collapsed church in which more than a hundred people, most of them women and children, had been killed. "They went to the church for refuge and the roof fell in. And the poor Italians — they would look at you and say, 'Why? Why would God do that?' That was tough."

When Andrea and Macu came to America, they had no skills, no money, no English; Andrea couldn't read or write. . . . One of the reasons the governor gives for believing New York City will make it — AIDS, crime and drugs notwithstanding — is that, aside from the fact that it remains the city where young people go to find their lives and their success (30 percent of New Yorkers were born somewhere else), the new immigrants come with skills and money, "better prepared to help in a city that has the water, the history, the people, the banks, the P.R. firms, the service industries. . . . They can buy brownstones in Brooklyn immediately, Korean fruit stores immediately" — whereas his father labored as a ditch digger in Jersey City (one can only imagine the iron necessity that drove people out of beautiful Naples to come to grimy Jersey City); he made trenches for sewer pipe.

The senior Cuomos moved to South Jamaica and opened a grocery store (and Mario Cuomo's belief in the durability of the American dream, as well as his feeling that he is a permanent outsider, can be traced to this time): "We had no bilingual education in South Jamaica. I didn't speak English well when I was young; in speech class I refused to give speeches; and it wasn't even an Italian community. At St Monica's Church we didn't even have an Italian priest. . . . You were born in South Jamaica? You probably owed my father money. Everybody owed us money. I still have the book. You'd come to the grocery store and we'd put your name in the book — a dollar fifty, seven dollars. When they'd get up to about forty, fifty dollars, no more credit. If they got up to forty or fifty and you didn't see them for a few days, that meant they moved to Newark."

Jamaica is part of the borough of Queens. "You never saw a movie about Queens. In all the movies they lived in Brooklyn — Brooklyn was the only place with ethnics, Brooklyn was the only place with neighborhoods. Brooklyn made it to the movies, Queens got nothing but disrespect. When you landed at La Guardia Airport — which was in Queens, in the city of New York — all the signs said TO THE CITY, like Queens didn't belong to the city. . . . I never left Queens." He says this good-naturedly, self-mockingly. . . . Success doesn't altogether obliterate past hurts.

One of three children, Cuomo was the only one to go to college, where, he says, he would have been "an odds-on favorite to be voted least likely to become a public person. Asocial. I was not a natural for public life, I never have been. I was a good lawyer and reasonably successful, and I never had a client in the house in twenty years. I never brought anyone home. Are you kidding? In my house? Forget it. My house is for my kids and my family. Friends, sometimes. But never a client or a partner. . . . Matilda is perfect at the public life. She goes to Italy, Spain, Japan . . . you put her anywhere, anytime — with the Rockefellers, with the Whitneys — she goes to the track at Saratoga and takes the governor's box; I went once and I didn't like it. They took my picture and put it with a horse. . . . If I can skip a speech, I will. I don't like giving up my privacy. Opening yourself to the world is not an easy thing to do."

They met in the cafeteria of St. John's College in Queens. She was a sober young woman, attracted to him, she says, because "he was very serious. My mother told me, 'He's very sincere, he'll never hurt you.'"

He had a scholarship to law school. On their third date he met her on the front stoop of her parents' house in Flatbush (stoops being halfway social gathering places in Brooklyn, neither within the defined confines of the home nor completely outside the sphere of parental influence); he had signed up to play baseball with the Pittsburgh Pirates. And she said, "Oh I'd never marry a baseball player." She still wears the modest diamond engagement ring he gave her when her when he received his bonus from the Pirates. For a combination of reasons — including, one supposes, Matilda's disapproval and his father's, combined with his getting beaned and finding himself in what sportscaster Red Barber used to call good old rhubarbs — Cuomo's career, especially after he was hit in the head and crashed into what Matilda (who has only a nodding acquaintance with sports terms) calls the back fence of the ballpark (he was taken out on a stretcher and spent two weeks in the hospital), was short-lived.

She was the breadwinner during his first year in law school; she thought that he would be a judge: "Maybe on the federal supreme court?"

Matilda's father was an immigrant, too; but he was a master carpenter, and "did very well for himself, God bless him. He spoke English well, and he went to Washington, and against a lot of competition he acquired big contracts for balsa-wood life rafts during the war. Then his whole factory went up in flames — could have been sabotage — and he lost everything. . . . He tolerated my husband's being Neapolitan" (Matilda Cuomo never refers to her husband by name or honorific; he is always "my husband"). "Nobody knew the Cuomos, nobody knew the family. In that generation, you married a fellow because you knew the aunt, the uncle. . . . I was very concerned that my dad didn't seem to care who this fellow was. But then I found out from my mother-in-law that her neighbors were coming into the grocery store saying that there was a man driving around in a big Cadillac asking who the Cuomos were. That made me feel good." When her husband ran for office, her father, who by that time was building supermarkets — Waldbaum, Key Food, Scoturo Brothers — would go to all the chain stores, "see a poster of Koch and knock it down, go get one of my husband."

But this was after success had come to the Cuomos. When they first got married, they lived in a furnished apartment. The only new thing they had, the governor says, was a green sofa, newly upholstered, given to them because "the landlady fell in love with Matilda. . . . And the only thing we had in the place that was our own was a mattress, because my mother wouldn't let me sleep on someone else's mattress.

"Then we moved to a third-floor walk-up," Cuomo says. "I hadn't finished school. Matilda was pregnant with her second child. I said, 'Pop, Matilda can't work anymore' — she was teaching — 'you gotta put me in your house.'"

On the evidence, Mario Cuomo assumed responsibility for his wife and children; if he applied for help it was to *his* family, not to her far more affluent one — he kept the conventional contract.

"Pop didn't even have a bedroom. So we slept for about a year on a sofa in the living room — we hung a blanket on an arch for privacy. When we walked in carrying our few possessions my father said [presumably because the Cuomos took seriously the Church's command against artificial contraception], 'You and that pope — I knew you were gonna get me in trouble.' He wasn't the world's most religious man. And then the walk-up — you hadda carry a baby carriage up three flights of stairs; and every time you had a baby you had to worrry about how you were gonna make it, how you were gonna pay for this kid. . . . We had a good life. But it was hard in those years. Especially for Matilda," who had never, in her single days, had to worry about money. Finally they moved to a $24,000 Cape Cod house. Mario finished the basement and the attic and added rooms — and they raised five kids there, with no outside help. It wasn't, by anyone's account, easy.

Cuomo came to prominence in New York City chiefly on the strength of his *pro bono* intervention on behalf of people in Corona, in Queens, who were fighting the city bureaucracy to keep their schools and their homes from the bulldozer. Thereafter Mayor John Lindsay asked him to mediate between the prosperous Jews of Forest Hills, Queens, and the city, which was planning to build housing for low-income and welfare families in Forest Hills. (He achieved a successful compromise.)

It wasn't surprising, given that in every marriage there is *his* marriage and *her* marriage, that there is a slight difference of emphasis in each of their stories when they discuss those days. In his published diaries, Cuomo writes of Matilda's being "understandably unhappy with the fact that I haven't been able to provide her with the things her friends have."

Matilda says: "The kids had to go to college, and he had that obligation, that responsibility. My father put five of us through college. . . . The Corona people, they started living in my house; instead of paying him, they were giving me sauce — tomato gravy — and more sauce, and more gravy. . . . I don't know what Lindsay would have done without him. But I was with the children, it took a lot of time from me. He said, 'Let's give something back.' Maybe it wasn't the right time. When *is* the right time? I believe in destiny. The right time is God's time."

She is wearing a perfume called Madeleine by Madeleine, given to her by her daughter Madeleine. The Cuomos have three daughters and two sons. Margaret, the oldest, is a radiologist; Maria is an entrepreneur; Madeleine is a lawyer with a small New York law firm, in her first year of practice — she likes litigation, the courtroom, "and the combat," her lawyer father says. The Cuomos have three grandchildren.

Maria is married to Kenneth Cole, the shoe designer — "factories in Spain, Japan, all over the world," the governor says. When he told his mother that Maria was going to marry Cole, he said, with some trepidation, "Ma, the first thing is, he's Jewish." His mother said, "Jewish? That's nothing, they'll work that out. But why did she have to marry a shoemaker?" When Ethel Kennedy — whose daughter Kerry is married to the Cuomos' oldest son, Andrew — met the governor's mother, she said, "What an extraordinary woman, so poised." "No, not poised, Ethel," the governor said. "What you mean is that she didn't fall down when she met a Kennedy."

*

Christopher, the Cuomos' younger son, was only four years old when his father entered public life; his parents worried about him: "We went through all these experiences as a family, and that was beautiful," the governor says. "But Chris was locked out — he was too young. . . ."

Christopher greets his mother in the executive mansion she has had refurbished with money from the private sector. (It is impossible to imagine the restless governor sitting in designer Mark Hampton's chintzy-flowery-tame dining room — and impossible to imagine Cuomo denigrating Matilda's tastes.) The good-looking young man is as sweet and loving and respectful as any parent could wish. He's a honeybunch. He's just finished reading his father's published diaries. "Man," he told his father, "you had a lot of guilt, always worried about not doing enough for us" — guilt that the six-foot-two, 211-pound Yale senior doesn't think his father earned. He's captain of the rugby team, and he's thinking about law school, struggling with the inequities of the legal system already; his fair brow is creased with concern. . . .

Cuomo men mature early. Andrew Cuomo is thirty-three; he's been working for his father for seventeen years. He started by putting up posters "and tearing down the other guy's — he had a couple of real big fistfights, it was terrible." By most accounts his is the political voice the governor most closely heeds; Andrew was running the Bronx mayoralty headquarters in 1977, when he was only nineteen. The governor likes to tell stories about him:

"'When he was thirteen, fourteen, he went into business cutting people's grass — tremendous with his hands, automobiles, engines of any kind. Took old lawn mowers, rebuilt them, used them. Went into business with Frankie Vitale, Pete the Cop's son from next door. Their slogan was We Clip You Good. He never took a penny from me to go to school. Went to Fordham, political science, and never took a penny. He worked on AAA emergency trucks all night every night; he'd sleep on the floor in the den next to the phone, with his grease-monkey outfit on, and if it rang he'd get up, jump in a truck, go out on a call, come back. If he needed four or five hundred dollars more, he'd go out, buy an old beat-up car, work on it for a week, two weeks, sell it, make a coupla hundred. Never once came to us for a penny."

Andrew builds transitional, affordable housing for the homeless and the working poor, with construction grants from public sources; his nonprofit organization, HELP, provides what he calls "a continuum of care" — day care, recreation, counseling, health and other on-site services. "The program works," he says, "because it works." It is a model of its kind.

Sometimes, Matilda Cuomo says, she and her husband "look at each other and he says, 'How did you do it?' Raising five children with no help. I opted to stay home till Christopher was in the third grade," and then she went back to teaching. "I don't know how any mother could say she's bored. The way feminists started turned off a lot of people because they were too strange — they almost wanted to make the homemaker feel guilty. My God! It is glorious, taking care of children. You actually have in your hands your child, whom you can mold. What is better? I mean, you have to be everything to that child. . . ."

Matilda Cuomo has some of her husband's speech patterns, but she wears them differently, as if she were holding an invisible pointer, gesturing to an invisible blackboard. . . . She used to make cupcakes for the Girl Scouts. In the renovated, blue-and-white-tiled kitchen of the mansion (she has cut the domestic staff far back; there were four chefs when she came, now there is one) she keeps neat books labeled "Summer Recipes," "Winter Recipes." She cooks her husband's favorite foods on weekends — lamb shanks baked till they fall off the bone, crisp potatoes. . . .

The governor uses the family as a model for governing; this image ignites passions; it antagonizes some people who are in unconventional living arrangements. "I'm not talking about a paterfamilias, a mother figure, a father figure," he says. "I use the analogy in a slightly different way. The essence of the family is you share blessings and burdens. Families were organized in primitive times to protect against the beast, against alien forces; that notion of community, that notion of serving one another's needs, simple as it is, that's the essential notion. It's what we've been missing in our national government the last ten years, when we had the period of the individual instead of the period of the community: 'God helps those whom God has helped. If He left you out, don't ask us to make the adjustment. If you're not making it, it must be that you did something wrong. All that the government will do for you is not get in your way, and protect you against foreign enemies. For the rest, you're on your own. And if you're homeless, you probably need to be. And if you're poor, it's probably because you're lazy. We're not gonna knock ourselves out helping you; you're supposed to help yourself. It's a government for the fit and the fortunate, and those not fit and less fortunate — that's not our concern.' That kind of individualism they dressed up — you know, the pioneer heroes and frontier macho — the whole image was the individual who did it by himself. 'I don't need you, and I don't need government.' Well, that's very nice. Except the world isn't like that.

"I have these five beautiful kids, five great kids. Now, if I had taken Andrew when he was two years old and emptied him out into South Jamaica as it is now, with people fornicating *on the streets* — I took the State Police to visit there — three o'clock in the afternoon, on the damn street, in the middle of the afternoon! Now, you put a kid out there where he learns to become familiar with the sound of gunfire before he ever hears an orchestra . . . and you tell me he's gonna grow up to be Andrew, who houses the homeless, who's charming, who marries Kerry Kennedy? If Margaret's mother had men over every night and was living on welfare, do you think Margaret was gonna get to be a doctor? What is the chance that they're gonna wind up that way? The difference between my kids and their kids is the accident of the environment. That kid you empty out into the street, he's gonna need something, he can't do it on his own. And that's my emotional family, sharing my blessings and my burdens. . . .

"Bush? Oh, Bush is a good man. He's American. He's honorable. He's sacrificing now to be president. I think his intent is good. I think he's probably a very civil kind of person. A man of great civility. . . . You say I'm describing a Wasp? Could be. It's a definition that conforms to lots of things. . . . He has to take abuse, he has to make terribly difficult judgments, he has to sacrifice his peace of mind, his family, he has to make his children vulnerable. . . . If his son had been the son of an oil dealer, it's one thing. It's another thing if the son of the *president* is involved in the S & L scandal. . . . He has to live with his conscience. He has to give the instructions to kill hundreds of thousands of people. Why should I assume that wouldn't bother him as much as it would me? I assume it would."

This is quintessential Cuomo: the compassion, and the irony that is like a gleaming dagger.

The governor's official plane has been forced down sixteen times because of mechanical problems. This is not reassuring. ("The helicopter's worse," he says.) The plane is taking the governor and aides to Pleasantville, New York. What would happen if the plane crashed, I ask. "From this height?" the governor says. "Splash. Splat. Listen, the worst you can do is get killed. Your daughter's a theologian — she's the first to understand that the ultimate vindication comes *after* the plane goes down. Am I scared? I used to be concerned that if, God forbid, anything should happen, it would be bad for the family. Now, they'd still miss me a little bit, but it wouldn't be so bad as when they were very young. Couldn't hurt, really. It happens to so many people." Death, he means. "You're gonna live forever? See, in my case, I have the exquisite-timing problem. If I wait too long, Matilda won't be able to marry again, and that's not fair either."

Chit-chat on a stuttering plane.

"Would I read my kid's diary if he left it around? My answer to you is no," he says, leaving no room for doubt that the real answer is yes. "How could you resist it? What, are you crazy? If they're still in the house? If they're eighteen, nineteen, even twenty? What would drive you to read it would be sick curiosity. Or healthy curiosity. What you would provide as a rationale is 'I have to know whether this kid is on drugs. Is he in trouble? I have an obligation to read it.' You don't really have an obligation to read it. The difficult thing is, what happens when you find out that he's got a girlfriend?

"Here's a true story that shows you how silly parents can be. The short version: Andrew is maybe seventeen years old, maybe sixteen. Of course he's a very attractive kid and he has a lot of friends — and I don't like to think about that. I've never had a discussion with any of my kids about sex. Why? Number one, they know more than I do about it, it's an embarrassment. I don't like to have a discussion with them where they have the advantage. Secondly, parents are not the best place to get it from. . . . So we don't get into things like that; but I know he has girlfriends, and that's fine. So. I get up very early in the morning, it's still dark.

[Now he enters the past, speaking in the present tense.] And I forgot to put my stuff out the night before, so I have to feel around in my drawer for my briefs. The damn thing is empty, no briefs. Where could my briefs be? Uh-*huh!* I go upstairs to Andrew's bedroom. Andrew's sleeping. I go to the built-in drawers where I know he keeps his underwear, and I reach in and I feel around and I pull out what I think are a pair of my briefs. I go into the hall, close the door to his bedroom, and turn on the light to see what briefs I've come away with.

"Here are a pair of bikini briefs. With zebra stripes.

"I go crazy. *Whaaat is THIIIS????* This is terrible. I open his door. . . . *Matildaaa!!!* Look what your son is doing!"

The roar of the plane, and his own laughter, drown the governor's reminiscences, but not for long.

"Maria kept bringing home these boys. 'Dad, she said, I don't ask you for a lot, can I ask you for one thing? Will you stop making those faces at the guys when they pick me up?' 'What faces?' 'Those terrible faces. Your face gets hard and cranky as soon as you meet them.' I said, 'Well, have I ever said anything wrong to any of them?' 'No,' she said, 'you don't have to. Just, "I'll be here when you get back."'

"They make you feel so foolish. What parenthood drives you to is really pathetic."

The governor gave a talk to Andrew's high school graduation class. "I hate commencement addresses, they're so presumptuous. Who am I to give these people advice? I'm reluctant to give my own kids advice; I always start the same way, by apologizing."

He is the father you wish you'd had.

"So I talked to the parents instead. 'Remember when they were getting older, remember when they started going out with that gorilla down the block, how you went crazy? The first time they were driving a car, how you worried? The first time they took a glass of beer? *God forbid they did what I did.* Remember all those nights when you promised them you wouldn't wait for them to come home? So you waited till you heard the car; then you turn off all the lights, but you listen to see whether their footsteps are sure — God forbid they're drunk. . . .

"'Let's face it. Who are we? Who are we to teach them about love when they heard us arguing in the bedroom? Who are we to teach them about making a better world when we gave them two wars? Who are we to teach them how to connect to God when we have failed so many times ourselves? Who are we to say, Don't worry about life, when we're still scared to death about them? And I'll tell you something. When they get married, we'll be worried; when they have kids we'll be worried. We'll never be confident that they can do it right. So let's abandon the notion of giving them any advice. Lemme tell you something. When I look at them now, they're bigger, smarter, and better than we were.'

"What I wanted to impart to them was: We love you. Forgive us. We worry about you all the time. We make dumb mistakes. We're clumsy about it . . . but that's the way we are; and probably that's the way you're gonna be."

He's the son and the husband you wish you'd had.

He writes in his diary — a journal of his inner and outer life — in his black, spiky handwriting, every morning of his life. The diaries were not written to be published. "We're not like that." Not public, he means. "I published it for one thing: for money. I told my publisher, 'I regret doing this. I'm broke after all these years in public life. We gave Margaret her wedding with our last $20,000. We were literally broke except for the house in Queens. I'll sell you the diary, but there are some things in it I will not give you, and I hope you understand that.' I took a lot of it out. . . . When does your obligation to your family end? Never. Not when you die. Never. There are things you don't share because your family wouldn't want you to share them."

He shares the good times, the telling anecdote:

"You have to understand the Italians. I'll tell you a story. My mother is now eighty-nine. She used to, when she was well, take a pregnant woman and say, 'I'm gonna tell you what the baby's gonna be, you wanna know?' 'Yes, Macula.' And she'd put a circle of salt on the floor and she'd say, 'Now I want you to sit in the middle of the circle. Now I want you to get up, but get up slowly' [he is interspersing this story with Neapolitan dialect]. So the woman would raise herself with her right hand or her left hand — 'Aaah.' And my mother would write on a card and put it in the jewelry box and lock the box, and she says, 'When the baby comes, we'll open the box.' And they'd ask her, 'Macu, what's the important thing? Whether you used the right hand or the left hand?'

OK. When the woman had the baby, at the appropriate time she'd open the box. She was never wrong. Twenty times, twenty-five times, she was never wrong. But once my older brother — only my older brother would have had the nerve — said, 'But Ma, how do we know that you don't go back and change the cards? I'm not gonna accuse you of that, we would never do that. I wanna hear you tell me you don't do that.' She says, 'Shut up.'

"She didn't *lie*. See, there's a lot of cleverness in their wonderful superstition. A lot of it was a high form of cuteness."

Some people would say that a high form of cuteness is a lot of what Cuomo's about. He doesn't lie.

"I *never* tell a lie," a seventeenth-century monk, Sarpi, said. "I *never* tell a lie, but the truth not to everybody."

We are talking about middle-class discontent. "I know middle-class discontentment, irritation, anger, better than *you* do," he says.

"Why?"

"Because I'm older than you. I've been middle class longer than you."

"Not by a lot."

"Hey. Am I older than you? I'm older than you. I'm older than you chronologically. I'm older than you spiritually. I'm older than you physically. I look older than you and I feel older than you."

While I am trying to absorb this, he segues into a story:

"My father and my godfather, Rosario, worked together. When my godfather quit the fish store and my father quit the grocery store 'cause he had a heart attack, there was nothing they could do with themselves, and they were irritated; so they came to me and said, 'We'd like to build a house. We wanna go in the house-building business.' My father can't read or write [his voice rings with pride], but never mind about reading plans. Rosario, my godfather, was a bricklayer, he had a skill, a real skill; and I was a young lawyer — so we got together: I bought a piece of land for two thousand dollars. We went to the old contractors that my father used to make sandwiches for from the grocery store. . . . We made a house. We lost twenty-eight hundred dollars. Then we made another house. We broke even. Then they made three houses. They made a four-thousand-dollar profit — and now they're going crazy. Then they made six houses, and they really made money, and they wanted to build an apartment house, and I stopped them. So they went back to the houses that they'd built and hired themselves out as patio builders for the houses.

"But they had these terrific arguments all the time — red brick, gray brick, what kind of design — they fought all the time. And they resolved the problem in the end always the same way, with my father conceding. And he always conceded in the same language: 'I'm gonna do it your way, Rosario, because you're older than I am. I do this out of respect.' Rosario was two years older. *I do this out of respect because you're older.* Perfect. It saved face for my father, it got the thing resolved without anybody admitting he was wrong."

There is that about Mario Cuomo which suggests a sense of guilt; he strikes one as a penitential kind of person — almost everyone who has spent any time with him remarks on this. Maybe it's just a finely honed sense of that inner dislocation and universal alienation we call Original Sin. Maybe. There are clues in *The Diaries of Mario M. Cuomo*, but it would take a hound of God to unravel their elliptical and opaque meaning:

> Has anything ever been so useless as the momentary acclaim of a world that does not know you, no matter how 'public'? Glory? The fear of shame and rejection is much more powerful a force than the desire for glory. . . . How you are troubled to think that even being troubled is cause for guilt. Because it's selfish. . . . As long as you are selfish — you are doomed to frustration. 'Me' is a bottomless pit which cannot be filled no matter how much achievement, glory, acclaim, you try shoveling into it. If only we were good enough to *do* perfectly what we know would work perfectly. But we can't. . . . Because being required to love denies me too many of the delights of being loved or liked or applauded or smiled upon? And if that *is* the case, then aren't you silly — as Matilda would say — because you know those delights don't last. You've tried them. You've had them. They don't work. . . . For God's sake, you know the truth! The truth is that the only way to make anything of your life is to be what you know you're supposed to be . . . "to fight the good

fight. To finish the race, to keep the faith." . . . I've not — truly enough — kept the faith. I've hurt people by bad example, even my own family. . . . That is part of the pain in my chest. . . . The desire for the transitory. . . . I have never had as much to undo as I do now and I have never had as much to compensate for as I do now.

I ask him if guilt is a form of narcissism, a perverse form of self-admiration. "No," he says. "Narcissism is seeing yourself as more beautiful than you are. Guilt may very well be your seeing yourself as uglier than you are. I think excessive guilt can be as disgusting as narcissism and as self-indulgent as narcissism, but I don't think they're the same."

"What makes you happy?"

"That's a hard one," he says.

"Would you rather be amused or amusing?"

An uncharacteristically long pause. "I guess I would rather be amusing so I could amuse those I love and make them happy — which would make me happy. And that's a perfect answer to both questions — if it's true."

In the state capitol — where he shows me the little hidden carpeted platform Governor Dewey built into his desk so as to stand on it and look taller than he was; and the desk scarred by FDR's wheelchair; and, from the window, the ugly ("Mussolini-style") multimillion-dollar mall Governor Rockefeller built — he appears before the television cameras for his weekly cable show; and he mixes it up as good as he does for prime-time network TV. A reporter asks him why he spent money during the last fiscal year when he was obliged this year to make drastic cuts in spending' "When we had it, we spent it. What are you saying? That we should have spent less when we had more? 'Save us from our expectations, Governor'? I hope you don't run your house that way." The reporter, hostile to begin with, is laughing with the governor now; and the governor scores the points he takes to America: there has been no *national* growth since 1989. The reason New York gets the attention is that New York is New York — and in New York, where "we all live in the same house," the problems are inevitably more visible. "This is a national issue. We have an umbilical connection with Washington. We are a nation. You can't handle drugs from New York City, poverty from Detroit, education from Arkansas. You need Washington."

He turns back $30,000 of his $130,000 salary to the state treasury. (Matilda contends that this is a gesture that goes largely unnoticed. Apparently she's right.)

The governor is a guest on a small radio talk show. "The whole country's going down the sewer," he says. A fellow named Chris calls in, surly, disaffected. The talk-show host keeps threatening to cut him off. But the governor wants to pursue his line of reasoning:

CHRIS: This state used to be called the Empire State. What a joke.
MC: Chris, what do you do, Chris?
CHRIS: What do I do? I drive a school bus.
MC: OK, are you driving today? . . . No? . . . Oh, good, 'cause you're all aggravated. God forbid you get behind a wheel.

Chris sounds apoplectic, increasingly incoherent with rage.

MC: Nice and quiet, calma, calma, Chris. . . . Go ahead.
CHRIS: We're seeing an insane crime wave in the time that you've been governor.
MC: Hold it a second, Chris. Hold it! Whoa! . . . Where does this state stand compared to other states?
CHRIS: This state is the disaster of the United States.
MC: Hey, Chris? Can I tell you something? Chris, simply: You don't know what you're talking about. We're about ninth on the FBI list. We have built more prisons, we have the best correction system in the United States of America. We don't have a single federal violation. I built twenty-seven thousand cells. Nobody even came close to us. . . . What would you suggest, Chris?
CHRIS: Get the chair back in Sing Sing, that's all you have to do. It'll cut the crime rate in half in six months.
MC: Hey, relax, Chris, you need a doctor, Chris. Listen to me, Chris. What do you think the crime rate was when we had the chair? Higher or lower?
CHRIS: The crime rate is ten times higher without the chair. Ten times higher.

> MC: You sure you drive a school bus? What do you do, take pills, you take Valium? Or how do you do it?

Chris curses the governor, calls him a hypocrite, and tells him to wash his mouth out with soap. The governor asks Chris if he's thin-skinned.

> CHRIS: You're a Judas Iscariot! You disgrace the Catholic Church!
> MC: This is good, this is good. . . . Chris, you're for the death penalty? Hold it. The Catholic Church teaches that the death penalty is wrong.
> CHRIS: No they don't. They approve.

Then for ten minutes the governor talks about the efficacy, ethics and economics of the death penalty, and his proposals for combating violent crime, opportunities he would have missed if he'd dismissed abusive Chris.

The governor is having a good time.

We are back on the airplane after a visit to the laboratories of a biotechnology firm in Tarrytown that develops products to treat degenerative diseases, a private-sector firm in which New York State invested $250,000 in 1988, as part of an initiative to expand the export capacity of the state's business sector. (A scientist's little boy asked the governor to sign a baseball; the governor asked the little boy what he thought of the Mets trading Ron Darling.)

He says he is *destrutto* — destroyed — operatic Italian for tired. Who wouldn't be tired?

He hasn't eaten all day; the executive kitchen, under Matilda's supervision, has provided bagged turkey sandwiches. We all eat; he doesn't. He is sitting across from a budget aide, a good-looking woman. He flirts with her with no lack of propriety — just enough to satisfy the demands of chivalry.

"What would you say if the plane went down, governor?"

"Goodbye. . . . Depends on whether you're an eschatologist" — someone who believes in final things, Death, Judgment, Heaven and Hell. "If you're an eschatologist you say, 'See you later. *Ciao*. See you in a little while.'

"*Mangia,* Grizzuti — eat. What are you afraid of? What's the matter with you? You're gonna embarrass us. Come on, this is nice, calm." The plane bumps along; he sings a Neapolitan song to distract me.

He anticipates a question I have it in mind to ask. (He's being awfully generous, considering he's *destrutto.*)

"How did you know I was going to ask that?"

"How did I know? I know you."

"How do you know me?"

"How do I know you? I've been married to you. I was a son of yours. I was a father of yours. I was a brother of yours. How do I know you. Ask the question."

The question has entirely slipped my mind.

The plane rackets to a landing, and he says: "See? We're home, we're safe — and you gave us credit for nothing, you shamed us as Italians. I'm gonna start telling people you're Norwegian. . . . *Harrison,* what's that? I don't want to know."

The governor does not take kindly to aggressive questioning about whether or not he will run. I don't ask him; I say, O.K. I've just been elected president; what should I say in my inaugural address?

He doesn't need prompting:

"We have to change course. We're great at winning wars, but we haven't been too good at anything else. I want to have a presidency that will culminate in a parade where we'll be rejoicing, rejoicing over the number of children we saved from drugs, the number of graduates from our technical colleges, four years of peace, the first national health insurance plan. . . . That's the parade I want to have, everybody waving flags and saying, Health at last! That's not a bad idea. I would write a speech about a parade — the parade I'd want after four years."

How I wish he'd run! For the pure fun — the absolute joy — of it.

"Life is motion, not joy." You can't demand joy or be reasonably sure you create it or grab a piece of it: "The one thing you *must* insist on and you *can* control is motion. You move, you function, you work, you don't run away, you don't despair, you don't quit, you don't die, you don't sit in a corner with your thumb in your mouth chanting your mantra, you don't slip under your bed and pull the comforter over your head so they can't find you. . . . How will I know that I'm justified? How will I know that I've done the right thing? There's only one rule that you can use with perfect assurance to measure yourself, and that is: I have to be sure I tried."

The man who might be president says his private life "would probably be regarded as so drab, so boring, so one-dimensional, it would surprise people.

"Public life is a strain. [New York City Mayor] Dave Dinkins is naturally public; he enjoys it so much, he'll make three, four, five stops a night, go to parties and stuff everywhere. At gunpoint I might go to a party in Manhattan. Not because I don't like the people. But to put on a tuxedo and sit for an hour and a half at a table — you want me to make small talk? No."

This naturally brings us to a question he couches in somewhat different terms than I would (we disagree): "Should you judge the individual by his or her private life? I think this is an easy question. I don't think it's a question of *should*. I think it's a question of *do* people judge that way; and the answer is yes. So many do that it becomes, therefore, a reality, and must be dealt with by the public figure. As a public figure I have to take that into account in leading my life, in becoming a public figure and deciding to stay a public figure.

"If your private life proves to be an embarrassment to you in your public life, then that's it, you asked for it. Gary Hart, Ted Kennedy, Barney Frank. . . . Can I make the argument that it should be irrelevant? Sure I can. I can make the argument that whatever the priest says from the pulpit, if it is beautiful and soaring and inspirational, that's what's important — not the fact that the priest is a good person. But if you discover that the priest is not a good person, it's gonna affect the way you judge the sermon, whether it should or it shouldn't. Therefore that becomes an operative fact. All the rest is nice, abstract, abstruse academic talk, should you/shouldn't you. . . ."

He has been talking in a lawyerly way. But his dryness yields to vexation: "Now that you mention it, it's something of a pet peeve of mine. I don't want to hear that Abraham Lincoln had constipation, that he drank purple fluid — some stuff that they gave him, who knows what. Maybe his form of grappa, I don't care what it was. Abraham Lincoln is larger to me than Abraham Lincoln the-grubby-individual-with-dirt-under-his-nails. Abraham Lincoln is an idea, is political poetry, is heroism, courage. I'm not interested in all that about Abraham Lincoln, about his feelings; and I don't wanna hear that St. Thomas More was not a great man, that he had debilitating faults. I have plenty of reality in my life; what I want is the symbolism of him. The inspiration. Don't tell me about Joe DiMaggio and his personal life. Joe DiMaggio is the ultimate in grace and skill and beauty in a ballpark and that's what counts. I don't wanna hear that he was a cheapskate, which he might have been. So don't bother me with that.

"Now, all this is anti-intellectual. Well, so what. Who said the intellect is everything? Doesn't emotion count? Do you have to be purely intellectual? What a terrible way that would be. Imagine. Would you cry? Would you laugh?"

His face is the face of a man who's laughed and cried a lot.

He is on the basketball court, playing with Christopher and with members of the staff. Naked to the waist, stripped of his elegant tailored suit, he is fit and he is fast. And he has that strange, intense look — both alert and inward-looking — that men have only in the sports arena . . . and in bed. "Play the game!" he calls out.

"There will always be more problems than solutions, more to be done than has been done, more quests than conquests. The game is lost only when we stop trying."

I was privileged to be in Eastern Europe soon after the people's revolutions. Happiness becomes people, even when they aren't practiced in it, even when charm is — as it appears to have been in Communist countries — an alien if not an odious commodity.

But you can't usher in the Kingdom of Heaven by Act of Parliament; something once done is — in the absence of grace — impossible to undo.

The story of Romania's Nadia Comaneci is a tragic one. People have asked me whether, given the same set of circumstances, any of us could have behaved differently, by which they mean better, than she. That is, of course, what none of us knows. I can observe and report upon a phenomenon — as Governor Cuomo says, Judge the product, and leave the man and the motive to God — I can't say what might have been . . . or, given a different past, what *I* might have been. Life is sad. (When I last saw Nadia Comaneci, she was a judge at a televised beauty contest, Miss Universe.)

The lust for absolute certainty takes different forms. Some are unwholesome. Some are fully evil. In Medjugorje in Yugoslavia that desire takes the form of a Marian cult, which is as much a political as a religious phenomenon.

Capitalism breeds its own kind of malcontents: in Island Pond, Vermont, the desire for certainty took the form of a messianic cult called the Northeast Kingdom Church. People sometimes ask me if I was overwrought when I wrote the story of Island Pond; and of course I was: I felt myself to be in the presence of evil. In the face of evil, detachment is a dubious virtue.

174

Budapest, Winter 1989

✦ ✦ ✦

IT IS DECEMBER; the snow is indistinguishable from the fog. Cocooned in white swirling mists (bone-chilling; delicious to the lips), one sees Budapest — as through an occluded mirror — dimly, as a city of water. The sky is heavy with water; the Danube, which divides the city nicely in two, is, while shrouded in metallic fog, always present to the senses; and the bridges that span it, from the hills of residential Buda on the Right Bank to flat commercial Pest on the Left Bank, daily claim one's gratified attention. Mineral and thermal spas, some of which have been in existence since the Middle Ages, dot the landscape, and one is subliminally aware of the thermal springs, 123 of them, that nourish Budapest's spas and give this East-West city a dreamy water life, offering the soporific warmth of healing waters democratically to all; even the Art Nouveau and Secessionist architecture of Hungary's capital, sinuous and curling, is like arrested liquid.

Budapest is Germanically crowded with statues and monuments; the 1947 Liberation Monument bullyingly towers over them all. But in the dense gray fog the 110-foot-high monument on the summit of Buda's Gellert Hill is softened, mercifully, its mock heroism rendered almost endearingly silly and (which is more than the sculptor had any right to expect) rather mysterious as well: on a limestone plinth stands a bronze woman dressed in flowing robes, a palm branch in her upraised hands (it looks like a giant feather); at the foot of the monument is a bronze statue of a Soviet soldier holding aloft the Red flag of "Liberation." The clouded heavens are mute. The whole thing is a metaphor for a futile imprecation.

And that is as it should be. In the summer of 1989, the Hungarian Communist party changed its name to the Socialist party, as if warning Moscow that the Soviet version of history was no longer acceptable; then, in October, on the thirty-third anniversary of Hungary's bloodily suppressed uprising against its Soviet bosses, Hungary proclaimed itself a republic. This is where history ended; this is where the world began to change.

But change is always slow and never complete. A maddening egalitarianism, for example, prevails on Malev, Hungary's national airline, when I fly in from Rome: Hungarians, Austrians, Italians, Japanese, West Germans — a polygenous lot, now that the borders are open — sit wherever they like, there being, in any case, no discernible difference between first and economy class except for the amount of hard currency one has shelled out for tickets. Sitting next to me is a German fashion model, who, wishing to exercise her thwarted first-class prerogatives, smokes although smoking is forbidden; rebuked, she strides to the cockpit, from whence can be seen the blue smoke of her Gauloise. When she returns to her seat, she gloomily announces, peering through a dense accumulation of clouds: "We are not flying over Hungary." And in fact we are not — though neither the pilot nor the flight attendants see fit to tell us so. Authority doesn't bend to the curiosity of the governed, it has lost the habit of graceful yielding, no matter that we grumble as we bounce through troubled air. When we land — at Vienna, 150 miles upriver from Budapest — some passengers are firmly convinced that they have achieved their destination and are in Budapest; confusion followed by good-natured complaining ensues, as we wait with our bags in the Lost and Found . . . for another plane? an overnight hotel accommodation? we don't know, no one tells us. We wait for several hours (the model — long legs count for a lot, anywhere — secures sandwiches for those she has chosen to claim as friends), and then we are in a bus, crunching on a surprisingly narrow, icy road, headlights illuminating a world decorated with hoarfrost, to a dark square, deserted except for taxis, in Budapest.

Taxis are so cheap in Budapest — a dollar will take you almost anywhere — one feels one has gotten away with something (and consequently overtips, to the amazed and histrionic gratification of the drivers, all of whom look like George Sanders or Attila the Hun).

My taxi deposits me at the glass porte cochere of the Hotel

Gellert, faintly damned for its "faded elegance." I love its faded elegance; it suits the pervasive melancholy and sentimentality of the city, its bittersweetness, which occasionally edges into mawkishness, and which literary historian John Lukacs calls "that blending of major and minor, of optimism and pessimism, of light and darkness" arising from the "Magyar temperament, in which a deep-rooted (and nonreligious) pessimism is often broken by sudden bursts of appetite for life, of a physical appetite stronger but perhaps less finely woven than . . . the French phrase *joie de vivre* suggests." Soviet monuments and new American venture capitalism notwithstanding, Budapest seems firmly located in the turn of the century.

In the brilliant warmth of my hotel, the city affords me the satisfying combination of outer ice and inner fire; chandeliers blaze, the suggestive lights of river ferries are reflected in my mirrors. My room overlooking the Danube is huge and cozy, threadbare scarlet carpets on the floor. Now violated by the largest traffic jams in Eastern Europe, the air of Budapest was once so sweet old men remember the fragrance of apricot blossoms and violets, and (a legacy of the occupying Turks) of roses carried by gentle winds. When I step out on the curving (almost plastic, Gaudi-like) terrace, I inhale the druggy smell of diesel fumes, which are met by the smell of the Gellert's thermal baths, vaguely sulfurous and not unpleasant. Light from streetlamps shivers on the Danube — a phenomenon that seems as if it should have some metaphysical significance or equivalent, like the ripples created by the tiny pebble thrown into a pond. I hear the sound of gypsy music — schmaltzy, sad, innocent, poignant, an old-fashioned hearts' suffering in which fear and anxiety play no part. Suffering as in a thirties film: Why are Jimmy Stewart and Maggie Sullivan not in the Little Shop Around the Corner, why does the world change and change and change and confound us with change? How can one wish simultaneously for change and for the comfort of stasis, the comfort of the past? What I wish for now, in this quintessential Budapest moment, is that the world, precariously poised to embrace hope, may keep its rendezvous with peace. While I am in this exalted mood, room service brings me thick pork chops smothered in onions and peppers, covered in a lardy gravy spiced with paprika; and pickled vegetables. I wish that I had ordered caviar instead. After one night in Budapest I understand that the best of my options is to live on Russian caviar, and cakes and pastries (in which the lard is disguised by thick whipped cream). Yellow trams swoosh/clack/clang — a mournful sound — on the water's edge.

I satisfy a sybaritic fantasy: I enter the lift wearing a mink coat over a bathing suit. (I would like always to dress this way and always to be on my way to warm waters.) The lift delivers me to the public anteroom of the Gellert's thermal baths; made for luxury but now shabby and dimly lit (two-penny sandwiches for sale), the cavernous, drafty room is occupied by dour old men and women sitting stolidly on leatherette banquettes. Their galoshes make puddles on the tiled floor I self-consciously walk across to gain access to the marble tunnels that lead to the exuberantly tiled, fabulous bathing hall — ceramic benches in Nouveau greens and blues, garlanded columns and incised pillars mimicking amusingly and acceptably those of ancient Rome, a retractable glass roof, like that of an Edwardian conservatory. Here, surrounded by Edwardian palms and Edwardian galleries — here, on the very spot where Romans bathed in the second century and the duke and duchess of Windsor frolicked in a summer of their love (their sepia images flicker on my television screen in documentaries sandwiched between soft-porn movies and, on the Super Channel, diatribes from American far-right religious fundamentalists), I swim with noncompetitive swimmers in kind waters.

Men are chivalrous though their flesh is withered. There is beautiful flesh and there is sagging flesh and it is all at home in the welcoming water. Ladies wearing shower caps paw the water, their necks erect, their heads held high like serious-minded dogs. Only an occasional giggle from a child hugging a stone griffin interrupts the mingled breathing of the silent swimmers. We glide in the regenerative waters, in the pale gold light.

A young woman with rubber flowers on her bathing cap and a handsome young American man in tow introduces herself to me as the daughter of the minister of justice: "Perhaps someday he will be elected president. Would you like to meet him? Will you have dinner with us?" I can't, sedated into diffuse benevolence, think of any reason to say no.

In a smaller, warmer, medicinal pool in the grand hall I float until I understand that the sound of purring I hear is the sound of heavy breathing — snoring . . . my own. So what. Water laps at my eyes. Pain floats away. There is nothing but this, breathing and floating, nothing else exists. There are no boundaries between bodies, and yet, I think dreamily, each of us is inviolate; I have a sense of wholeness and of separateness, of absolute integrity. . . . I am betrayed by my romancing water: I receive unwanted attention from a Libyan (I know enough Arabic to understand his hoarse assumptions, and I understand the obscene language of his proposing thigh.) How rotten of him.

Later, in the café of the Gellert, I comfort myself with seven-layer butter-cream-and-chestnut cake and pause to chat with a young American who is reading *USA Today* with sweaty hands. He has undertaken to learn Hungarian, which is related to no language other than Finnish — no easy task. He is enrolled in Budapest's Karl Marx University. Poor thing, what a time to be an American Communist abroad. Like the Libyans invited by the old regime, he has missed his moment in history, he has got it all wrong.

Not knowing the language makes life simpler; it's hard to make a fool of yourself when you don't have words to command or contort. . . . That is what I tell myself at first. But I find it increasingly odd, and then uncomfortable, to exist on this nonverbal — pre-verbal — level. Then, much against my word-oriented will, I remember, as if understanding this for the first time, how much can be conveyed without language; and this makes me question all kinds of things — for example, falling in love without words: I had forgotten that I did that once, when I was young; now, in a country where practically nobody speaks any language I do, I remember that long-ago falling-in-love. Perhaps experiencing this form of nostalgia is the reason so many foreigners perceive Budapest as a romantic city. I felt at first as if, without words, I was submerged, living an underwater life; and then I felt liberated, unburdened by words.

The chambermaid has oiled my electronic typewriter with my moisturizing cream. She bobs and nods and smiles at me, pleased to find herself so enterprising. I haven't the energy to get angry without the words to express vexation.

I am having a facial that combines the properties of shiatsu, dental torture, and a caress with the flesh of a silken flower. (Facials were not costly even during the bad old days; there are so many cosmetic and facial establishments in Budapest, one sometimes gets the feeling Hungary invented skin.) All kinds of things happen to me without my prior knowledge and consent. I find my eyelashes being "permanently" blackened — the immediate side effect of which appears to be blindness. I am peeled and waxed and vitaminized and creamed and slapped. *I you speak English me?* the facialist asks. *Hmmmm,* I say; what else is there to say? Something blue and buzzing is coming toward my face. *What's that?* I ask, alarmed into speech. Chrissie, the facialist, says: *Used orgasms.* I cannot imagine what she thinks she means. My skin tingles with the electric discharge from the buzzing blue machine.

The West Railway Station, a magnificent urban palace of glass and steel, was built in the 1870s by the Parisian firm of Eiffel. The National Geographical Institute boasts blue Hungarian Art Nouveau ceramic tiles with quasi-Oriental and Transylvanian folk motifs. (Orange, yellow, brown, the decorative colorful tiled roofs of monumental buildings look like geometrical embroidery translated into ceramics. They are gay and jaunty, like Ukrainian Easter eggs.) The State Opera House is neo-Renaissance. The Parliament building, completed in 1922, bears a more than passing resemblance to its neo-Gothic counterpart in Westminster, and is furthermore a winsome combination of Magyar medieval and French Renaissance. The serious and the whimsical, large-scale and small-scale, neobaroque, Italianate, Turkish, Victorian, neoclassical, Empire, Art Nouveau and Art Deco amiably coexist to provide a startling kind of unity; and architecture is not only influenced by the Vienna modernists but is reminiscent of Gaudi. Eclecticism is one word to describe it. Serendipity is another.

Pest consists of broad semicircular rings intersected by broad boulevards, one of which is Nepkoztarsasag utja (Street of the People's Republic). It is this street of beautiful old villas and embassies and palaces and cultural buildings that is most suggestive of Paris — of the Champs Elysées — and down this thoroughfare my guide, who is full of quirky facts, is pleased to drive me. ("In this Plague Hospital Dr. Ignaz Semmelweis found the cure for puerperal fever.") All the ancient oaks and the horse chestnut trees that were once the glory of this now sad but still imposing boulevard have been chopped down to midget height, in what is surely a vain attempt to allow the sick trees, killed by automotive pollution, to breathe again.

When it was called Andrassy Avenue, Nepkoztarsasag utja was paved with huge wood blocks, and the provocative sound of horses' hoofs filled the dust-free air.

The boulevard empties into Heroes Square, a huge public space with a histrionic and ineffectual monument celebrating the Archangel Gabriel, and seven equestrian statues of Hungarian tribal leaders. (One is occasionally reminded that this was once a barbaric land.) I see the Changing of the Guard — five or six soldiers, listless, tatty. More to be reckoned with in the imagination is the solitary old woman with a flowered babushka who makes her slow and tidy way around the forbidding square, cleaning it with a shovel and an orange Day-Glo brush.

Across the square, the Art Gallery wears the accoutrements of mourning: its façade is draped with an enormous black veil of net, which manages to be showy and classy, elegant and theatrical and sincere. In the summer of 1989, one thousand men and women killed in the 1956 rebellion, and ignobly buried in common ground, were reburied here, in honorable proximity to Hungary's Unknown Soldier. *Temetni tudunk,* the Magyars say: "We know how to bury people, that is one thing we know."

Beyond Heroes Square is the City Park, once the hunting fields of kings, where now, on what was once marshland, on an artificial lake strung with bright electric lights, young people skate (the amusements of this city are of water and are cheap). They are chanting *Gor-by, Gor-by, Gor-by* as they skate. Elephants are housed under mosaic domes of Nouveau splendor. Hippos become fertile in these warm waters, and breed, as they do nowhere else in captivity.

A faded billboard advertises the fleshy delights of a vaudeville show from London — giant flamingo-pink breasts, wine-red nipples, erect.

All over the city there are posters of bright red condoms.

*

Workmen remove the Red star from the roof of Parliament as cleaning women sweep. Amazing how people continue to hope — men and women over sixty in this country have endured the ravages and crimes of two alien dictatorships; and yet they smile and exercise a sanguine belief in symbols — out with the old and (glasses are raised in rathskellers) in with the untried new. It is the season when hope is born.

Budapest's underground electric subway line links the City Park Zoo with the Inner City, where it stops in fine Vorosmarty Square, just near Gerbeaud's, the most famous pastry shop among hundreds of patisseries that lend the city an air of harmless, Arcadian hedonism. A kind of solemnity reigns in the enfiladed red-and-green-papered rooms; at the marble tables, the gossip of women in furs, now proud to declare themselves among the bourgeoisie, is hushed, intense. The dedication to treats and sweets is intense, too; marzipan Santas and Santas' boots are a more substantial proclamation of the coming feast than are the rather wispy Christmas trees that have begun to appear (the trees, for forty years a hidden vice, look defiant for all their frailty). I treat myself to an open buttered caviar sandwich with goose liver, and a Sacher torte, and a double coffee and a mineral water, and with tip this comes to under five dollars.

Nearby is Vaci Street, a pedestrian shopping promenade, off which are tiny squares and mews and narrow pokey streets full of big, jokey, happy Art Nouveau buildings, dusty boutiques and antique shops: old lace, fur boas with beady predatory eyes, old crèches, and shops with fur caps and muffs, serviceable against the bitter cold. The pickings are slim. There are only echoes of the days when prosperous-looking men strode purposefully in fur-colored greatcoats that smelled of new money and rosy girls in furs shopped to satiety in glove shops and confectionery shops and flower shops, the days when "women smelled like oranges in Japan."

"Have you ever been behind the Iron Curtain before?" the daughter of the minister of justice says to me — a sentence that restores me with a jolt to my faith in the power of words: I had never once said to myself that I was "behind the Iron Curtain"; and now all the facts, and all my impressions, begin to arrange themselves differently — around those potent words.

We are eating, among marble columns and hazy speckled mirrors, in the tired glory of the Astoria. Thin linen cloths are held together by starch. I sometimes have the strange impression that I am walking through an old illustrated coffee-table book when I am in Budapest's cafés — the smell of cabbage is a homely haunting, the gypsy violins play songs I swear I heard in movies starring Carole Lombard. We are eating duck and heavy things in sour cream. In this hotel in 1918, a National Council proclaimed the Hungarian October Revolution, and the Austro-Hungarian Dual Monarchy began to crumble.

Tunde, my guide, is always sending me to restaurants "where the people eat" — to the Kispipa (lentils cooked with sausage, linoleum floors, a lighted Marlboro sign), and to the Kis Borostyan (Hungarian fried chicken, red-and-white paper tablecloths, and high-backed booths made for whispery assignations, where I eat in isolation). The joys of Hungarian cooking escape me. But the pleasures of Budapest's Tolbuchin Indoor Food Market, across the river from the Hotel Gellert, do not. The vast 1875 iron-ribbed glass building is a cross between Victoria Station and (narrow alleys winding through walls of food) an Indian bazaar. Great ropes of red paprika peppers and yellow peppers and creamy garlic in parchment jackets hang in wrought-iron stalls. Offal. The rear quarters of animals. Cabbages in net sacks. Bloody fresh fish with conscious-looking eyes. Goose livers, pale and obscene. Ubiquitous pickled vegetables. Men in jeans: "Wanna change money?" Sides of mutton. Tinned goose liver with truffles; Christmas tree lights. Cooked sausages on crusty bread, golden grease. I like this place because of its combination of openness and mystery; it is wholesome and it is exotic and it is hard to be unhappy in a food market.

The elevators of neoclassical buildings smell of garlic.

"There are two kinds of people," Tunde says, "those who live in Buda and those who want to live in Buda," hilly and green. She lives in Buda with her family and her boyfriend (our driver, Stephan), there not being enough money between them for an apartment of their own.

On Gellert Hill, where witches once met in labyrinthine caverns in dolomite cliffs (Tunde crosses herself, a practice she likes publicly to indulge in now that it carries no disapprobation), pleasant Hansel and Gretel villas and miniature palaces lead the way to the summit and the nineteenth-century fortified citadel, Nazi headquarters during World War II.

On Castle Hill the Royal Castle sits atop ten kilometers of honeycombed caves, horribly useful in horribly many wars; thirteenth century in origin, destroyed and rebuilt many times, it houses four museums, some (Museum of the Labor Movement) with off-putting names; a permanent exhibit, "A Thousand Years of Our Capital," which displays objects of daily life in use over the centuries, provides the quickest way to imbibe Budapest's history, poetry and practicality both dwelling in the common objects of our common lives.

The medieval character of the Castle District is somewhat ersatz, but its pastel charms are real; and the human urge to rebuild and thus reclaim its past is not to be despised. It is estimated that only twenty-six of every hundred houses survived Allied bombing and German/Soviet house-to-house fighting, which was most ferocious in what was once a sweet village and is even now wholly successful as counterpoint to monumental architecture. On winding streets of pink and Hapsburg yellow and gray houses (the colors, also, of Milan) shops are identified by iron symbols (so hospitable): leaves for tobacconists, mortar and pestle for chemists, a teapot for cafés . . . in one of which, the small and intimate Ruszwurm, I had a confection that surpassed my dreams of gustful sin: *somloi kocka*, a combination of chocolate pudding, chocolate mousse, sponge cake soaked in Hungary's sweet Tokay wine, and whipped cream.

Two houses, one yellow, the other pink, are joined with a common roof to symbolize the marriage of two neighboring families.

At 32 Uri near Ruszwurm, there is a gray house with a courtyard in which there are Gothic niches where servants used to wait, standing unobtrusively, for their masters. It makes the past seem less sweet to think of them.

I like the neogothic St. Matthias Church in the Castle District a lot, its dark spaces and its polychromed interior, its vaguely Oriental/arts-and-crafts flat olive, honey, sand, turquoise, mauve, pale green mannered style. I went to hear a Mozart organ concert but heard what sounded very much like Methodist hymns, sung by a baritone/organist in a well-worn overcoat, instead. Outside, in Trinity Square, I did hear Mozart played — by an organ grinder wearing a black derby. Behind the church, on Fisherman's Bastion, I heard a man sing "The Battle Hymn of the Republic."

It's interesting to watch Hungarians genuflect in church. They have the furtive look of solid citizens caught eyeing pornographic magazines; they are not yet used to doing openly what was so openly censured before.

Mencken said Budapest looked like an empty ballroom, and one knows what he meant: in certain moods and certain weather, the city has an air of the forlorn, grandly dressed and forsaken.

For all its glory of stone, Budapest comes back to me always in images of water:

One day Tunde and Stephan took me to self-consciously picturesque little Szentendre twelve miles north of Budapest, an eighteenth-century artists'-colony town that has been "discovered." The trip was instructive in a civics-lesson way: we drove through Obuda, where shortly after the birth of Christ the Romans set up camp and where now concrete blocks of buildings loom over scraps of ruins; we drove through diesel-choked industrial suburbs and coal-mining country where lace-curtained cottages of patterned stucco still remain, haystacks on their verandahs; we passed a cemetery of Allied forces' war dead and the barracks of Russian soldiers who, forbidden to fraternize with Hungarians, were never a real part of Budapest, and are probably just as glad to be going as the Hungarians are to see them go; we passed Budapest's Williamsburg — Skanzen — an ethnographic open-air museum of furnished peasant houses from all of Hungary made of wood and mud and straw (closed in winter — not so much an empty ballroom as an empty stable); we passed fields where once Hungarian kings and now rich Italians hunt for boar and rabbits — but it was not till we reached the old town of Esztergom that history came alive. And not because the Magyar kings reigned here, nor yet because the wife of King Matthias, Queen Beatrix of Naples, caused marble fountains to spout red and white wine here, in a castle that is ruined, black and jagged against the sky.

And not because Esztergom is the seat of the Catholic prince-archbishop of Hungary and the site of the country's most magnificent cathedral:

From the promenade of the ruined castle we look across the Danube and there is a bridge that from this height looks like a child's toy snapped in two. It was snapped, bombed, in World War II. On the other side is Czechoslovakia, the part that once belonged to the Austro-Hungarian Empire. The monarchy of the Danube is past, and Hungary has shrunk with the geographical division of the spoils; it is no longer surrounded by water, surrounded by the Baltic Sea. But the Danube — never blue and now an industrial sewer — still excites the lyrical imagination: we drive around a horseshoe bend in the river and Tunde and Stephan see what they have not seen since they were children (winters were colder then): the Danube has frozen over, there are skaters on it. Tunde claps her hands in excitement; Stephan cries. *It is like a picture in a book*, he says. *A lost book*, Tunde says, and she cries too. I feel as if I am tactlessly intruding myself into their lost childhood, found.

The history of Budapest from Roman times is quite literally written in water. Turkish pashas cultivated roses and built steambaths and thermal spas; the most beautiful still in use are the domed sixteenth-century Kiraly baths, adorned with golden moon and crescent; but more homely Turkish baths, cozy, clean, allow one to find dreamy peace for almost no price at all. Some are single-sex, and in some baths men and women swim on alternate days — the social and class history of Budapest is found in Budapest's waters, too. There are all kinds of treatments and cures and all kinds of claims made for these waters: they are said to remedy stomachaches and footaches and nervous disorders and muscle spasms and heartaches; a seventeenth-century Turk called the waters "beneficial for the French sickness and for seven other ills." Of course, water is a drug, the most potent drug of all, more potent than opium — surely Hungary's conquerers knew this. To enter these warm waters is to forget all else, to feel submerged in life's origins, to experience a natal calm.

In City Park there is a bath that seems made to be a landmark in dreams. It is called Szechenyi. In dreams one censors the flaccid flesh of cigarette smokers in soggy electric-blue woolen bathing suits, the mustard-colored peeling walls of the bathing hall, the smell of cabbage that has insinuated itself into it, God knows how. One remembers this: A freezing day. Furs. An outdoor thermal pool, hotter than body heat. Icy snow on the deck around it. Great billows of blameless steam issuing from it. Men and women sitting in these waters and, on bobbing chessboards, playing chess. In dreams men and women, always young, always kind, gracefully promenade to these lovely waters, which disregard time and exist in their own eternity of space; they are born again in water.

Dubrovnik:
Spell of the Moonflower (1989)

✦ ✦ ✦

I was in another walled city, Lucca (sunny and safe), when I heard of the bombardment of Dubrovnik. "We are a pinpoint of darkness in hell," a Croat said. No paradise is secure; none has been since angels barred the entrance to the first one. — 1992

IT IS SO SAFE HERE.

Beguiled and soothed by boundaries, I am in a little square, as comprehensible and logical as it is charming, drinking apricot liqueur (a lovely soporific), in a café fast against the Venetian-Gothic/Renaissance Sponza Palace. My eye, from this pleasant spot, traverses the whole of the gated main thoroughfare, the Placa, a street paved with creamy stones worn to the smoothness of satin, lined with creamy, monochromatic seventeenth-century houses. This is containment without claustrophobia. The city walls circle, embrace, shelter and protect. One wishes the topography of the unconscious were like this — harmonious and orderly. Dubrovnik extends an invitation to believe that life, the contours of a life, can be ordered, rectified, serene, and willed. Once inside the walled city, one forgets towers and dungeons and ramparts and battlements; one even forgets (and this is odd) the presence of the Adriatic Sea, which surrounds Dubrovnik on three sides. The sea here is a ghostlike presence — not even the smell of brine invades these walls, in which, it sometimes seems, a weather-unlike-the-weather-outside is begotten not made.

I always approach the walled city — yielding to its insistence on logic (which results in habit) — from the eastern gate, the

Ploce; the introduction to the old walled city is gradual: I cross a stone bridge over a redundant moat; I pass a little park alongside the Old City port, small craft bobbing, an opening in the walls revealing the always surprising juxtaposition of pine and palms; I enter iron-studded wooden gates, their massive machinery rusted. I have by this time passed under two arches, on one of which is a bas-relief of St. Blaise, the patron saint of Dubrovnik, holding the city-in-miniature, as he always does, on what appears to be a platter. I descend a few steps, pass a frescoed and vaulted clothing boutique and a chrome pastry shop built into the walls (unexceptionable reminders that we are, medieval lanes notwithstanding, in the twentieth century); and I am in the comely square. I have gone from the narrow to the wide into a place which is an antidote — one is held here — for agoraphobia . . . into safety.

I always stop in this square before I explore the narrow side streets, which ascend on the south, in steps lined with plants, vertiginously to the ramparts; and which, to the north, march in flat patterned lines to the walls. (Sometimes the pattern is interrupted — by a piazza, a market, a cloister — and the grid becomes, briefly, a maze: comfort and excitement coexist.) On these streets are houses as close together as tenements, with carved portals and balconies and pots of flowers and dubious plumbing and gray shutters against the buttery yellow façades; clothes flutter on clotheslines. . . . To the south, above the beautiful city, the wooded hills, crowned with spiky cypresses; to the north, unseen, the sea, a pearly haunting. . . . Bells. . . . A fifteenth-century clock tower rebuilt, its sun-ray hands keeping perfect time. . . . The Sponza Palace, once a customs house and mint. (Amazing to think of such ethereal Gothic arches, such lavish Renaissance loggias and generous atrium constructed for such homely activities as the delivery of parcels, the minting of coins, the storage of wheat — it makes one question the meaning of "progress.") Facing the Sponza, and in pleasing contradiction to its airiness, the massive baroque Church of St. Blaise, standing stolidly on a balustrated platform, as if to earnestly remind the citizenry of the supremacy of the sacred over the profane. And also in this square — Luza Square — Dubrovnik's glory, the Rector's Palace, a simple two-story building, as delightful and unified a mixture of the Gothic, the Renaissance, and the Baroque as can anywhere be seen. One sits in the shadow of the baroque staircase in the cool atrium drinking Dubrovnik's silky apricot liqueur thinking of the days when this city was a republic and a rector was appointed to serve for a month — a nice curb on temporal power — during which time (dressed in a toga of red silk and a stole of black velvet) he was not allowed to leave his palace except for state occasions. Confinement in such a place could not have been a punishment. (It implied, of course, that corruption could not be found inside but had to be sought outside — one of the sweet fallacies bred in a walled city.)

I have never seen pigeons so aggressive.

Dubrovnik is exquisite, elegant — and anomalous. It is, given that history and nature have so little favored Yugoslavia, a lily in a cabbage patch. It is very nearly perfect. And one feels — if one ventures into the wasteland of the forbidding interior and exposes oneself to the bleakness of the terrain, and of the economy — that it almost has no right to be perfect. It is in this way not decadent by design, but by sad happenstance. It was — and in appearance now is — an aristocratic city; when what we now call Dubrovnik was the Republic of Ragusa, all power rested in the hands of nobles. A caste system prevailed: there were nobles, there were commoners, and there were workers. There was no marriage between classes, no social relations at all. The workers could not vote; they were without voice. That was then (in the nineteenth century Napoleon annexed Dubrovnik, and it came under Austrian rule); this is now: Now, in socialist, nonaligned Yugoslavia, all enterprises and services are, in theory at least, owned and managed by the people who work for them; this is called "workers' self-management."

Of course it is not safe here.

Nowhere in the world is it safe; but here, in Dubrovnik, in spite of the sense of bodily integrity its ordered space imparts and the sense of bodily well-being the benevolent climate imparts, one might be in the eye of a hurricane. It is perfectly possible while in Dubrovnik to ignore the problems besetting Yugoslavia; but that in itself is spooky — just as being on the sea, in the walled city, and being able to forget that one is on the sea, is spooky. One can exercise selective vision here . . . just as one immediately trains one's eye to avoid registering the prickly television antennae that sprout incongruously from the red slate roofs of the lovely houses.

Here, where scampi and strudel and good wines are almost as cheap as the perennial sunshine and where tourism enriches the local populace, it is burdensome to stop to think of the bread-lines in the province of Serbia, of the dark "people's bread" that has replaced the ordinary bread ordinary people cannot afford. Here, where Yugoslavs are informal and almost uniformly amiable (though the faces of the men are the faces of martyrs and adventur-ers), it is difficult to think of the bitter antagonisms that exist among Serbs and Slovenes, ethnic Albanians and Montenegrins, between Roman Catholics and members of the Eastern Orthodox Church, in this patchwork country. Uneasily unified in 1918, and given its present form by partisan hero Marshal Tito (whose like-ness can be seen in huge posters in the surrounding hills), Yugo-slavia is the Tower of Babel. (Dubrovnik is Eden.) Eight years after the death of Tito, whose grateful country made him president for life, the Balkans appear to be sliding into chaos. There are two dozen ethnic groups in this country. Before Tito worked his manly magic, *balkanization* was a synonym for the terminal division of a state, for the ungluing of several imperfectly bonded parts. Now, in one of history's peculiar twists, Yugoslavia's leaders proclaim they are resisting *lebanonization*.

Serbs accuse ethnic Albanians of rape and pillage. Albani-ans — whose birthrate is the highest in Europe — fear the rebirth of Serbian nationalism. Croatians, some of whom collaborated with the Fascists during World War II, are regarded with contempt by the Serbs, some of whom collaborated with the Nazis during World War II. The Serbs are hungry for bread and for power; the prosperous Slovenes shop for fashions in Italy. The Croatians (Dubrovnik is on the Dalmation Coast of Croatia) sympathize with the Slovenes. There are three and a half million Moslems in Yugo-slavia; the rise of Islamic fundamentalism is a source of concern to the government — which is as cumbersome as a government can be: it is a federation of six republics and two autonomous prov-inces, each of which has its own Communist party hierarchy and its own administrative government. Power is decentralized; the presidency of the Federal Chamber rotates annually. In this it is reminiscent of Ragusa's Rectory. But it is not orderly. It's messy and it's not working.

There are even two alphabets, Latin and Cyrillic: Babel. Workers in Titograd and Belgrade and the Serbian province of Kosovo protest and strike and riot. How much of this disequilibrium and unequal distribution of wealth is due to history's frivolous and terrible quirks and how much to geography — the interior is nearly impossible to traverse — it is difficult to say. One is tempted to believe that God either lacked a blueprint or rested prematurely when the Balkans were created. This is a banquet for tourists, but funeral meats for the divided Yugoslavs.

In 1940, Rebecca West wrote (in *Black Lamb and Gray Falcon*) that in this land, scene of so much tragedy and bloodshed and madness and heroism and bravery — and so many assassinations — was to be found "the primal stuff of humanity." Her determination to see in Yugoslavia a metaphor for all of Europe is perhaps an example of the perversity of genius; but her pessimism is confirmed if one regards the Tower of Babel as a metaphor for the suffering world.

Meanwhile, in Eden, people swim in the cerulean sea.

The sun shines seductively out of season, at the ragged end of Yugoslavia's summer, but even the hardy British will not swim in the icy sea.

My hotel is east of the walled city on a stony beach. It is a great lumbering modern thing, white; it feels at all times of day like an ocean liner well lit after night has fallen . . . and it is for all practical purposes deserted: seventy people occupy its two hundred rooms. Its red walkways and terraces and eerily empty shopping malls are meant to echo and are a parody of the noble ramparts of the Old City. At night the fragrance of flowers, intensified by moonlight, wafts up to me. The sea is silent. Few pleasure crafts ply their way through these waters; the splendid cities of southern Dalmatia are walled cities — it is as if the sea, here, is perceived by Slavs as a source of danger, not of hedonistic pleasure. Sometimes I hear voices from a lonely rowboat; voices gain definition in moonlight across expanses of water — they are voices in bell jars. I hear a man clear his throat on a balcony three floors above me. From far below I hear a pretty little English boy who has lately discovered the joys of alliteration: "Mummy, may I pee in the pomegranate planter after pudding?" The bright lights of a distant village blink unsteadily. This is a holiday-resort ghost town.

But it is not generous to complain of anything near the generous sea, a friend says; and he is right. The Adriatic is not the Mediterranean, it is true. The olive grows here (one could argue that it is not possible to be unhappy in the vicinity of a silvery green olive tree); the myrtle, oak, and pomegranate flourish. But the Adriatic does not have the heady abandon of pastel houses on lush terraces climbing — amid almond trees and flowering limes and broad beans and orange blossoms — to the sea, which one finds in Positano; or the Moorish gold and blue of Amalfi; or, for that matter, the kaleidoscopic white of the Aegean. The Adriatic is not so fecund nor so floral nor so gay as its mother sea, the Mediterranean; the Siren has not sung here. It is grave and grand and stern, severely beautiful.

In part densely wooded with maritime pines and in larger part deforested, this coast, denuded of great trees hundreds of years ago, bulges now with tiddly boulders and outcroppings of raw limestone disguised imperfectly by weedy bougainvillea. The sea is dotted with islands, none of which have the gorgeous inevitability of Capri's Faraglioni; they have, instead, a kind of awesome loneliness — almost as if rock could yearn. I like it best just before sunset, when the water stretches toward the sun and shines silvery like a bolt of shot silk. The sun sinks theatrically behind wooded Lokrum, an island gift from Emperor Franz Joseph to Empress Carlota and Emperor Maximilian. My balcony faces Lokrum. It is not too cold, then, to stand naked on my protected balcony wreathed in rosy failing light — the light the Welsh hymn calls the "praising light."

And it is never too cold to swim in the huge domed pool, an Olympic pool enlarged and squared. Often I am alone in the pool for hours; I see myself mirrored in the retractable glass roof above. Sometimes I share the pool with two blond English twins with yellow water wings; sometimes with two unsmiling matrons, also twins; and sometimes, with the little boy who likes to pee in the pomegranate planter after pudding and his nicely indulgent mother.

I can sit in deep water — Billy Rose's swimmers were trained to do this; I do it by happy accident of gravity and distribution of weight — and I can stand perpendicularly in water above my head without treading water. These accomplishments, though I have done nothing to earn them, are a source of vanity to me; and afterward, tingly/toasty with cold, I sunbathe on a terrace overlooking the beach, I drink apricot brandy, the Old City in view.

Inflation approaches 250 percent. My "Continental" breakfast consists of two slabs of strudel, hams and cheeses, rolls, butter, jam, coffee; this is considered a light breakfast. The phones work intermittently. It rained (an event) the day I arrived; my ceiling is streaked with wet. The Yugoslavian Tourist Office calls me from Belgrade, and, with a kind of bullying inefficiency combined with a patent desire to please, keeps offering to take me to places I do not want to go to; my acquiescence is taken for granted. In my sybaritic room there is a sign on black oak advising me that if I insist on using "foreign appliances" they will be taken away from me for the duration of my stay; I feel chided, I feel like a ward of the state. There has recently been a fire on the third floor of my hotel. Guests were evacuated. (I am on the fifth floor; the road and the entrance to the hotel are on the sixteenth floor — as the concierge says, "Everything is upside down and backwards here.") The air still smells of char. I try the fire exits, they are locked. I am meant to extract a key from a glass case beside the door in case of fire: *Oh, no,* I say. "Never mind," says the concierge. "We have earthquakes once every three hundred years and fires we do not have twice in six months." Nevertheless, I want a fire key of my own and will sleep in my clothes till I get one. "But we will save you," says the concierge. Given that the people of Dubrovnik were wily, clever, and strong enough not to be eaten alive by the Maritime Republic of Venice, or Hungary, and that they managed to ward off the Turks for four hundred years, closing Europe to the Ottoman Empire while much of what we now call Yugoslavia came under the heel of the Ottoman Turks, perhaps they will save me. Any suggestion that they will fail to come to my rescue is taken as a reflection on their manhood. Their speech is not mellifluous. They do not set great store on flattery or charm; but every man and woman who works here smiles, no one is unpleasant. Dresses I send out to be ironed come back in three hours. In France I have sometimes paid more for a dress to be ironed than I paid for the dress itself; here, the price of laundering is so low I think they must have made a mistake. These are reasons people offer for coming to Dubrovnik: it is cheap, people are obliging. The Italians come, too, Capri and Positano notwithstanding.

The day before I leave, my bill is $683. The day I leave, it is $659: the cashier cannot — nobody can — keep up with inflation and the foreign exchange (bills of larger and larger denominations are printed every day, no one knows what grotesqueries of finance the next day will bring). "Let me understand this," I say. "My bill is *less* today than it was yesterday?" The cashier shrugs. "So that means if I stay two weeks more, you'll owe *me* money, is that right?" "Something like that," he says.

People cope.

Inflation, this rate of inflation, is like a tidal wave; and people react to it according to their natures. I say to a blank-looking waitress, "I must have a receipt . . . for my office, my boss." (The words *office* and *boss* invariably produce results.) She identifies with me immediately — she is a worker, she has a boss — and, with conspiratorial goodwill, she writes a receipt for approximately twenty times the amount I have paid. As this would oblige me to claim I have paid forty dollars for a cup of coffee, I ask for a receipt for the proper amount — which, ruefully, she provides (a worker's defeat).

A taxi driver has overcharged me. (Why are taxi drivers always the least agreeable people one meets?) When I ask him for a receipt, he snarls, grabs my notebook, and spits at me. He is going for my throat — shouting *Spy! Spy!*, he thinks I am a government agent — when a hotel employee pulls him away. He scrawls a receipt for 12,000 dinars; I have in fact paid him 14,000 dinars. Spiteful to the end, his spite is now greater than the fear which gave rise to it.

A waiter charges me 8,000 dinars for coffee. When he gives me the receipt I ask for, it is made out for 6,000 dinars; and he gives me back the 2,000 dinars he has blithely overcharged me. We both laugh. "Well," he says, "I tried. I tried to cheat you but it didn't work out. What can a poor man do?" He is so good-natured, cocky, and unremorseful we both feel that we have come out ahead. (I tip him 2,000 dinars.)

There are two Dubrovniks — the one I try, in this elegiac season, to imagine: the hurly-burly Dubrovnik of sun worshipers and nudist beaches and tantalizing coves and beach umbrellas and summer entertainments spontaneous and contrived in government hotel complexes and in private *pensiones* and genteel, terraced villa-like hotels and faded hotels in the grand fashion and flocks of tourists like gaily colored birds; and the walled city, separate from the beaches, inimical to the sea, a world apart.

It is a city cut from stone. From marble, some guidebooks say. From limestone, "homely as cheese and splendid as marble," Rebecca West says. It is so worn it retains the mystery of its origins. It is so pale it ought to be a palate for the shifting colors of day: but it is always the same color; even at night, when the lanterns are lit in orderly progression, the stone gleams creamily, unchanging.

The sweetest spaces of Dubrovnik are the cloisters, those of the Franciscan Monastery and the Dominican Monastery . . . for if one is "held" in a walled city, one is held twice over in a cloister, that womblike (and, without evident contradiction, seraglio-like) form of architecture in which one is quintessentially safe.

To be a cloistered monk was to enjoy the physical world without risking contamination from it. The small, silent Franciscan cloister with its faded frescoes and its capitals ornamented by wholly original faces that look like cheerful satyrs, its fragrant orange trees and frilly palms and high hedges, is a world within a world. . . .

Dubrovnik is like a set, one within the other, of encapsulating boxes . . . eggs . . . nests.

But it is not a fairy-tale city: the sea pulls us back to our origins, reminding us of the beginning of life, and (in its ebb and flow) of death; and all of Catholic architecture reminds us, not only of the resurrection and the life which it celebrates, but of the leveling inevitability of death. In the cloisters of St. Dominic are buried bishops, archbishops, monks, historians, philosophers, theologians, poets, painters, mathematicians, merchants, artisans, soldiers, politicians; we tread upon them, their ornamented tombs are underfoot. Indeed, a just appreciation of this place is contingent upon a fine appreciation of memento mori, for in the monastery museums (and in the six-hundred-year-old Franciscan pharmacy) are to be found an effigy of a nameless saint, one breast lopped off; miniature reliquaries: tiny bones and bits of sanctified cloth enclosed in intricate lockets and glass vials (housing is all —

just as the grave shall be our home and we shall be forgotten, it is no longer remembered to whom these bones belonged); the blackened forearm of St. Thomas the Apostle wrapped in cotton wool; bones on which the accordion-folded flesh has mummified; a picture of St. Vincent roasted over coals; votive plaques of legs and limbs and hearts; the skull of St. Damian, overlaid with chased silver; the middle finger of St. Dominic sheathed in gold — and raised in a universal gesture not generally understood to be one of sanctity.

Thank God for a Titian of St. Blaise blessing a plump and earthy Magdalene; and for a picture — reminding us of the indivisibility of the holy and the mundane — of a beautiful woman gazing at the sea, a useful occupation inspiring no guilt. . . .

In the cloister of St. Dominic, among the amphorae and the lemon trees, there is a tree of white lilac that blooms through October; and there is a moonflower bush. The moonflower remains obdurately closed by day; at night it opens — it is white and shaped like a trumpet — and it has unusual properties: If you sleep with a moonflower under your pillow, your sleep will be long and sweet. If you sip its nectar, you will sleep forever.

Outside the cloister, the bright laughter of children, the smell of frying fish. . . .

I have caviar for lunch.

The days are long and balmy, the elements are kind. Wearying of predictable perfection, I take a day trip north to Mostar, a Moslem town in the interior, in the district of Herzegovina, a province of Bosnia-Herzegovina.

I might be in a different country.

Lying in a limestone gorge, Mostar — a settlement of no account until the Turks conquered it in 1440, after which it became the crossroads of the spice trade — rests on both sides of the Neretva River, which empties into the Adriatic; to reach it one drives steeply from the sea through a ruptured limestone plateau, a forest wounded and exploited for timber to build the splendid cities of the coast.

"From childhood," Rebecca West wrote, "when I was weary of the place where I was, I wished it would turn into a town like Mostar."

Mostar is a kind of dream city — a city of sugared figs and pomegranates and slender minarets and graceful mosques and graveyards with ornamental tombstones (the men are buried vertically, the women horizontally); and one structure of enormous beauty, the Old Bridge that spans the rushing waters of the Neretva. Its many steps, smooth as glass, meet in an improbably steep Gothic arch unsupported by pillars (but defaced, now, by a rusty iron railing, presumably for the clutches of the faint of heart). For thirty dollars young boys from the town will jump into the Neretva from the bridge; for sixty dollars they will dive — a theatrical sight but not a happy one.

Cats scud across slate roofs; clutches of gypsies swarm and extend listless begging hands.

My unofficial guide, a young woman who, having come here on a tour, stays on for reasons of lethargy and lust (Yugoslavian men are handsome), shows me, in the winding streets of the bazaar, the local "head shop," where opium pipes are put to more than decorative use.

Mostar is exactly what a child — a child reared on Disney's fantasies — might imagine a Turkish bazaar to be. Stagey. Cute. Obscurely sinister. One can imagine it stripped of its coy and crass commercial trappings (art galleries; instant antiques), and the censoring eye can see the anatomical purity and beauty of the (now gussied up) architecture. Poor Mostar, tarted up for tourists, reminds one of a fifty-year-old woman who uses makeup in order to look thirty and succeeds in looking sixty-five. Better to leave well enough alone.

Still, it is pleasant, however much one doubts the authenticity of the restored Turkish merchant's house, a house of fretted wood balconies and elaborate wooden doors, built on pillars over the Neretva, to sit in a broad room under coffered wood ceilings and bulbous brass chandeliers on banquettes covered with bright rugs, listening to the slippery sound of the river on one side and the splashing sound of the fountain in the whitewashed cobblestoned courtyard on the other. The house in all its parts — with its disregard for comfort, which coexists with a true regard for the aesthetics of minimalism — confirms the observations of Charles Eliot, who wrote (in *Turkey in Europe*) that if the Turks had "quoted from the Bible instead of the Koran, no words would better characterize their manner of life than 'Here we have no continuing city'; for a room in a Turkish house is scrupulously clean, but bare and unfurnished," so that a European visitor might conclude that "a party of travellers have occupied an old barn and said, 'Let us make the place clean enough to live in; it's no use taking any more trouble about it. We shall probably be off again in a week.'" In this house, with its steep and narrow steps and its pretty green-and-white latticed balconies, lived many wives and concubines, their view restricted to the green waters of the Neretva — no neighborly over-the-balcony chats for them.

It is pleasant to stroll along the flowering banks of the river and to sit under a crab apple tree, lunching on *burek* — a spicy meat encased in layers of delicate pastry.

This is said to have been Tito's favorite town.

For Moslems green is a holy color. All the posted death notices in Mostar are printed an ardent green.

The trip back to the coast takes us past vineyards and tobacco fields and gypsy encampments, and through the moonscape of the *karst* — the denuded limestone outcroppings that make so much of the interior of Yugoslavia a stony open-air prison.

It is afterward hard to believe that we have been in a real town and not in a fiction created for tourists. And yet the Ottoman Empire determined the fate of the Slavs for two hundred years; Serbs and Croatians speak of the exquisite and ingenious tortures of the Turks as if they had happened yesterday. And we are, in Mostar, only thirty-five kilometers from Sarejevo, where in 1914 a Bosnian student fired a shot that was heard around the world and changed the political configuration of the world. It is hard to get realer than that.

I bring with me tangible evidence that Mostar is not wholly contrived — from the market I have bought, from an old woman in a babushka, paper spills of lavender and citron and juniper and camomile, folk remedies for insomnia, "nerves," respiratory ailments, circulatory and kidney and heart problems (and a silver filigree box to keep them in).

The outdoor markets of Dubrovnik speak of abundance — it is not food that is hard to come by, it is the money with which to pay for it. I see, in the open-air market tucked behind the cathedral, produce that I never see on restaurant tables. (Perhaps the Slavs — who are determined that tourists shall eat iceberg lettuce — think that because they can afford these greens, they are weeds; my immigrant Italian grandmother told me that when she first came to America, broccoli was thought to be an Italian weed. . . . She didn't live long enough to see arugula become trendy.) Purple broccoli (fourteen cents a bunch); watercress, scallions, kohlrabi (all eight cents a bunch); also necklaces of dried figs (fourteen cents), and persimmons (five cents each). . . . Also lavender water, and rosemary ("for sinus and for migraine"). . . . One egg costs thirteen cents; a loaf of bread, fifty cents; a liter of quite nice wine, a dollar; a kilo of margarine, a dollar; a two-pound chicken, three dollars. . . . The average white-collar worker in Yugoslavia earns $116 a month. . . .

Which may account for why, late at night, two miles west of the city in the restaurants of Gruze, broody workers sing, in mahogany voices, dark and mournful songs under the pergolas. (I eat grilled red mullet, and drink Zilavka, a dry and fruity white wine from Mostar: fourteen dollars.) Gruze was once a suburb of summer palaces in the Venetian-Gothic style; the palaces were looted and burned in the Napoleonic wars. Now a commercial harbor, it is also the home of Minceta, a state-run department store — $20 for a bikini, $1.30 for a Matchbox car; $22 for a child's blue jeans; half a month's salary for a child's winter boots (thirteen cents for a child to ride on a mechanical pony); $5.50 for a Cyndi Lauper tape, *True Colors.*

Dubrovnik is in part a dreary consumer wasteland (fatty, sweaty sausages hang on hooks in every butcher shop) and in part a setting for the food of sultans — melons, persimmons, figs: a Turkish delight.

Purple and rose and peach are the true colors of the exquisite old shawls and rugs in a shop off the Placa owned by a woman who, passionate and incoherent, reels off names of Montenegrin heroes as familiar to her as Washington and Jefferson and Lincoln are to me; she is forty-seven, and she has lost her chance to have "eleven children, so as to outdo the Serbians. . . ." She is an ethnic Albanian. . . . Montenegrins are among the most beautiful people in the world. "One thinks one is visiting a movie set all the time when one is in Montenegro," an acquaintance says; "such beauty in such a lonely place." So I go there.

*

Along the coast, past the medieval walled towns of Kotor and Budva, both devastated by earthquakes in 1979 ("Kotor is under the protection of UNESCO," my guide says glumly; "so it will take years to restore it"; "Budva is not under the protection of UNESCO," he says, "so it will take years to repair it" — he has no gift for irony, in general Yugoslavs do not), past the narrow Bay of Kotor, finger-fjords that thrust into the flanks of pale mountains; and inland by means of a spiral road (reserved for tourist coaches that negotiate its harpin turns like moray eels), a serpentine "ladder," which, in seventeen dizzying loops over a distance of nine kilometers, takes us to the plateau town of Cetinje, once the capital of Montenegro — a drive of several hours; and we find ourselves in yet another world.

Until 1851, tiny windswept Montenegro, now one of six Yugoslav republics, was ruled by a succession of prince-bishops, the Eastern Church and the government being indistinguishable and indivisible. This oasis in a petrified sea of stone was a darling of imperial Russia — its daughters went to Russian boarding schools. The odd thing about Montenegro is that it was a fierce state and a joke state, simultaneously. For hundreds of years, Montenegro kept the Turks at bay (heads of Moslems were regularly served up on platters); and during World War II, partisans in these blank and rugged mountains waged war with absolute bravery. (Gladstone once compared Montenegro's heroism to that of Thermopylae and Marathon.) And yet, after it became a sovereign state in 1878, no ambassador could have seen a posting here, to the kingdom of King Nicholas — first and last (and self-appointed) king of Montenegro — as anything but disgrace. For Cetinje never was, and still is not, anything more than a one-street town, a broad but not a noble street, which was, in living memory, lined with hovels and with palaces. One begins almost unconsciously to hum the "Merry Widow Waltz" as soon as one arrives; for surely this preposterous and pretentious and yet jovial little kingdom was the inspiration for Ruritania, a musical comedy principality. Nicholas was a buffoon ruling over a kingdom of rocks and huts and foreign embassies, no less a simpleton because one of his daughters married Vittorio Emanuele III, king of Italy; another married the king of Serbia; and two became grand duchesses (one of whom introduced Rasputin to the Russian court). Another of his daughters gave birth to the future king of Yugoslavia. In embalmed Cetinje are the lost kingdoms of a lost world embalmed.

Faded embassies — French (a Nouveau structure apparently made of Silly Putty and glass), English, Austrian, and Italian, line the dusty streets. The modest salmon-and-white royal palace, with its toylike sentry boxes, its portraits of royals, its absurdly unimportant marcasite medals, its rather more impressive guns and sabers, its time-bleached military and ceremonial costumes (tarnished epaulets) and court dresses, its superfluity of gilt mirrors, its ridiculous Javanese furniture, its crimson dining room with gifts of plate from Napoleon and Josephine (a dining room that resembles, with its motley silver, an Anglo-Indian mess), its silk-covered walls and grimly gray-white lace curtains, is a visited tomb. Even the royal brass bed looks as if it were made for comic performances — though twelve royal children were conceived here.

This is the poorest part of the Balkan peninsula, its history gnarled, its location in a stony crater dramatic but unenviable — "like a town set inside the brainpan of an enormous skull," Rebecca West called it. And yet (in Yugoslavia there is always an "on the other hand") our trip back to the coast takes us not only through a wilderness of stone, but past quince orchards and occasional basins of alluvial soil upon which sheep and cows and goats graze; and past Lake Scutari, whose legendary beauty we must take on faith, for this lake that resides partly in Albania, an outlaw state (there is a certain frisson in passing it), is wreathed in mists.

This journey to another land, another time, has taken just a day.

The prince of Wales and Mrs. Simpson once had occasion to call on the resort town of Budva; and — while I have no great affection for those two — I am glad of that; I am glad that Budva was the source of sunny pleasure, for I still cannot quite grasp the relationship of Slavs (all these walled and fortified cities) to the nourishing and healing sea. (The Yugoslavian government, on the other hand, has more than adequately grasped the importance of sea and sun to foreign tourists; the houses of whole fishing villages have been gutted and made determinedly picturesque and habitable for visitors.) It is perhaps because of the ambivalence I perceive that I spend my last day in Yugoslavia at the aquarium in the walled city, like a child on a school outing.

It is nicely cool here. Crabs tap-dance. Sea anemones with long purple tresses (remarkably like those of the murdered woman pictured on the cover of my penny-dreadful mystery novel) and sea anemones like velvet radishes and a scarlet starfish and a wrinkled albino scorpion fish and fuchsia net coral and tangerine twig coral and iridescent fish — blue, silver, pink, speckled, blotched — slither and insinuate. A conger stands on his tail and appears ready to address me, like a character in *Alice in Wonderland*. A lobster, like a bloated orange cockroach, waves. This place pleases me.

Outside, everything is subtly different. The warm air, lately threaded with cold, has turned positively nippy. My square has changed. There are few tourists now. The children of the town, hitherto not much in evidence, are out in force. Skateboards and bikes zip by on the glassy stones of the Placa. The children crowd the cafés as if reclaiming an occupied zone. The waiters serve them solemnly and with evident pleasure. From the direction of the Pile Gate comes — it is twilight — a marching band. Red jackets, brass buttons; trumpets blare. I take this unexplained display of ceremony and good cheer as an omen. When I reach my hotel — which seems to me now like a white city upon a hill — I see to my amazement someone snorkeling in a wet suit. All I see of him (her?) is an orange snorkel, bright blue fins (like the tail feathers of the bird of hope). I go to the swimming pool, from which I see the snorkler, who glides along, hugging the coast. I regard the snorkler's presence as an invitation to return. In summer when the shining water is warm.

Nadia Comaneci (1990)

◆ ◆ ◆

SHE SOARED through the air with insouciance and with the delicacy of apparent ease; we loved her. She swam and danced through air as no one had before her; and what we read in her movements was joy. She was fourteen, and she combined an exquisite elfin fragility with tensile strength; her body defied mental categorization, challenged our ideas of gender and of physical law — it seemed to belong neither to a boy nor a girl nor an androgyne; it was *sui generis,* a Nadia-body, just as her fleeting smile was a Nadia-smile, unique to her, and indecipherable. Beautifully alien and improbable (her performance was called "biochemically inconceivable"), grave when she accepted her three gold Olympic medals, a preternaturally solemn child, a little girl whose charm lay precisely in her failure to exercise facile charm, she became, in a few short days, both more and less than human: she became an icon.

Time passed. (It was unlikely she gave serious consideration to the passing of time; she is not given to introspection, analysis, or metaphysical inquiry, and metaphysical inquiry was not encouraged in Romania, which was, during the years of her glory, ruled by a monster who made critical thinking a crime, cannibalized his country spiritually and materially, and enshrined evil as good.) Fourteen years after Nadia Comaneci won three gold medals, one silver, and one bronze in Montreal, the twenty-eight-year-old perfect 10 — the first person ever to be awarded a perfect 10 in Olympic history — defected from the demon state of Romania. America took her in. We were prepared to love her again — we'd never stopped loving her, she'd given us no reason to. (And it is in the nature of icons to stay fixed, to remain trapped lovingly in time.)

Almost immediately she tested our desire to embrace her. She was accompanied by Constantin Panait, a thirty-six-year-old Romanian immigrant, a self-employed roofer who had planned and overseen her escape. Nicely romantic. Except that Panait (who at first told reporters that he was French, an apparently gratuitous lie) was a married man with four small children, two, four, five, and eight. Asked at a press conference in Pompano Beach, Florida, whether it troubled her that her presumed lover was a married man, Nadia replied matter-of-factly, unwisely, and unendearingly: "So what?"

Soon Nadia and Constantin — a coarse fellow with gorilla good looks — were on the road, sleeping in motels from Florida to Cleveland to Los Angeles. Constantin, who had abandoned his wife, Maria, in the Romanian community of Hallandale, Florida, became known, not affectionately, as the Adulterous Roofer. Nadia became known as a homewrecker.

Nadia sold her story to the *London Mail*. (So did Constantin's impoverished wife.) With the blunt and interfering Constantin acting as her "manager," Nadia interested David Frost in producing a movie about her life. . . . Ah, capitalism! How quickly she'd caught on to the art of the quick buck, the main chance, the immediate fix. Well, who could blame her? Nadia's life had been dominated, not only by dreary Communism, but by a surreally eccentric villain, Nicolae Ceausescu, and his bloodthirsty regime. Nadia, and, before his own escape to the West twelve years earlier, Constantin, had been for all practical purposes not subjects but slaves. All Romanians were slaves . . . except for the masters.

Nadia made her escape a week before Ceausescu's government, was, in one of history's crackerjack surprises, overturned. After forty years of suffering, Romania seemed to be giving birth to itself as a free nation, in a series of actions as reality-defying as one of Nadia's double twists or somersaults. For once the light at the end of a tunnel was not the light of an oncoming train; it was the spirited will to hope, the flame of freedom from tyranny.

Her timing was bad. She had left just before the party began.

Well, anyone can make an error of timing, that's the story of most of our lives. But there was much about her guarded past that gave rise to unhappy speculation: she had been exorbitantly privileged in a country where most people subsisted on nettles and chicken feet and dry biscuits, and many people died of starvation. . . . Yes, but who, offered life's necessities — or luxuries — as a reward for one's (astonishing) work, would have the courage to refuse them? Who, in the name of the commonweal, would have the strength of character to resist? In Romania, a vocal dissident was a dead saint. Perhaps she was an appropriate subject for pity?

But there was more: she had been part of the inner circle of a demented ruler who obliged women to line up for gynecological examinations and forced them to bear future workers for the state, as a consequence of which hundreds of thousands of children were abandoned by mothers who could not feed them. They lived a half-life in sub-Dickensian orphanages, from which Ceausescu recruited the secret police, the Securitate, thus becoming their father and eliciting their loyalty forever.

There was more and more: she had been by all accounts the mistress of Nicu Ceausescu, the son of the dictator, a polymorphously perverse torturer and rapist, his father's political lieutenant, a man as like unto his father as made no difference.

If this terrible thing were true, the Nadia we loved — the child who inspired us to joy — was lost in the woman she'd become. And her affair with the Adulterous Roofer paled.

I caught up with Nadia and Constantin in Los Angeles.

I came to think of our meeting in Los Angeles as a meeting on one side of a warped and cloudy looking glass. I think of my later trip to Bucharest as a passage to the other side of the looking glass — the side where the graspable truth about the strange life of Nadia Comaneci is to be found.

"How fat and ugly you are," I said. I meant of course that she was not. She was pretty. A little used-looking, perhaps, but — one wanted so much to see the incandescent child in her — pretty.

"I am fat and ugly," she said, her wary eyes, exaggeratedly penciled in black (1950s Cleopatra style), darkening. She pouts. The enigmatic smile she wore at the Olympics still hasn't gotten itself right: it is part grimace, part grin, part reluctant acknowledgment of praise. Sometimes she emits a high-pitched giggle that has nothing to do with a smile.

She is wearing a blue blouse of some shiny stuff, a black leather jacket, a black leather miniskirt, black nylons (her good legs are shown to good advantage), black stiletto heels on which the price sticker still remains. Her leather jacket cost four hundred dollars. (Constantin knows the price of everything and likes to talk about it.) She wears dangling rhinestone earrings, overlapping circles that remind her of the Olympics logo. She bought them in Disney World. There is a smell that clings to her — impossible not to notice, something both sweet and rank, feral.

"How long this interview will take?" Constantin asks, bullying with a smile, his notion of how to do business American-style. He wears a diamond cluster ring on his pinky finger, a gold ring with the Mercedes-Benz emblem on the fourth finger of his left hand, a shirt shot through with silver threads. He dyes his hair.

In the dining room of my hotel, Nadia orders sweet champagne. I have reserved a table where we are guaranteed privacy. This is a mistake. Nadia covets attention. All those thousands of eyes that have adored her every move, the lush applause that met her when her little feet touched the ground, the voices crying her name: *Nad-ya Nad-ya* — she craves that now. She does not like the location of the table, she feels cheated; she looks sullen and unanchored. When the waiter pays her court — and spills champagne on me — she responds with feigned indifference . . . and a tight little triumphant smile. Her sense of entitlement is voracious. "Give me more champagne," she says, "more meat." This deficiency is not one of language — we speak Italian together as well as English, and I never hear her say Please or Thank you in either language. It owes nothing to shyness. It is a deficiency of grace. At the 7-Eleven near her apartment, she says: "Coca-Cola." The clerk looks at her hard, wanting to form some human connection which she is determined to withhold.

Her appetite for food is voracious. She eats her own food and Constantin's too. After each course, she goes to the bathroom. She is gone for a long time. She comes back, her eyes watery, picks her teeth, and eats some more. She eats mountains of raspberries, and my crème brulée. She makes her way to the bathroom again. When she returns, she is wreathed in that rank sweet smell.

*

They live — provisionally — in a modest one-bedroom apartment in West Los Angeles that resembles a medium-price motel. The predominating colors are gray and black; the bed is king-size, rumpled. They make a giggly to-do about Nadia's liking to cook. (Constantin has grasped, if belatedly, that "image" counts.) The cupboards are bare. Nadia "cooks" coffee, instant. Against the drawn vertical blinds (the sun doesn't enter this room) there is a headless tailor's dummy covered with black felt on which are stuck glitzy brooches, gleaming dully. All the plants are dead. The television is always on. They like this place.

We watch a tape cassette of Nadia being interviewed in 1984 by an ABC reporter in Los Angeles. She can be seen at one point in the interview to frown, stumble, falter; her answers become forced and staccato — she has glimpsed, from the corner of a watchful eye, a member of the Securitate strolling (like a movie extra) behind her. All her life she has been followed, observed.

Next to the television set is a cardboard cutout of Shirley Temple.

According to myth, as we have come to accept it, coach Bela Karolyi discovered Nadia in a village kindergarten class in Muldavia, three hundred kilometers from Bucharest, when she was six years old. *Who wants to be a gymnast?* he said. *I do; I do!* Nadia said. Thereafter he fine-tuned her body to perfection.

Karolyi defected to America in 1981. Nadia was the gymnast "most mature and closest to my heart," he says. He told her he was going to defect, whereupon the nineteen-year-old Nadia cried: *Take me with you! Take me with you!* He didn't take her because "she was 'not finished,' kind of spoiled by fame and fortune. I couldn't expose her to the frustration of an uncertain and confused future, a new culture, a new language. I couldn't give her family warmth.

"Nadia is still Nadia, tenacious and restless, hard and strong, harsh, superaggressive, hard to change. People like Nadia start to feel that because everything is granted to them they deserve everything — they don't feel the pain of anyone else around them.

"Of course I have heard that she was Nicu's lover. I have no specific knowledge. I will say that she was ambitious. She wanted the highest social ranking in the country and all the doors were open to her. . . . She was always a hungry girl."

Nadia denies that she and Constantin are lovers. Nadia denies that she and Nicu were lovers. Nadia — "Hero of Socialist Labor of Romania" — now denies she ever led a privileged life. Nadia hates Bela Karolyi.

In 1984, a movie called *Nadia* was made, according to Nadia with Bela Karolyi's collaboration: "He makes many lies. He wants to be the star," she says, "he wants to be the best . . . so he makes many lies. He is not my first coach. He is only my fourth coach. My first coach was Israeli. He doesn't discover me, it's a lie. My mother brought me to the gymnasium. He tells people I try to commit suicide because I have a boyfriend who doesn't love me. I never had a boyfriend. I never liked boys. When I was twenty-five I start to like boys, not before. He didn't give me no time for boys. He doesn't tell me he's going to defect, I know it only when he is not on the plane to Romania. I am the star."

A star so bright she was in danger of eclipsing Ceausescu, according to Nadia, who says that if her picture appeared on the front page of the official newspaper too often, Ceausescu would halt publication, preferring to see his own face. "Why shouldn't I be on the front page? I do something. Ceausescu doesn't do anything."

She smiles dreamily. She is thinking of Ceausescu's wife, Elena, executed along with him by the revolutionary government, the Council of National Salvation. A vile woman said to have bugged every hotel room in Bucharest so that she could entertain herself by listening to what people did in bed, Elena was also an ugly woman: "She is beautiful now," Nadia says with a high giggle. "She is very beautiful dead. Now she is beautiful. Dead."

Nicu she dismisses: "Why people are telling these lies? Because I work for him at the Young Communist party — only to make the money. And I am famous. I am the famous one. So when people see Nicu and see me, they think we are lovers only because they know me. All lies."

It has been reported that Nadia was engaged to a soccer player who was beaten to a pulp by Nicu and his thugs at their engagement party. "What party?" Nadia says. "What party? There was no party. There was no party. He didn't come, he didn't come, he didn't come. . . .

"Maybe Nicu will be dead like his father, too," Nadia says.

Constantin says: "Maybe Barbara will be dead. Maybe the Securitate will follow her and kill her and she will be dead."

"Yes," says Nadia, who has watched me trip over a step in her kitchen and ignominiously fall without batting an eyelash, "maybe you will be dead. . . .

"Why, if I lived so good in Romania, I came here?" Nadia asks with plausible logic. "I work for the money and I buy the house." With the money she received from the Ceausescu government for winning at the Olympics — $1,700 in American money, Nadia says — she bought a big house ("because I like it," she adds, as if that explained everything); but the house is not entirely paid for, and she had no money to pay for gas to warm it, and her electricity was rationed just like everybody else's — in Bucharest a forty-watt bulb was considered sufficient to light an entire flat — and she too had to have ID to buy food: "I have no money in the bank."

One of the first things she did when she came here was to buy a 1990 Camaro convertible with a sticker price of $20,300. It is now in the garage, either because — they are unable to settle on a reason — Constantin's license has expired or because the car needs repairs.

The phone rings constantly with people wanting to make deals. Constantin makes all the deals. Nadia is going to do commercials on Italian television. Constantin agreed to an interview with ABC's Connie Chung largely on the grounds that "she is pretty." Soon Nadia — or Constantin — will have money in the bank.

I draw a crude graph: "Here are the rich people," I say, "here are those who live so-so, and here are the common people in Romania. Where are you?" Nadia points to the line that separates the common people from those who live "so-so." . . . "Almost so-so," she says.

Constantin tells me where, when I go to Bucharest, I can exchange dollars on the black market at ten times the official rate of exchange, where I can find a shearling coat cheap: "The system can be beat if you play right, if you are a little smart," he says.

Nadia says she likes him because he's smart.

She doesn't love him, that's what she says. He doesn't love her, that's what he says. They have no plans to marry. They "stay" together, they do not "live" together.

After their initial gaffe, they told the American press that they were together but chaste and would remain so until their marriage. When this was greeted with cynicism, they changed the story again. According to the re-revision of the story, Nadia "knew he was married, he told me. So what? He is my manager. A manager can be married or not married."

They are sitting together on the gray couch holding hands.

She has been called unknowable, a Garbo of sports. She tests the prevailing winds. She gives people what she thinks they want in the way of a line (her training has equipped her for this superbly); her voice is flat and uninflected, it lacks the color and ardency of truth. She performs grudgingly. Reading what she has said over the years is like walking through halls of mirrors: she issues denials and counterdenials, she writes and rewrites the script, editing all the time, contradicting her contradictions. This time she has a collaborator: Constantin. Perhaps she has always had a collaborator. Or a director. Sometimes her face in its orangy makeup looks both tough and frightened, and very small.

Constantin explodes: "It's bad when you take a walk and people say, Hey, look at that guy — he left his wife and four children. How you think I feel then? It's nice when you know people love you." Constantin says that it is his heart's desire to return to his wife and to the children he loves, but that his wife, embittered and unsympathetic, will probably not have him. He stays with Nadia out of gallantry: "We have a lot of protection when we get to New York, twenty policemen, and in Miami we have state police; now we have nothing. I can't tell Nadia I am worried because then she will be scared. She needs protection. She is here all alone. I must take care of her."

When it was known that Nadia had escaped, she says, Nicu ordered the Securitate to find her and bring her back dead or alive.

Nadia truly believed that when Romanians heard she'd defected it would be "like a bomb. A bomb for the government. Because what will the people think? That even Nadia leaves Romania. They thought I had the good life . . . but I didn't, I lived just like the others. . . . But they thought I had the good life there, and they will think, If *she* leaves. . . ." Constantin wants the Romanian people to know that he is happy to have been of use to the revolution. Nadia actually believes she catalyzed the revolution by leaving Romania . . . for a "freedom" she cannot in any language define.

Some people need to hate just as others need to love.

And for some people life outside the spotlight is death.

I am going to tell the story as Nadia tells the story, as if truth — which is the first casualty of tyranny — is still in her.

Nadia lived away from her parents (an office worker and a car mechanic), who divorced after the Montreal Olympics, and away from her younger brother, in a gymnastic training school in Moldavia, two girls to a room. She saw her parents once a week. She trained eight hours a day, seven days a week, with two hours for classroom lessons from eleven to one in the afternoon, and homework at night, Sunday mornings off.

Nadia did not go to church for fear, she says, of being observed. Nadia did go to church one morning — "the day Jesus was born." She does not know the word for *Christmas* in any language.

She was happy to have won the Montreal Olympics — and also bewildered: she couldn't see what all the fuss was about. She'd just done her job. She'd done what she'd been trained eight years to do. She expected no less of herself. She knew how good she was. It was strange, all that attention. She wanted to go home.

When she competed in the 1980 Olympics in Moscow, she fell off the bars. Wrangling among judges and officials about her score delayed the games thirty minutes. (She won the silver). She blames herself: she fell off the bars. She blames photographers: their flashbulbs blinded her. She blames the Soviet Union: Moscow would never have allowed a Romanian to win.

She can't live without winning; but the cost of winning is high. She can't live without being in the spotlight; but the spotlight blinds her.

Once, before a European competition in Strasbourg, she did not eat for seven days. She had to get her weight down from 140 pounds. (Five feet three inches, she weighed eighty-five pounds in Montreal.) After the fourth day of her enforced fast, Karolyi gave her food, but her stomach had shrunk and she couldn't eat; she gave the food away. Her muscles cramped. She was dizzy and seeing double when she competed. She won.

("How did you feel?"
"Happy. I won.")
When she was fifteen she tried to commit suicide by drinking bleach. (She has heretofore denied this.) She does not regret having tried to commit suicide; she does not regret having failed. She was tired. She rested in the hospital for two days, and was therefore "glad — glad because I didn't have to go to the gym for two days, so I am happy."

No one has seen her cry. Previously it was a source of pride to her that she never cried. Now she says she cried when she retired before the 1984 games. She cries, she says, when she watches herself perform.

It was not the same for her after 1980. Her situation deteriorated until, toward the end, she went into a kind of official limbo, coaching a little in Romania, being permitted to attend the '84 and '88 Olympics, but only for a few days. She does not like to speak of this murky time.

She met Constantin at a party in Bucharest. He had, he said, already helped a cousin to escape. He had escaped by means of swimming across the Danube clothed, a feat he practiced for six months; he spent eleven days in a Yugoslavian jail until sympathetic guards showed him the way to freedom. Thus he appeared to Nadia in the guise of a hero. He offered to help her escape; two years later, he returned to fulfill his pledge. (Why the Ceausescu government allowed him a visa to get back in is a mystery.)

Dressed only in jeans and a jeans jacket, Nadia and five others walked for six hours to get across the border into Hungary, where Constantin, who had driven ahead of them in a car rented in Hungary, met them by arrangement at a police station. There were glitches — the six had trouble finding a police station where they could make themselves understood — and it was bloody cold; they made it. What has happened to the five people who escaped with Nadia they do not know (nor do they particularly seem to care), having seen the last of them in Vienna, where Nadia was granted asylum by the United States government. Little Nadia Comaneci.

We are on Muscle Beach in Venice. Nadia is posing, reluctantly, for the camera. Constantin is bumbling into other people's fields of expertise. The last time she was here, in 1984, Nadia was surrounded by police and helicopters and adoring fans. Now she is surrounded by homeless men and women sleeping on the sand, by bums in gazebos drinking wine from Dixie cups and hacking terminal coughs; about them she expresses no interest at all. Nothing in this wide beach world interests her.

She eats a huge plate of Mexican food and goes into the bathroom.

Riding back home she snuggles against Constantin in the car; her smell is ripe. Her giggles seem to arise from a faraway place.

We are in a Romanian restaurant in downtown Los Angeles. There is a private party going on, but the owners are persuaded to set a table for Nadia anyway. Introduced, she thanks "American and Romanian people." Her characteristic brevity is like her smile — one suspects it contains many warring things. There remains an inclination to love her. Americans and Romanians pay her court. Her half smile comes into weary play. She eats two bowls of tripe in a milky white sauce with vinegar and liquid garlic, and her sausages and Constantin's sausages, and pickles. She goes to the bathroom. The Romanians tell her that the first thing you need in America is a public relations man and the second a lawyer. This is the kind of talk Constantin likes. David Frost's executive producer is with us. He wants to cast Holly Hunter as Nadia. I think Nastassia Kinski. And Tommy Lee Jones as Constantin.

Nadia and Constantin hold hands under the table.

Nadia has promised to give me the addresses of her brother, Adrian, who lives in her house in Bucharest, and her mother; I will take in the coffee and cigarettes Nadia will buy. I wait for two days for the addresses I have been promised. "I want my brother to come here. I want my brother," she says; "my brother."

On the first day Constantin calls several times with several different excuses for the delay. On the second day he does not answer the phone. (I imagine them feverishly writing a new script, the Bucharest script.) On the morning of the third day, when I am about to leave for Bucharest, he calls to tell me that he has given the coffee and cigarettes to fellow Romanians to bring in. He tells me Nadia's family is scared, scared of retribution from remaining

Ceausescu loyalists, and scared of Libyan and Syrian antirevolutionary terrorists, too. Afraid, they have left Bucharest.

This, as it happens, is untrue.

Constantin will give me no addresses. Nadia defers to Constantin. I go to the apartment to say goodbye; they do not answer the doorbell, though shadows move behind the drawn shades. On the phone, I collect from Nadia a dull goodbye.

Bucharest is dark brown and bitter yellow. Black smoke blankets an undistinguished skyline — Ceausescu tore down houses, churches, and synagogues to make imperial palaces for himself and monolithic high-rise buildings for the Securitate.

But in this Orwellian city the hope and cheer of the people, troubled though they are by the vacuum of leadership, to say nothing of the lack of food, is palpable. The soldiers at Passport Control and the young women who carefully and apologetically search us accept congratulations for the revolution with charming smiles, though their jobs require them to be stern. It is like being present at a birth — one is full of trepidation and of joy, pity, terror: life. People grin. For forty dark years they had no access to information about the outside world except that which they could gather from clandestine radio: the BBC, Radio Free Europe. Now the world, in expectation, is coming to them.

On the way to our hotel (where gypsies stop us in the lift and ask us if we want to change money), we see makeshift memorials — candles and heaps of dried flowers — to the thousands Ceausescu killed on the night of the spontaneous uprising of December 20.

In Bucharest everyone has a story, and Ceausescu's thievery of Romania's material goods and its soul takes bizarre and consequential form.

Ceausescu — a worthy successor to Vlad the Impaler and Dracula — once decided to allow the discipline of transcendental meditation into Romania under the auspices of the Institute of Pedagogy. Then, just as capriciously, he declared it heresy, and punished the people he had appointed to sponsor it, firing everybody at the institute, research scientists, professors, all. Having lost their party membership, they became manual laborers: street cleaners, toilet attendants.

Ceausescu devised something called the Hymn to Romania, which seems to have no earthly counterpart. All of culture and the arts came under the umbrella of this "Hymn" — folklore, symphonies, books (the authors of which had not only to register their typewriters with the police — privacy threatened his absolute control — but to acknowledge Ceausescu as their father and inspirer).

The liberated people spend hours rehearsing Ceausescu's madness . . . and hours berating themselves for the compromises they had to make in order to survive. One marvels at the durability of the human spirit, the courage and intelligence of those who survived and endured, damaged but decent and rejoicing.

At night there is television. Ceausescu allowed only two hours of television a day — and he usurped the larger part of that time. One night there is footage of a Bucharest orphanage — children with soiled clothes in dirty white iron cribs, children under three rocking their unwashed bodies back and forth to tranquilize themselves, hitting their heads against walls with autistic precision.

One night on Romanian Free Television, against the background of this horror, there is a news item about Nadia and Nicu: hotelkeepers in an elite Romanian mountain resort speak of having seen the lovers together on holiday.

"The thing about Nadia," my driver, Romeo, says, "is that she was not very smart."

"The thing about Nadia," Emanuel Valeriu, a sports journalist who led a double life for over twenty years as a reporter for Radio Free Europe, says, "is that she was stupid."

It is probably true that while her body possessed a kind of genius, fate denied her symmetry: the muscles of her imagination were shrunken and slack. Nadia Comaneci is not, and probably never was, very bright.

"A selfish little girl," Valeriu says. "Getting packages of sweets and never sharing them with the others. And vomiting, too."

And, one hears, getting hormones and endocrinologic drugs as well.

Could she, given all this, have been other than she is? God knows.

(The Securitate got Nicu everything he wanted, and of course he'd want her, she was Romania's "only celebrity.")

"She was a horrible character, became just like Ceausescu,"

Valeriu says. "Prototype of zero. Tried to elope with a folksinger, an actor — a homosexual. Ceausescu decreed a state of emergency — airplane and surface traffic was stopped, they thought she'd been kidnapped. Then she lived with Nicu — he's just as stupid as she is; and then — who know why? perhaps another lover? — she fell into disgrace. She did better than some of Nicu's lovers. They just disappeared."

Her mother and her brother are in Bucharest; Romeo finds them. (Romanians are practiced in conspiracies and in getting news from word of mouth: mouth-to-mouth resuscitation.)

We drive through empty streets in brown fog, flames licking at shallow puddles of kerosene oil at the improvised memorials. It is not safe at night: the Securitate still hides in sewers and shadows and occasionally emerges to shoot. One can see that the city must once have been beautiful — there is a hint of old beauty in the curve of certain streets, in Art Nouveau confectionery and pastry shops (empty, however, of goods), in noble and handsome villas that Ceausescu did not get around to destroying.

In one of them, on a quiet street of villas near Ceausescu's huge and ugly unfinished palace, lives Nadia's brother, Adrian, in the house that belongs to her.

Bowls of grapefruit and lemons perfume the cream-colored French villa, so pretty with its white shutters, its gingerbread, its charming French doors. It is toasty warm inside and full of light . . . and full, in a depressing way, of Nadia. (If, as Nadia says, the Securitate has been here to vandalize, there is no sign of it.) Middle European mahogany antiques are scattered, along with stiff brocaded furniture groupings, on blond parquet floors. Vases of ruby and cut glass are everywhere. Her bedroom is that of a virginal whore; it is a contradiction in terms: the drapes are made of screaming scarlet cloth; the double bed, unpillowed, is covered in screaming scarlet cloth. The room is as neat as a convent girl's.

Twenty-three-year-old Adrian's wife, pretty and mousy and soft, takes me by the hand to show me the house. There is a trophy room. Cups and medals. Like a museum. Lifeless.

There is a room, painted acid green, filled with stuffed animals and dolls — three hundred, Nadia has said she collected; there are perhaps a couple of dozen here, some still in their origi-

nal boxes, some — porcelain — of value (and one of jade, a foot
high), some simperingly cute and cheap; and one of Nadia.

Her brother is a skinhead. He holds the Nadia doll. A twang
of incestuous longing is in the air. Adrian, holding his sister's
image and idol in his arms, says Nadia is "difficult and sentimental. . . . She must always be told that she is beautiful and good . . .
but I am only her brother, she will not believe me. . . ." I think
perhaps he is the only person she believes. I think Constantin will
go the way of Nicu and of Karolyi: she will not love him anymore.
I think she loves Adrian. He loves her. A visitor asks him to wear
Nadia's gold medals. He recoils, reeling: "Nadia worked for
them," he protests, his oily black eyes, slick with fanaticism, hazel
in the light, sparking; the visitor has defamed an icon.

And defames it further by asking if the rumors about Nicu are
true. Adrian looks so sad. He says only that Nicu was "powerful
power" — as if to say: She was coerced.

In the dining room — an unsuccessful copy of an American
suburban breakfast room — we drink a disgusting mixture of
white wine and Pepsi-Cola. And we watch a tape cassette on
Adrian's VCR of Nadia's last birthday party, November 12.

Nadia dances with bloated men and cadaverous men, not a
good-looking man among them. A long table groans with food.
(The hotel has run out of milk; the country has a five-day supply
of meat.) Adrian keeps up a running commentary, from which I
conclude that they miss each other as much as two people who
have almost never seen each other can miss each other, which is to
say very much and romantically. They look alike. In my experience
one either hates or absolutely loves a sibling one exactly resembles.
It was my impression that Nadia's love for her brother was the
most authentic, least corrupted part of her. I think as I watch
Adrian gaze at his sister's flickering image — the television is a
shrine — that they are searching for the mystical lost half of each
other in each other.

Adrian does not know his sister's telephone number; he does
not know where she lives. She has not called him. She has not
written him. (Ah, and there is such a frenzy of calling all over
Romania now, when voices almost forgotten can once again be
heard.) He does not hold her in ill-regard for this. (He is amazed
to be of this flesh, the flesh of a Hero.) He is wistful. And he hates

Constantin. "Is it only for the money she lives with him?" he asks. "Perhaps such things are different in America?" His sister's life is incomprehensible to him. It always has been. She has said she saw him once a week. He looks at me in sorrow and confusion: how he would love to have seen her as often as once a week! Please will she send him airplane tickets?

"I saw her at the airport, I waited with all the other people," Nadia's mother says, "never once a week. . . . How does she live? Where does she live? In what city does she live? She is happy? She is happy *now*, perhaps, but Constantin. . . ." Nadia's mother, Stephanie Alexandrina — Steffi — makes a sour face. Men have their uses, but their uses are ephemeral, she implies; in the bedroom she jerks a painted thumb at a wedding picture and says *Comaneci*, investing the name of her husband with contempt. She sticks her tongue out at the picture and kisses me on the lips. "Bad man, Constantin." (Thumbs down.) . . . "Will Nadia send me the airplane tickets? Will she call me? . . . He wants her money only. . . ."

Is it true that her daughter became interested in boys only when she was twenty-five, I ask. Steffi regards me with astonishment and asks me if I am mad.

Steffi Comaneci, a cashier in a bank, lives in a comfortable three-room apartment near a row of embassy houses guarded by police. (Nadia's villa adjoined a small military compound — this family was well protected.) She is a bottle blonde, she smells of garlic and of used-up sex. She wears high heels and a black kimono. She is full of forced vitality. She flirts. She serves us sausages — it is midnight — and mashed eggplant and white bread and goat cheese; she eats pickles. "I drink only white wine," she says, red wine being an aphrodisiac. In fact she is quaffing quantities of red wine; there are two men in the room. She changes from her kimono to a dress of some crepey turquoise stuff, offering us all a glimpse of a still good thigh and bikini underpants. She is proud of her body. ("She should be," Romeo says; "she has used it enough for the pleasure of the Securitate.") In her bedroom — a luxury to have a separate bedroom in Romania — lights flash blue and pink.

The living room is full of dolls. Nylon curtains tacked to a pink stucco wall frame a mural of palm trees and white sand and blue sea. She is a fantasist. She is an idea of sex, not the thing itself, a campy parody. She gives me a letter to mail to Nadia.

For all her brass, she is unable to bring herself to ask for her own daughter's address.

Tanks are in the ruined square where Ceausescu ordered the army to shoot his own people; tanks crushed hundreds. From all over Romania people come to see the buildings pockmarked from gun-fire, the memorials to the brave young dead. Students stand on line for the cinema. Men and women stand on line for coffee and sugar and meat. For years starved of news — "Our only hope was that we were not as bad as North Korea, we had further to fall," one woman says wryly to me — people read and talk voraciously, their hunger unappeasable. Now they can talk without worrying that they are talking to a spy, without guarding every precious word; imagine rationing words, rationing friendship and loyalty for forty years. The future is unclear; the present is perilous but delicious, too.

To all these things Nadia, Adrian, and Steffi seem perfectly indifferent. They think of things in terms of usury; if revolution means anything at all to them, it means chocolate and hatred. They are entirely, tragically, self-absorbed.

I listen to people young and old measuring the moral dimensions of the compromises they were forced to make. I listen to them speak of Nadia — a young woman who lived an extravagantly privileged life, and knew it. They call her a moral nonentity. Do they feel sorry for her? "No. . . . Her friends were butchers. There were cruel butchers and butchers not so cruel; but they were butchers. From them she got favors." And even then, they say, it wasn't enough for her. And what if she were to come back? She won't come back, they say; she is irrelevant, a woman to be de-spised.

Is it possible, I wonder, to think of her as a captive — a captive of a diabolical regime; a captive of a wicked man, Nicu; a captive, once, to a gymnastic training that stunted her mind as it perfected her body; a captive, perhaps, to loneliness and self-delusion (all icons are lonely, being denied the common fate).

Perhaps if I had not gone to Bucharest I might have seen Nadia in this light; I might have seen her as a victim. She was a casualty. My pity for her was tempered by my admiration and love for those men and women who had resisted tyranny and maintained their integrity through dark and bitter years. They miraculously embody the truth that the meek will inherit the earth: for them, to whom nothing was given, the future is rich with hope; having once tasted freedom, they can never look back. To them, much has been granted, not the least of which is their souls — "no longer on sale in the black market," says a woman who lost six of her family in Auschwitz, an official "nonperson" who never sacrificed her essential dignity for material gain.

Poor Nadia. What will become of her?

On my way to the airport, the road lined with tanks and soldiers, I remembered something she'd said. I'd asked her why she'd chosen to live in Los Angeles. "Because it is easy to park the car there," she said. It was as good a reason as any she could come up with; it was the measure of her life.

Mary: The Stars in Her Crown (1989)

✦ ✦ ✦

NOON IN MEDJUGORJE, a grass oval in front of the parish church of St. James.

A two-by-four cuts through the air in a wide, controlled arc, culminating in the pulpy sound of opposing wood meeting passive flesh. An orange mongrel dog — whose flesh and fur and bone are being assaulted — yelps and whines and then is declaratively silent; stale-looking blood trickles from the animal's mouth. The tall, martyr-thin man who is responsible for this violence on a sunny day strides confidently off, apparently in the consciousness of good work well done. A young American man kneels beside the stricken dog, a rosary dangling from his hand, and intones the Mercy prayer: *Lord, through your passion on the Cross, have mercy on us and on the whole world;* then he recites the rosary over the convulsing dog: *Hail Mary, full of grace.* . . . Onlookers join him. Some cry.

I retreat to a nearby outdoor café to mull over this small potent happening . . . imagine saying a rosary over a mangy dog. . . . All violence is lamentably absurd, but this is absurdity piled upon absurdity; there is something edge-of-the-world about this, it is cartoon-crude, adrenalized, surreal. In fact, I find the display of piety almost as disquieting as the violence that gave rise to it.

Two American women who are known to me by sight — in the village of Medjugorje greetings with strangers are routinely exchanged — approach me, one grim, the other (her shadow) pale; they are hot with indignation that is indistinguishable from

222

pleasure. "I've never felt the presence of Satan so strong, I've never felt the presence of Satan so strong," says Grim, the presence of Satan being, for her, proof of the presence of God, and of the Virgin Mary. "Poor dog," says her pale shadow. "Poor man," say I, an unprepared, uncalculated response that gives voice to what I am feeling: how tormented he must be to need to exert mastery over such sad flesh, to take joy from such a predictable triumph. "The Devil!" Grim says, through clenched teeth. "Don't you believe in the Devil? He was the Devil."

I do believe in the Devil — it is, after all, not so difficult to believe in the Devil if one believes in God; one has noticed that there are opposing principles operating in this world — but I am not so lucid or so ardent in my beliefs as to satisfy Grim. (For in my experience, good and evil are as often intimately braided as they are violently opposed, and it is sometimes impossible to tell one from the other; in any case it seems highly unlikely to me that the dog-beating man is the Devil.)

"Hell?" she says. "You believe in Hell?"

"Yes," I say, "I do, but I don't know what Hell is like, or Heaven."

"Who asked you?" she says (having asked me), and then she screws up her face and wags her tongue at me, she a gargoyle (her tongue must hurt at the root, she is sticking it out so far), I, in her mind, the Enemy. While I am taking this in, she dangles a large crucifix in front of my face — exactly as if I were a vampire and she an exorcist.

The man who struck the dog is a church custodian, and two reasons are offered for his action: the dog desecrated holy ground; the dog appropriated someone's bologna sandwich. "How is the custodian?" I ask the American who said the Mercy prayer. "No one seems to care," he says — he is kind — and: "I've lost my backpack." The man to whom he handed it, so as to release his hands for prayer, has disappeared into the crowd.

The dog will live. The young man will not find his backpack.

What a very strange Church I belong to.

Medjugorje is a small mountain village, invariably described as remote, a two and one half–hour drive from beautiful Dubrovnik, in one of the poorest of Yugoslavia's six provinces, Bosnia-Herzegovina. In this place of bald limestone hills (the landscape of alienation) the Virgin Mary appeared, or is said to have appeared, to six children, their ages ranging from ten to sixteen.

Since the Queen of Heaven first appeared to the dazzled but apparently unsurprised children (two boys and four girls) on a hilltop in 1981, she has continued to appear, almost on a daily basis, to at least two of the "visionaries," as they are popularly known. This is a very long run for Mary, who played a far more limited engagement at Fatima and at Lourdes. Her messages to the children were and are simple in the extreme: Live in Peace; Fast; Pray; Attend Mass; Convert. She has entrusted ten "secrets" to the children, some of which, they say, regard future grave punishments due to befall the wicked.

Bear in mind that this is happening in a troubled Communist country where there are three major religions — Roman Catholic, Eastern Orthodox, and Moslem — and two dozen ethnic groups, and that Yugoslavs are not at the moment, and have not been since Tito's death, living together amicably, ethnic and religious rivalries being exacerbated by economic disaster. (Inflation approaches 300 percent.)

Conveniently for the hundreds of thousands of tourists who have transformed Medjugorje into a bustling place of cafés, souvenir shops, and frenetic building development, Mary now appears to the visionaries in the church presbytery. She appears, they say, nightly, from 5:40 to 5:45. One could set one's watch by her; and indeed, church services at St. James are scheduled to accommodate her appearances.

Bear in mind also that the Roman Catholic Church, while it recognizes the apparitions at Lourdes and at Fatima as becoming to faith, does not regard disbelief in these apparitions as a sin. The Church, cautious and prudent, has not recognized the apparitions at Medjugorje, nor does the Church authorize or acknowledge pilgrimages to Medjugorje. This does not discourage Catholic Charismatics and Marian devotees from going to Medjugorje (over a quarter of a million Americans alone have made the voyage), which they refer to (attaching great freight to the word) as a "Journey," capital J.

On one such trip last fall [1988], I joined a group of forty-three Catholics organized by the St. Pius X House of Prayer in Plainview, Long Island. The trip itself (there is one or more a month) is organized by Peter Purpura, owner of Chosen Ventures in Bay Ridge, Brooklyn. Mr. Purpura has been organizing group travel to Lourdes and Fatima for twenty-five years. He was introduced to Medjugorje by his sister, Marcella Purpura, a Sister of St. Joseph, who is, coincidentally, codirector of the Plainview House of Prayer. An average price of $1,000 buys the travelers a substantial package: they fly Yugoslav Airlines to Dubrovnik, where they spend one night in a hotel, and are then driven by bus to Medjugorje, where they spend five days in private homes (all of this includes the services of a local guide), then back to Dubrovnik for a few hours of sightseeing and a night in a hotel, and home.

Travelers are instructed (so, presumably, as not to defy the Vatican) to regard this as a retreat, not a pilgrimage. They are also advised by Mr. Purpura (whose arrangements leave little to chance) that "Many people compare present-day Medjugorje to the beginnings of Lourdes. . . . You will be part of a great historical event in the history of our Church. . . . It is difficult for one not to anticipate the Church's approval. . . . Bring snacking foods . . . dried fruits and nuts." Mr. Purpura treats everyone as if he or she had never crossed the Atlantic before, which is just as well, because it is, generally speaking, the case.

I meet members of the group at JFK's Delta Airline Terminal at 8:30 P.M. JAT Flight 511 does not take off till two A.M., giving me ample time to observe my fellow passengers. One of them, a determinedly upbeat kind of person, tells me not to fret over the delay, as we will be "borne on wings of eagles," which is not how I have come to regard flying.

There are, as I count, eight men to thirty-five women, all of us in the competent hands of group leader Sister Marie Coleman of the Plainview House of Prayer, a center for "Charismatic Renewal." One of the men wears a Mets/Red Sox World Series T-shirt. One of the women entertains with a roll of toilet tissue ("unused, I bought it at a garage sale") on which jokes and trivia are printed. "Former Jobs of Famous Men" — it reads, in part: "Gerald Ford, Male Model."

Two of the men, brothers, are Travolta-handsome, dressed for Saturday-night fever. Pleasant and open, they have come out of a breezy curiosity. Two of the women — who smile but do not talk — are Sisters of the Precious Blood, a semicloistered order.

They are permitted, now, to watch the evening news on TV, and that is the sum of their knowledge of quotidian worldly life. An aura of otherworldly piety (of the sort that attaches more often to women than to men) coexists with idle domestic chatter, talk of the suburban comforts left behind, and "won't it be funny without TV?"

The women are extraordinarily autobiographical. No sooner has M., the upbeat person next to whom Sister Coleman has seated me, buckled her seat belt than I learn that one of her six children has worked for Father Bruce Ritter's Covenant House (a refuge for runaway kids) and Operation Rescue (a passionate antiabortion group), and that her husband had a stroke two years ago and then a heart attack, which, she says (disturbing my mind), "brought us together."

Shortly after her husband became ill, M. joined — reluctantly at first, she says — the Charismatic Renewal and began to attend services at the Plainview House of Prayer. Having become part of what is sometimes referred to as the Catholic Pentecostal community, or, less politely, as Catholic born-agains, she "received the Holy Spirit." She received the gift or charism of speaking in tongues. . . . Oh dear. This is going to be a very long plane ride. "We all have charisms," M. says. "Yours is that you are friendly and bouncy." Who, me?

There is turbulence, damn it. I white-knuckle it. M. prays over me — in tongues: It sounds like *Shaboom-Shaboom* to me. I hate this. Why is she setting herself above me? I'd like her so much better if she were scared too. "Breathe in the glory of the Lord, breathe out the peace of Jesus." I do as she says. M. makes the sign of the cross on my forehead. I feel refreshed, how odd. I'm grateful to her, beholden, odder still.

Nine hours after takeoff we arrive at Belgrade, where we will wait six hours for a connecting flight to Dubrovnik. Sister Coleman, calm and efficient, manages to secure us a courtesy meal. "What, no beverage with this?" says D.: He has been on a package tour of the Caribbean; he has learned to expect a free beverage with his meal. The waiter regards him blankly.

Belgrade is Eastern Orthodox; its people are ethnic Serbs who are currently insisting on their ethnic identity, setting themselves in opposition to the ethnic Albanians. In recent weeks, there has been rioting in Belgrade, rioting and strikes and breadlines. People cannot afford to live — the government issues staples — coarse dark bread, chicory coffee — to supplement a meager diet.

Security police in plain clothes stalk the airport, cadaverous, unsmiling. They are like secret agents in movies, caricatures, how funny. Their presence gives rise to a speech by one of my companions: "Liberals talk about rights in our country, we have rights, we're soft, we've never had to stand up for what we believe in. . . ." I resolve, on the spot, to secure a single room for the night.

A Medjugorje-bound group (moneyed, spiffily dressed) from San Diego passes the time by singing Marian songs and ostentatiously displaying rosaries. They call this "giving a witness." I call it foolish and dangerous, for it is clear that the Serbs are simmering in their own antipathy — a chaotic economy and born-again nationalism do not engender ecumenism or tolerance.

"In 1937," Rebecca West tells us in her monumental work about Yugoslavia, *Black Lamb and Gray Falcon,* "the Serbian parts of Yugoslavia were up in arms because the Government . . . signed a Concordat with Pope Pius which gave the Roman Catholic Church immense advantages over the Eastern Orthodox Church." This rankles anew; Serbians are hostile to the phenomenon of Medjugorje.

Though they seem perversely thrilled to be in a Communist (Satanic) country, these specific political realities do not intrude upon the minds of my companions. In the face of discomfort, Communist bureaucratic inefficiency, and exhaustion, they buoy one another up: "We are climbing the mountain. . . . This is part of our Journey, putting aside our little amenities, whatever. . . . This is a test."

I offer the manager of the empty, dreary restaurant five dollars to open his doors to me, and derive such comfort as I can from cups of strong sweet tea. As we board the plane, two members of my group are extolling the virtues of American chicken-salad sandwiches over English chicken-salad sandwiches. How peculiarly the otherworldly and the mundane are mated here, and how reassuring this quaintly parochial discussion is.

We are on our way by bus to Medjugorje, having had dinner and spent the night at a hotel in a state tourist complex in Dubrovnik, on that part of the peninsula where Napoleon once had a summer palace. Bubbles of intimacy, unguarded revelations, rise above stagnant clichés. (The clichés: "If you have faith, no explanation is necessary; if you don't have faith, no explanation is possible.") I have been made privy to the particular pain (fears, dreads, discontents, sour marriages, feckless grandchildren, ill health, despairing children) of half a dozen people. It is, of course, impossible to dislike someone who is, without guile, confiding in you.

We drive along the severely beautiful Adriatic, past chapels and pomegranate trees, stone houses and bougainvillea, cone-shaped haystacks and lazy canals that meander to the sea, women in black babushkas astride donkeys, the great wall of the fortified mountain village of Ston, salt pans and vineyards and tobacco fields.

Mary's life was rooted in dailiness, in the physical world. Seeing is a form of praying. So it drives me nuts that these women — into whose terms of reference I slip in and out — disregard landscape, the physical world in which we find proof of God's existence. (If there is no God, why isn't the world dark brown?) We are in a harsh and rocky land. We have passed oyster beds and the summer villas of the Socialist elite and state-run hotels for old people, and now the Dinardi Mountains are between us and the sea. An hour away from Medjugorje, the women, following the lead of Sister Marie (whose voice is twenty years younger than she is), begin reciting the rosary. I feel claustrophobic, trapped in alien concerns. Why aren't they looking out the windows?

As we enter Medjugorje, everyone sings.

Mirella, our guide, has wide green eyes, the perfectly amoral face of a cat. She is beautiful. She makes the equivalent of $116 a month. She has despaired of Americans pronouncing her name correctly, and invites us to call her Mickey or Marybell. She appears to have contrived a persona composed in equal parts of platitudes, pragmatism, magical thinking, and superstition: "Mary comes to tell us 'Peace,' not just from war but within ourselves, because unless you love yourself and find yourself you cannot bring peace to others." Thank you, Whitney Houston.

"The Blessed Mother tells us to convert. Conversion doesn't

necessarily mean you have to change from Orthodox or Moslem — as long as you believe." To say this is nothing more than politic for someone whose continued employment and career advancement depend on maintaining the goodwill of the state. Mirella tells us — with relish — that when the Turks ruled Bosnia and Herzegovina, which they did for four hundred years, they tortured Christians by impaling their bodies on a spit ("they were kept alive for days"), and that they stole Christian children from the mountains here and brought them to Turkey and converted them and sent them back to kill their parents: "So there are no Moslems here, there are only converted Christians." This information is well received, but in fact, Bosnia-Herzegovina is one-third Moslem.

"Barr-barr-a," Mirella says, "tell me one English word for crazy."

"Nuts."

"Tell me one other word."

"Fruitcake."

Every once in a while I catch Mirella staring off into space and under her breath muttering: "Frrut-cak."

Mirella has split the group of forty-three and placed us in three different houses. In my house there are fifteen people with whom, for the next five days, I will share breakfast and dinner, and with one of whom I will share a small whitewashed room — twin beds two feet apart, oiled wood floors, gay Yugoslavian scatter rugs. Six people will share one bath. Privacy will become a luxury. For some of these people, I will come to have feelings approaching love.

T., my roommate, alerts me, the first night, to what she calls her "little habits": she puts her hair up in paper curlers, she sleeps with a hot-water bottle at her feet and a pillow covering her face, she doesn't fall asleep till first light of dawn. I could not have wished for a sweeter, more tolerant, more amiable roommate. She has five children. (I have two.) We talk about our children, those mysterious familiars upon whose happiness our peace in large measure depends. We giggle together like girls in a dorm. T. approves of everything I do — at least she disapproves of nothing I do, how nice. Sometimes she sings — she has a high, clear voice like that of a child (little hands like that of a child, too). She sings songs as simple as nursery rhymes. She asks Jesus to "help us to live day by day"; she sings about "turning it over, letting it go." I have always wished for a sister, and this is sister-talk, and sister-ease.

It was T. who entertained us at the airport with the roll of toilet paper.

If anyone knows, no one is prepared to say how much each host family is paid to house and feed us. Peter Purpura of Chosen Ventures says "they get enough." If the talk in the cafés is true, our hostess, who seldom appears before us, her daughter, Elena, and her son, Mischa, receive about $51 a day to feed and house fifteen people. For this we get, in addition to our comfortable beds, peasant breakfasts of sausages and local cheese, rolls and margarine and jam, and coffee and tea and fruit; and fine full dinners eaten on a long linen-covered table — roast chicken, saffron risotto, fresh tomatoes, pork chops, french-fried potatoes, lamb stew, roast peppers — and rough bread, and Elena's father's wine, and coffee, tea, and mineral water and plenty of it. It is a mistake to include food in a package tour; eating becomes an occasion not only for gluttony but for petty anxiety (have I got my money's worth?) and visible greed.

That first night, from our bedroom window, T. and I see a man walk across the fields and enter the woods carrying a suitcase. This is strange.

The next morning T., whose soul is pure, says to me, "Barbara, is all Europe like this?" What she sees from the window is a fringe of woods, straggly oleander bushes, a muddy field strewn with the impedimenta of construction work, a concrete platform on which Elena stands to hang the wash, plastic buckets, chickens pecking over debris.

We are far from Paris. For that matter, we are far from Dubrovnik. And we are very far from Dix Hills; and from Uniondale and Commack and Setauket and Hampton Bays and Floral Park and Glendale and Huntington and East Quogue.

Medjugorje is a boom town, complete with a Duty Free shop and a Rent-a-Car. Cafés and concrete houses that double as *pensiones* sprout up everywhere, and to old houses are added extensions, new floors, baths, internal and external staircases. Everything seems improvised, it looks like grown-up Lego. Solar panels and front yards planted with homely cabbages coexist. Almost everything here — a sandwich, a pizza, a taxi ride (no matter how short or long the distance) costs three dollars; and American money is preferred. The taxis are all Mercedes-Benz — symbol both of new wealth and old poverty: the men of this region, until the Marian phenomenon brought a wholly unexpected bonanza, had to find work in Germany, leaving the women, sometimes for as long as twenty years, to till the unpromising soil. Belching vile emissions, an old red London double-decker bus, "St. Johns Wood" still its destination sign, carries British travelers to the ugly, capacious, buff-and-institutional-green twin-steepled church.

Medjugorje is a Coney Island/Disneyland of religious kitsch, souvenir shops everywhere selling combination key rings and beer-bottle openers with representations of Mary (whose eyes move); rosaries that glow in the dark; anything remotely Marian that can be made of seashells and resin, pastel drawings and needlework cushions of a long-necked, simpering Mary; sun hats, Yugoslav scatter rugs, ersatz peasant skirts and blouses; and stones from "Apparition Hill"; also a Balkan Cookbook ("offal stew"). Altogether an invitation to reconsider the Reformation, an invitation to Protestantism.

The air is fresh, country sweet. Scented roses grow in fall.

Masses are concelebrated by as many as forty priests in English, Italian, German, French, Croatian, and occasionally Latin. The rosary is said at five. Mary is never late; according to the visionaries, who assume Bernadette-like poses, she arrives promptly at 5:40 P.M.

I take pleasure in the choral music, in a local wedding ceremony that lasts for only moments before the rosary is said; in the people — from so many countries — singing "Ave Maria" in the soft twilight, their faces lit by a crescent moon. Most of all, when I am in church, I take pleasure in the way Europeans have of regarding the church as an extension of their living rooms or kitchens — they stroll and talk, they touch, they are both stolid and curious.

Outside of the church, candles flicker against a darkening sky. Local children form balls from melted candle wax and use them to play soccer with. Lined behind the candle stand are rows of portable toilets. At one English mass the closing song is "The Battle Hymn of the Republic."

It is possible to spend as many as nine hours a day in church.

I do not. I like to sit in outdoor cafés — chrome and black faux-marble cafés, cafés with reed canopies, red and white and orange molded plastic tables and chairs and grapevine pergolas. I never know what I will hear in these cafés — Joe Williams singing the blues, "Ave Maria," or Doris Day singing "If I Give My Heart to You." I like to sit, drinking strong, rich-smelling coffee, listening to the sound of many voices mingling with the sound of church bells and the sound of guitars playing folk music, sacred and profane.

T. returns one night from a church healing service to tell me that prayers were said for AIDS sufferers; the congregation was instructed to love their sisters and brothers who were ill. A young man whose dear friend died of AIDS said that while he loved, he also judged, and judged harshly; he asked for forgiveness for presuming to be another man's judge. This is the most encouraging thing I have heard since I came to Medjugorje.

T. would never presume to judge motive. Her love loves the doer even when it disapproves of the deed. I am able to tell her, and no one else, that I do not believe Mary is here (any more, that is, than she is anywhere else). T. giggles. "You should hear my husband," she says. "He thinks I'm cuckoo. Am I cuckoo?"

"I don't know, am I? Everybody's cuckoo."

"God put us together," T. says, and who am I to disagree? If we're cuckoo, we are making a pleasant thing of it.

On the second morning we are here, the travelers make the difficult climb up Apparition Hill — breakfast at 6:45. I have a lie-in and read a mystery.

Men and women, the fit, the halt, and the lame, snake up the rocky hill as others snake down. At the bottom there is a souvenir stand. Halfway up — the treacherous climb takes an hour for the most young and able — there is a boy selling orange Crush.

T. says climbing the hill is the hardest and most exhilarating thing she has ever done, hard as giving birth, and as wonderful. She also says: "The Lord died so *you* don't have to climb a mountain if you don't want to." What could be kinder?

There is substantial anecdotal literature — but no empirical evidence — of rosaries changing from base metal into gold on the mountain, of the sun wheeling and dancing in the sky. No one in my group has experienced these phenomena, though someone thought he might have seen a shooting star. No one has been — or will be — in a demonstrable, physical sense, healed. In fact there is absolutely no hard evidence that anyone has ever been healed in Medjugorje.

At dinner: "How thrilling it was to be where Mary walked," they say. They need no proof. But T. prays: "Lord Jesus, forgive me for not giving to the beggar on the hill, perhaps you were that beggar, Lord Jesus."

Three generations of women. P., the mother, has a thriving pizzeria on Long Island; she is a diabetic who injects herself with insulin three times a day, she has had many surgeries for a bad back; she chain-smokes and wears a Budweiser T-shirt; she is solicitous of her divorced daughter, with whom I happily talk about hairstyles, clothes, men, and children. C., the daughter, looks nineteen — and is having a nice flirtation with one of the Travolta-handsome boys — but has a nineteen-year-old son. C. is solicitous of both her mother and her grandmother; each woman thinks she is taking care of the other; in fact this is true, they take care of one another.

G., the grandmother, is seventy-eight. She comes from the south of France. "Shit, we cooked clean food," she says. "Son of a bitch, our frogs were never muddy." She has seen Jesus. When she was sick and fevered, Jesus came to her "like cotton candy." Her hand turned red and her arms turned yellow. Jesus didn't have much to say. This happened in Huntington Station.

"Did Jesus say anything about your filthy mouth, G.?"

"Crap, no."

She has also climbed the hill. Her granddaughter is exhausted as a result. She is not.

It occurs to me that the women with whom I am spending this disjointed time have come to feminism by, as it were, a back door. Those who are the most insistent upon their identities as wives and mothers are the most vocal about Mary's having come to Medjugorje to save the world (a place reserved, in orthodoxy, for Christ, a man). These women, while they make a great point of their obedience to the pope, speak of him, in various degrees of sadness and disdain, as someone who, for whatever unconscious motives or cultural reasons, has missed the main chance, the chance to honor Mary by acknowledging the apparitions at Medjugorje. For the male clergy who do not promote Medjugorje, they have thinly disguised disgust. So, while continuing to present themselves as passive and obedient, wifely and subordinate, they nevertheless enjoy the consciousness of superiority over men because they have taken the main chance, they have rededicated themselves to Mary, Mary as Savior.

R. has come here hoping to throw her crutches away. (She will not, but she will leave saying that she has achieved peace.) How will she climb the mountain?

Her roommate, a German woman, answers: "I'll pull her by the hair."

A. has emphysema. She has with her an apparatus for breathing that she calls a lung cleanser. The electrical-current adapter she brought with her doesn't work. This necessitates a trip to the nearest small town, a prospect which — though A.'s ankles are swollen and her feet blistered — she faces with remarkable equanimity. She is brave. A.'s husband is given to such speeches as: "New York is a socialist city . . . the homeless want to be homeless." But he is immensely loving and kind to his wife. All night long I hear her, painfully coughing and wheezing; it sounds as if she will never catch her breath. And above the sounds of her distress I hear his voice murmuring, soothing.

They all yearn to be made whole. Yearning, Teilhard de Chardin writes, is the quality that distinguishes humans from stones. It is because man yearned that he evolved. In the company of these good people I will go — on the fourth day of our Journey — to visit the visionaries.

Published reports say that Vicka has an inoperable brain tumor. Marella says Vicka has a "water cyst," not a brain tumor. Vicka, who was sixteen when she experienced whatever it was she did experience, says that Mary has told her she will be cured. Of all the visionaries, it is Vicka the travelers want most to meet. But today, Marella says, Vicka has the flu.

Even Vicka's house is an object of fascination. It is a stone house with a terrace and a grape arbor, surrounded by a low stone wall, much prettier than the brazen new "villas" going up in

Medjugorje. Travelers walk around it — there is a steady stream of traffic — as if they could draw some message from it, or from the silent girl within. Nothing about it suggests that it houses anything extraordinary: soccer team stickers on the lace-curtained windows; pots of flowers; baskets of laundry; clean clothes flapping on the clothesline, gathering dust from the dirt road crossed by cows and Mercedes taxis. In the fields, bent women in black weeds. Birds sing in pomegranate trees.

Jacov was ten when he saw Mary. It is he that we meet. Jacov is fey. He attends a technical school in Medjugorje. His sweet face provides no clue to his interior life. He stands, in front of his villa, on a rock, naturally assuming the pose of Michelangelo's David. He accepts written petitions (he will commend them to Mary's attention), and he answers questions from the travelers. Mirella translates.

"How many stars are in Mary's crown?"

"He hasn't counted."

"Can you convey her beauty?"

"She has brown hair and blue eyes and she wears a gray dress."

"Can you tell us what Heaven, Hell, and Purgatory are like?"

"He doesn't want to say at this time."

"Has the Blessed Mother said when she will make her last appearance?"

"The last time he asked her that, the Blessed Mother said, 'Are you getting tired of me?'"

"Mirella [I ask this question], is Jakov worried about the unrest of his country? Does Mary speak of it?"

"No."

"How has this changed your life?"

"I don't know," Jacov says. "I was ten. I grew up with her — in her. I don't know anything else."

Ivan is twenty-three. He left the Franciscan seminary when the work became too difficult. He is handsome — sexy. He wears a football jersey, works on his family's farm, and stresses, in all his answers to all our questions, family and prayer, prayer and family. Mary, he says, in response to a question posed urgently, has not spoken about abortion. When he is asked what his future plans are, he replies that the question is "too personal."

"Can you tell us about the secrets?"

"That's what a secret is — secret."

Someone asks Ivan why the Blessed Mother has chosen to appear in Czechoslovakia. . . . *Czechoslovakia?* Mirella's lips form the word: "Frrut-cak."

However one regards these young people — as dupes, as prophets, or as freaks — they are by definition abnormal. But it is their ordinariness they insist upon. And indeed they speak of the Mother of God as if she were their auntie come to tea. I frequently wondered, in Medjugorje, where God and Mary seemed almost an extension of the villagers' families, what would happen if a film or rock star came to town. Is it possible that they would be more overwhelmed by Bruce Springsteen than by Jesus Christ?

What has happened to the others? Of the remaining three visionaries, Mirjana, twenty-three, studies agronomy in Sarajevo; she sees Mary only on extraordinary occasions.

Ivanka, twenty-two, lives in Medjugorje with her baby and her husband; she was married in 1986. She says she receives a vision on the anniversary of the first apparitions.

Marija, twenty-four, has said she sees Mary daily. She believes that she has been called to a religious vocation. In February 1988, she went to Italy for a religious retreat, and no further information is available about her.

Rebecca West called Slavs "addicts to spiritual pursuits . . . believers in magic and the existence of a reality behind appearances who . . . perform any ritual and carry on any argument that promises a revelation of the truth." Bosnians, she wrote, have a history of incorporating into their worship "pre-Christian beliefs and customs, including such superstitions as the belief in the haunting of certain places by elemental spirits."

These practices have been used, she said, to further nationalistic or ethnic claims. West was writing in 1941. "Isn't it nice," says a café habitué almost fifty years later, "that the Blessed Mother appeared on our side of the hill and not on the other, where the Serbs are."

In 1941, a short-lived Croatian fascist state was created in Herzegovina. Roman Catholics are said to have inflicted unspeakable atrocities upon their Serbian Orthodox neighbors. Hundreds of Serbian women and children, including babies, were marched to a cliff on the other side of Apparition Hill and thrown to their deaths.

The provincial government in Sarajevo — where the assassination of Archduke Franz Ferdinand by a Bosnian student set off World War I — interpreted the appearance of a Croatian-speaking Mary so close to the scene of the 1941 butchery as a right-wing plot in religious disguise, a revival of Roman Catholic separatism. Officials who did not take kindly to the crowds at the hill issued statements that there was, at the time of the so-called apparitions, a burgeoning of signs saying CROATIANS UNITE! and also that Nazi swastikas had been seen. At the very least, they said, religious fervor was being manipulated to support political goals. Apparently, though, the government no longer sees a threat in Medjugorje, which brings much-needed tourist revenues.

When the children first saw the apparitions, Father Jozo Zovko, the Franciscan pastor of St. James, was away. Upon his return, he questioned the children and concluded that the apparitions were inauthentic. A few days later, having received an "illumination" — he heard "a human voice that rang all over my life" — he reversed himself, and acted to protect the children, who were being pursued by the authorities. The children moved into the church presbytery — and so did Mary.

The union of the very handsome, charismatic Zovko (a soft-spoken master of the dramatic pause) with peasants already inclined to see the world superstitiously — in terms of miracles, visions, omens, and predictions — was extraordinarily potent. After Zovko gave a homily about the conversion of a man who had lived forty years in sin, which government authorities took to be a comment on forty years of Socialist rule, he was imprisoned for eighteen months, his "martyrdom" adding fuel to the fires of religious fervor. (He is now the rector of a prosperous parish in Thaling, forty miles northeast of Medjugorje; he gives lectures several times a day to tourists — like the man with the albatross, he is compelled to tell his story over and over and over again.)

Pavaso Zanic, Bishop of Mostar, in whose diocese St. James lies, initially defended the children from charges that they were lying, and later appointed a commission to study the phenomenon. The results of the commission have never been made public, but according to unofficial sources, eleven members of the commission voted, in 1986, against the supernatural character of the events; two voted in favor; and one said that the apparitions might originally have had a supernatural origin (he was apparently negatively impressed by Mary's thousands of appearances — in Lourdes she appeared exactly eighteen times); and one abstained.

In January 1989, Zanic discussed the phenomenon at Medjugorje with Vatican officials and with Pope John Paul II, expressing a desire that the Church would soon make a public judgment, so that travelers might stop "deluding themselves." Publicly, Zanic would say only that he felt "supported and encouraged" by the pope's response.

It has been suggested that the events in Medjugorje are an echo or a continuation of a hundred-year-old internecine Church battle in Herzegovina: Zovko is a Franciscan. Yugoslavian Franciscans take credit for having kept the faith alive during the four centuries of Turkish rule. They symbolize Catholic and Croatian identity. They have, according to this theory, been bitter ever since Pope Leo XIII appointed secular priests to their parishes one hundred years ago.

None of the doctors who have examined the children has concluded that they were anything but healthy and sane; it is inferred that they were not deliberately lying — but this still does not speak to the authenticity of the phenomenon.

If one does not believe that Mary appeared, it follows, then, that what *has* happened at Medjugorje is a result of the coming together of many factors: a grave dissatisfaction with forty years of Communist rule that has resulted in extreme economic hardship; the rebirth of Catholic nationalism and of ethnic nationalism; the vanity and egotism of Franciscans; the fragmentation of a once monolithic Church and shock waves from the Second Vatican Council, which deemphasized Marian worship (the recitation of the rosary and the making of novenas); and, of course, the simple desire to know by seeing, combined with the Slavic predisposition to accept the supernatural as natural.

Medjugorje also signifies the birth of an obstinate, convoluted and inarticulate feminism. The centrality of Mary to Catholicism — the centrality of a woman — has never been in question. But Mary Immaculate, Mother of God, Queen of Heaven, has been viewed, by many Catholic women who nevertheless love her, as an instrument of oppression, for she has been held up as an example of perfect passivity, childlike purity, subordination, and blind obedience — the perfect tool, in fact, for browbeating ordinary women who dwell in their (ordinary) bodies.

Now feminists and liberation theologians are finding, as they reinterpret the symbolism of Mary, a source of renewal and refreshment in her: in her innocence can be seen not weakness but (as Mary Gordon writes) "the absence of the desire to inflict pain." In her consent, asked for by God and freely given, can be seen a radical openness to experience, an "attitude of expectation, of readiness, and receptivity to grace," as Karl Rahner writes, which need not, for the rest of us, find expression in virginity.

Latin American theologians see Mary, poor and unlettered, as "a mirror of identity" for the downtrodden; her discipleship was perfect, William Behringer writes, because she understood what the word of God meant "in terms of the life of the poor and the slaves of whom she was representative." Nicaragua's Sandinista Catholic women, familiar to sacrifice, see Mary — who did not oppose her son's prophetic mission though it led to his death — as a sister and a liberator. For these and many ordinary Catholics, Mary is the antithesis of withdrawal; she has become a spur to creative involvement in the problems of a suffering world.

A., who cannot breathe and is brave, says: "The closer you are to God, the more you suffer." I find this symptomatic of the unwholesomeness of Medjugorje. Surely God does want us to be happy? Suffering is inevitable, but surely it is wrong to court it, or to regard it as a kind of reward?

Sister Marie sees a bent old woman in black. She thinks the old woman is Mary — it is, she says, in any case the way Mary will be revealed to her.

"Stop singing, we're praying," Grim says to T., who, brimful of joy, is singing "He's got the whole world in his hands." Charismatics are schismatic, Grim says. She has met a doctor engaged in AIDS research — a believer — and she hates him, she thinks AIDS sufferers are being punished for their wickedness. She wants a return to pre–Vatican II — no vernacular liturgy, reduced emphasis on the Bible; she wants nuns in habits if not in hair shirts;

she wants hellfire and (in human relationships) ice; she wants novenas and no involvement in social issues. And she seems to feel that it is her duty to dampen the spirits of everyone else.

All this talk about the Blessed Mother. Mother. I think so much of my own mother, two years dead. I think of my failures, her failures, our failures, of imagination and of love. I try not to think. I grieve, I mourn, I cry. I cry easily with T., who accepts tears as a gift. "Weep with those who weep," said St. Paul. "Laugh with those who laugh."

A remarkable thing has happened: I still — frequently — feel spasms of irritation; but with some of these women (with, for example, Sister Marie, who works with abused women and children) I have moved from a position of cynicism and indifference to one of trust. I feel that they have a radical inability to harm. There are nuns in this group (I didn't, for days, know they were nuns, they wished no one to know) who are nurses; healing is their desire and their vocation. I experience their presence as a healing one.

Everyone (except me) on the bus, on our way back from a visit to the now-adored Father Zovko, breaks into a loud and militant version of "God Bless America." The faces of Mirella and the bus driver are carved in stone.

The kitchen is sunny. Elena and her mother are preparing dinner — cannelloni stuffed with Parmesan, Trappist and pecorino cheese. (This, in fact, is how the women of Medjugorje interpret Mary's exhortation to fast — two days a week they abstain from meat.) I help. In this room I feel very great ease and pleasure.

Elena, modest, innocent, and rural, is an invitation to redefine simplicity. She has a remarkable tolerance for difference and diversity, and while the moral and practical consequences of her acts engage and concern her, the contemplation of consequences does not paralyze her. Her smile and her laugh are completely honest. It would bewilder her to be spoken of in these terms; it would bewilder her to be regarded as a subject of discussion at all.

Elena believes absolutely that Mary comes to Medjugorje, she is buoyant with belief, transparently receptive to grace. Elena moves in light.

I believe that for days I have been witnessing the consequences of fraud.

I believe that Elena believes.

Her belief is as moving to me as the unconditional love of a child, but it can't transform Medjugorje, and it can't change me. Elena is as authentic and lovely as Medjugorje is spurious and sleazy. Yet she is part of the phenomenon of Medjugorje, her shining intelligence informed by a belief that is inseparable from the machinations and manipulations (and treacly nonsense) that I wholly distrust and allow myself to despise.

Good and evil are inextricably bound.

I want to go home. I want to be in the world.

As I was pondering the events at Medjugorje, my parish priest called me. He was in Wisconsin talking with Erma Bombeck. (This delights me; I am back in the real world.) He had read that one of the visionaries had come to a southern American city — he couldn't remember which, Erma Bombeck was making him laugh too hard — to get medical attention for her brother. Mary came to visit the visionary while she was there (staying, in fact, with the organizer of package tours to Medjugorje). First Mary appeared in the living room of the travel agent. Then she appeared in the branches of a tree in a parking lot.

Horror at Island Pond (1984)

✦ ✦ ✦

In 1971 a carnival barker in Chattanooga founded a church. Elbert Eugene Spriggs, who had studied psychology at the University of Chattanooga, first called the group of troubled young people he gathered to himself the Light Brigade; later — when they removed themselves from the mainline churches — Spriggs' commune became known as the Vine Christian Community. In 1978 the church — which has small branches in Dorchester and in Clarks Harbour, Nova Scotia — moved, having run afoul of authorities in Tennessee, to that part of Vermont known as the Northeast Kingdom. It now calls itself "the Church in Vermont" or the Northeast Kingdom Church. Spriggs now lives in France with a handful of followers.

LATE AT NIGHT, Jan Montford sits at the Common Sense Deli drinking Red Zinger tea. She is not a member of the Northeast Kingdom Church, the cult that owns and operates the all-night deli, but she likes it here. An "ex-hippie brought up by hippies," she is reminded of Woodstock (macramé and candles and rough-hewn wood benches and apothecary jars full of spices — a stylized simplicity). She likes it here and she doesn't like it here; sometimes, without seeming to notice it, she lapses into local slang and calls the Common Sense the "Yellow Deli." Nobody knows who started calling it that; few people in Island Pond call it anything else. As epithets go, "Yellow Deli" is not particularly harsh; and perhaps that's the uncalculated point: when you suspect or believe that there is something malignant in your midst, the instinct is to trivialize it, to rob it of its black magic.

Jan smokes furiously in the deli she calls "so peaceful" — so peaceful compared to the bar at the Osborne Hotel, at the other end of Main Street . . . the bar that is known, even to its habitués, as "the Zoo"; and to which we now walk.

"I am in a sunny sweet-smelling meadow," Jan says, "vibrant with yellow wildflowers. The children and I play 'roll about.' We roll down the slope, and at the bottom there are two huge iron doors. The doors swing open and women in babushkas grab us by the throat and on the other side of the doors it is all darkness and smoke and the air tastes of sulfur. When my eyes grow accustomed to the dark I see a lake with tongues of fire playing on its surface. I crawl back to the iron doors and now there are peepholes in it and I can see, all over the sunny meadow, women in long dresses and babushkas, tearing at the throats of children. . . ."

"What does the dream mean?" I ask, knowing what it means, but wishing to break the frightened silence that surrounds her words; and thinking, How eloquent Jan's unconscious is, how simple and urgent and spare — elegant — the nightmare is, how nicely fact and symbol dovetail in her dream.

"My husband says the dream means I shouldn't talk to you," Jan says.

"Is that what you think?"

"I'm tired of thinking," Jan says; "I'm afraid. . . . Find out what 'the training' is. They send their children to 'the training.' When the children come back, they're terrified. Find out what it is."

"Why don't you ask them?"

No longer eloquent, suddenly listless, Jan shrugs. "I don't know," she says, her voice drained of feeling.

In Nazi Germany, dissident or distressed Germans censored their own dreams. They automatically awakened when anything in their dreams signaled to them disaffection with their rulers. Sometimes their startled awakening was triggered by the appearance, in their dreams, of a uniformed Nazi hovering over their beds demanding that they cease to dream. This is the ultimate violation of privacy — the dreaming mind internalizing and incorporating a censor; but if one is frightened enough, one will choose so to violate oneself . . . and whether this is schizophrenia or self-protection (or both: madness as a response to madness) it is difficult to know.

Jan is not afraid of me, she has sought me out. It must be

clear to her that her dream owes its urgency to her fear of the cult that occupies so much of her waking life, eliciting from her an uncertain response in which attraction and revulsion both play a part.

It does not require genius to interpret Jan's dream:

The women of the Northeast Kingdom Church in Island Pond wear babushkas. Their children are beaten with rods; they are also forbidden to entertain fantasies. Members of the cult believe that we are living in the "end-times," and that only those living a sacrificial Christian life — which is to say, them — will survive; the rest of us will be consigned to the Lake of Fire. Jan has seen children abused. The cult has sworn to "get" her husband, which is to say enlist him; and while he plays hard to get, he frequently goes to their "Celebrations" and defends the cult's "disciplining" of their children and sees something admirable and pretty in the submissiveness of their women. Jan deplores — she says — the "discipline," and the submission; but she often goes to the deli because, she says, she has good friends among the cult members, and also because, she says (not altogether convincingly), she wants "to see what's going on and to set an example to them of how you're *supposed* to raise children. . . ." Her own words sound slightly mad to her: "Dammit," she says, "how many contradictions can one person stand?"

It is Jan's very ordinariness that makes her convulsed and convoluted response to the cult so distressing.

It would not be a gross exaggeration to say that the entire town of Island Pond has gone haywire. Paranoia, anger, hopelessness, apathy, hysteria, bitterness, and fear are everywhere in evidence.

And yet haywire seems almost too thin a word to describe what I truly believe (and in this belief I am not alone) to be the contagion of evil.

Fancy religions have become almost as American as apple pie. Millenialists and doom-proclaimers and utopian communities come and go, and unless they directly impinge upon our lives, we tend to regard them with little more than distaste or bemused curiosity. Anybody, after all, can wear saffron or sacrifice to Baal — and, provided that it isn't *our* children who are the sacrificed or the sacrificers, we take refuge in the First Amendment (which, after all, protects *our* right to worship as we please); we dismiss all such groups as aberrant but not dangerous, or as emblematic of our freedom and diversity.

We are right in thinking that fringe groups either disappear or are, ultimately, absorbed into the mainstream (the 1984 Miss America is a Mormon; what was once regarded as pernicious is now, most Americans would agree, wholesome). We do not spend our lives anticipating Jonestowns. We are a sanguine people. We mind our own business and allow others to mind theirs; and we call this innocence.

The people of Island Pond have lost whatever claim they may once have had to innocence. They've lost what nobody can afford to lose — a sense of the fundamental decency and rightness of things. Being neither rich nor foolish, they always had good reason to know that injustice exists. But experience of injustice is not the same as apprehension of evil. When Elbert Eugene Spriggs' commune moved, three hundred or so strong, into Island Pond from Chattanooga, Tennessee, the town's fifteen hundred residents had no way to anticipate the traumatic events of June 22, 1984. Now they have no way to recover from them.

Before six thirty on the morning of June 22, some ninety state troopers and fifty state social workers, empowered by a warrant from a Vermont district judge, removed 112 children, all under the age of eighteen, from twenty communal homes of the Northeast Kingdom Church. The children, together with 110 adults, were taken in chartered buses and police vans to Orleans District Court in Newport. State officials, armed with affidavits (most of them from former members of the cult) alleging that the children of the Northeast Kingdom Church were brutalized — stripped, lashed, whipped — sought to gain temporary custody of the children to examine them for signs of abuse.

Judge Frank G. Mahady called the action "grossly illegal" and refused to detain the children, who were returned to their homes.

For most reporters there were two overriding questions: Were the children in fact abused? and was the "raid" constitutional? (The second question is, of course, contingent upon the first: The courts have consistently ruled that children's rights supersede

First Amendment rights in cases of flagrant abuse: children of Jehovah's Witnesses, for example, have been taken in temporary custody when their parents denied them blood transfusions; children of other sects have been made wards of the court when their parents, acting out of religious [faith-healing] principles, refused to allow doctors to administer life-saving drugs.) But these questions, both flashy and important, are not the only questions.

To whom do the children belong?

Can the cult be said to damage human lives, and can it be said with any certainty that such damage will escalate?

And (this is not a very "reporterly" question, but it is nevertheless at the heart of the matter): Are they truly evil?

Why do people choose to join a group that lives in tribal isolation? What does it offer them? (Is *choice* the operative word?)

These are questions that might be asked, in one form or another, in regard to almost any cult. This cult operates in Island Pond, Vermont. So the related questions remain: How does the cult regard — and deal with — the townspeople? Confronted with perceived evil, how does a town of 15,053 souls react to the cult?

A cult is not an abstraction. We are talking here of flesh and (possibly broken) bones. The Northeast Kingdom Church claims to be "in the world but not of it" — to have come out of the world. This is on the face of it nonsense: there is not one soul in Island Pond who is not affected by the cult . . . and that is the story. It is not a tidy one.

The main (and only, by urban definition) street of Island Pond is ugly. It takes ten minutes to walk up and down the main street, a thoroughfare so bleak, so devoid of charm and lacking in New England grace, that even the Green Mountains and the pond from which the town derives its name — a pond with a 22-acre island in its center — do not erase the impression of blight.

Island Pond is poor. Three hundred and forty-four Island Ponders live below the official poverty level; 192 people receive food stamps; 25 households receive Aid to Needy Families with Children. Even these statistics don't accurately reflect its poverty: people hunt (bear and moose), and fish, and gather blueberries and apples, and can fruit and cultivate gardens in order to survive;

in the hills, high above the white steeples of the Roman Catholic and the Congregational churches, marijuana is a cash crop, grown and harvested by people whose underground economy escapes statistical analysis.

It's remote — two hours from the Burlington airport and sixteen miles from the Canadian border; and Island Ponders will tell you that the Northeast Kingdom Church established itself here — after the group left Chattanooga with $8 million derived from sales of property, according to Galen Kelly, a private investigator who teaches at Rutgers — precisely for this combination of circumstances.

The Common Sense Deli is at the north end of the main street; the 125-year-old Osborne Hotel is at the south end of the street. An anthropologist might tell you that there are four forces operating in Island Pond — forces represented by the Common Sense; the Osborne (where the drinking and the living are hard and where the amenities are practically nonexistent); the communes — Madbrook Farm, Frog Run, Earth People's Park — that anachronistically thrive in the hills of Essex County; the folks who go to Congregational picnics and to Grace Brethren Fundamentalist Church and the Roman Catholic and Episcopal churches. Most Island Ponders will tell you there are only two forces: *them* (the Northeast Kingdom Church) and *us*.

In this town, the church has purchased twenty-two houses . . . no, twenty-three: When I came to Island Pond, there was a FOR SALE sign on a ramshackle house between the Osborne and the Common Sense; a week later, I saw five children staring out from a second-floor window of the house. They were cult children. Cult children are not like other children. (And it's more than a matter of their not being allowed toys or coloring books.) Their expressions are both vacant and watchful; they are preternaturally grave. It reminded me — the old house, the silent children — though I am not usually given to hysteria, of a scene from *The Village of the Damned*.

When I walk into the Common Sense Deli, I am greeted pleasantly and served by a young woman called Donna. Donna wears a babushka over long blond hair, and a loose, peasantlike dress; she has the pasty look of someone whose diet consists only of starch. She does not wear a watch. None of the women of the church wears a watch, which seems to me more significant than wearing a babushka as an outward sign of submission to men: If your time is not your own, your life is not your own; you have given both your time and your life over to someone else. The elders of the cult — all male — have watches and timepieces; their time does belong to them, as does every decision, and every initiative. Donna, upon hearing that I have come to Island Pond by bus from New York, tells me, when I express a weary traveler's displeasure with New York's seedy Port Authority bus depot, that "the angels of the Lord" gathered around *her* when *she* was at Port Authority: "Nobody had any intention of doing me harm." It is a characteristic of religious fringe groups to see the hand of God in every temporal event, to lay special claim to understanding the ways in which He works. All believers have the conviction that God is present in the world, brooding gently and mysteriously over us all; but members of the cults so particularize God's activities you'd think the Almighty had nothing better to do than see them safely across a street.

Donna does not chat with me long. Cult members have no small talk — a casual remark about the weather will invoke a sermon on the bounties of the Lord and the saving goodness of their commune, proselytizing being to them second nature. When I tell Donna that I am a writer, she sends a man called Isaac over to talk to me. I extend an unsmiling Isaac my hand. He places his own hands firmly on the table that divides us: "I'll wait," he says; "I like to see where you're coming from. . . . Of what benefit is it to you to write?" he asks. Although Isaac is neither cross-eyed nor wall-eyed, I have trouble focusing on his eyes, which seem to want to bore into me rather than to see me, to make a statement rather than to observe. I try to answer his question thoughtfully and honestly; my answers sound foolish to me.

"Why are you on earth?" Isaac asks. I give him the catechism answer — "To know God and to love him," I say, which is in fact what I believe. As this response elicits nothing but an unblinking stare from Isaac, I add, feeling as foolish as he intends me to feel, "and to try to be good, and to work, and to suffer — that's the easy part — and to raise children who are better and happier than I am."

"Your children can't be happier than you are — they live in the world. You're not happy."

Oh, well; I've heard this line of talk before — from Werner Erhard, from the Moonies. . . . Isaac has to insist upon my lack of happiness to establish his own happiness.

"Why do you paint your fingernails that passionate red?" he asks.

"How do you know I'm not happy?" I ask.

"Because I'm looking at you," Isaac says. "I don't want to shred you, you're a human being. . . . *Worthless*," he mutters. . . . "You don't know God."

"How can you be sure of that?"

"If you loved him, you'd serve him. You would leave the world. You would die. You would be living with us. You are not my sister. If you were, you'd serve God."

"Tell me how you know I don't?"

"If you served God, you'd know the truth. If you knew the truth, you'd serve God. Are your fingernails part of your fantasy? Your fantasy is that you are Lois Lane. You come here in the guise of a writer. You're looking for Superman. . . . *Worthless*."

This cloud-cuckooland conversation is tiresome, discouraging, too: One wishes to believe that there is something in every man and woman that words and goodwill can reach. Nothing can touch or disturb the certainty of Isaac and Donna, their sense of me as worthless, which reinforces their own sense of salvific worth. (The conversation accomplishes its aim, though; it makes me feel frivolous.)

So: "Do you abuse your kids?" I ask.

"We do and we don't."

"You *do*?"

"We don't. We spank them."

"Why?"

"And we don't send them to school. Why should they salute a piece of cloth, a rag?"

I have been told — by an eyewitness — that a boy of three has recently been consigned to a dark, airless closet for one half hour because he pretended that a block of wood was a car. Seen in this light — as a monitor of fantasies — Isaac is both silly and dangerous. "Fantasies," he says, "steal the person you are" — a surprisingly sophisticated and ornate thought. But how can he know when the children are fantasizing? "If you get down on all fours and bark like a dog, you're fantasizing," he says.

Thinking of their children's impoverished separateness from the world of other children, remembering how my own childish fantasies nourished me when adults and the real world hurt me, thinking of the castles (the refuges) in the air I built when I was growing up desperate in a religious sect, I ask: "What about sand castles? Would they be permitted to build sand castles?" Isaac is stumped (as he is when I ask him to tell me the difference between wish, hope, imagination, and fantasy): "I don't interpret the heart," he says; but — he makes a quick recovery, taking refuge in instantly concocted certainty — "We don't build sand castles. We live in reality. God is the only reality. Sex isn't love," he says (once again regarding my fingernails with inordinate interest).

"I used to be a pervert," he says, "due to reading pornography." He asks me to define perversion, an invitation I decline. "My knowledge of perversity is deeper than yours," Isaac says. "Roman Catholics are perversions. Garbage and corruption and baloney. You are a pervert." And — perhaps anticipating that women of the town will later tell me that he has said he will make them "queens, empresses," if they will sleep with him — he says: "I left the church for two years. I was not in the Spirit. I was sleeping around, stealing . . . an outlaw." The Butch Cassidy of the Northeast Kingdom Church. Isaac has long greasy blond hair and fingernails bitten to the quick.

Children circle around Isaac as we speak — as Isaac speaks now compulsively of homosexuality — "a form of global birth control," he calls it, also an interesting, if not a wholly original idea. The children express no curiosity. They are without animation. They do not speak. A beautiful girl — ten? twelve? — approaches Isaac in a controlled storm of apprehension. He turns an icy countenance toward her. "I was supposed to return the Spannel bottles," she says (her name is Phoebe), commencing a conversation I cannot at first decode. Isaac's silence is stony. "And I failed," Phoebe says. Poor Phoebe; there is a question implicit in her confession. Isaac allows her to stand there, humiliated for reasons I don't understand. Then he rewards her, when it seems no longer possible for her to withstand the severity of his gaze. "I have seventeen cents," he says softly; "you can buy popcorn." Phoebe, I now understand, wants seventeen cents (but cannot ask a direct question — none of the children may ask a direct question or make a choice: if they are offered an apple and an orange, their response must be, "I'll have what you know it is good for me to have"); she wants seventeen cents to buy a bag of popcorn the deli sells. She kisses Isaac's hand.

Another child, Madeleine (are they all beautiful?), sits next to Isaac. She looks like a hurt animal, her enormous eyes swivel in her head, attaching their regard to no one and nothing. "Are you afraid of this woman?" Isaac asks, turning her palpable terror to his advantage. ("Of *me*?") "She doesn't live with you," Isaac says to me; "you are not part of the body of the Messiah." Madeleine says not a word. He dismisses her with a glance.

And Donna, the Good Cop — says: "You can't be comfortable at the Osborne. We want you to be comfortable. Will you stay with us? Stay with us for three days. Will you have dinner with us on Thursday? At Pleasant House?"

Three days is the standard period of time for what is variously called brainwashing, persuasive coercion, mind control. I do not believe I am susceptible to their bullying or their blandishments — nor do I have complex yearnings for a simple life — but I won't spend three days with them; I will have dinner at Pleasant House.

Ten A.M. The drinking starts early at the Osborne. And all the talk is of the cult, Yankee reticence having yielded to obsession. Teresa, the pretty young bartender, says: "If *we* didn't send our kids to school, we'd get our asses in jail. Somebody in that church" — this is the majority view at the Osborne — "bought the state officials off." Jackie, who works at Ted's Market down the street, says: "One of the church women came in yesterday with a dollar and asked me how much chicken she could buy with it. She wanted to know if a dollar's worth of chicken would serve twenty people. She bought a can of mackarel and said she'd stretch it with potatoes. . . . The other day a kid came in to return a bottle. Then an elder came in to ask the kid what he had to confess. The kid said: 'I stole one grape.' Well," Jackie says, "I'd want my kids to be that honest, too. But, oh my God, I was scared for that kid. I worried about him all night. The next day I wanted to lift his shirt to see if he'd been hit."

Lise Grimaldi, who shares a five-by-ten room without bath at the Osborne with her cat and the man she expects to marry, and who calls this old railroad hotel, which severely tests her patience, "a cross between Tennessee Williams and Mayberry RFD," is one of two women in town whom I have seen wearing makeup. Twenty-four-year-old Lise is a New Yorker; in this town she is *sui generis*, proud to be a misfit. Down on her young luck, an actress out of a job, a waitress without money for a Manhattan apartment, she came here — "as a stopgap" — because her sister lived at Madbrook Farm, and then she fell in love with Lenny, whose sister owns the Osborne, and now she's here, defiantly wearing New York designer rip-offs and high heels in a town where women wear jeans, and not because Calvin Klein told them to. Lise feels a kind of vexed sympathy for the women of the cult — a feeling she shares with almost every woman in Island Pond — but, as for the men of the Northeast Kingdom Church: "They were out for me. I was a fat bird they were trying to get their claws in. When I started walking down the street with Lenny, they stopped talking to me. They're looking for the wounded — for people they can re-create, people with soft minds." Living at the Osborne is bound to give you a skewed view of Island Pond. The Osborne and the Common Sense are Lise's Scylla and Charybdis: "The women who come to this bar are barracudas. Any man is fair game. If you stay long enough, you'll see people bust pool cues over each other's heads — they turn their guns over to the bartender before they start drinking, if that comforts you. What's better — unwed mothers on welfare whose kids crawl on the barroom floor or those nuts down the street? What is this, the Hotel Romper Room? I've seen women in this bar beat up and kicked in the stomach — and you can't call the cops because they'll go right back to the son of a bitch who beat them. So who's worse? . . . I saw those state troopers the morning of the raid. I was waiting tables at Jennifer's Restaurant down the street, and they came in — big fat barbarians — eating ten-pound breakfasts and laughing, like Southern vigilantes. You think those guys were protectors of children? And how do you ask a kid of five to believe his parents are bad? On the other hand, their mothers — if they *are* their mothers . . . you can't figure out who belongs to who in that church, they all change their names whenever they feel like it — they stood around, the morning of the raid, with shit-eating grins on their faces, like they'd just found glory. I don't know who's right and who's wrong."

Vickie Guthrie, who owns the Osborne, has no doubt as to who's right and who's wrong. Vickie parades through her bar and her hotel barefoot in a blue flannel nightgown. She lives here in a room of hot pink ruffles and lampshades and geegaws. Her morality is conventional, her life is not. Her ex-husband, a diabetic given to bouts of what Vickie calls "insulin temper" lives down the hall; they seldom converse. Vickie, like some maternal hyena, dispenses money and advice in a barbed roar, offering her opinions and her largess, solicited or not. And it is her opinion that cult members, who offered her $35,000 for the Osborne, are Communists. When they were courting Vickie, she says, they gave her a copy of what they called "the Love Bible — nothing but hell-fire and hate in it." Vickie has been told that cult members pray for her death. She says: "The way they're taking over the town — it's killing me. . . . How dare they tell me I'm not a Christian," she fumes.

A cult woman walks by the hotel. When they are together at the Common Sense Deli, the women of the church are perpetually smiling, eager, buoyed by communal faith ("drugs," Vickie says darkly; "show-and-tell," Lenny says wryly); when they walk the streets of the town, their posture is one of dejection, they shrug into themselves, heads bowed, as if heavily burdened. . . . "Assholes! Moonies!" Vickie yells out. "Your blood pressure, Vickie," Lenny says.

The Northeast Kingdom Church pays property taxes, sewer and water rates. They are registered with the IRS under a provision of the tax law called the Apostolic Order; they file returns as if they were one family, a family vowed to poverty. They do not send their children to school, nor do they register births, deaths, or marriages. It is a measure of the induced apathy of the townspeople that Island Ponders feed off the persistent rumor that the cult has its own graveyard, in which bones of children were found. In fact (a single call to the town clerk provides this information, which church elders will not provide, preferring to keep their captive audience on the ropes), the Northeast Kingdom Church does have a registered private graveyard; bodies of children were found; one baby was stillborn, another died, apparently, of spinal meningitis. Children of the cult are assigned names "when the Lord reveals their true nature to the elders." The children are

moved from communal house to communal house, defeating efforts of social workers to act on allegations that they are beaten.
Baptized members of the cult are assigned new names. (André
Massey, to whose house the Chattanooga group first moved, is
now known as Cephas.) What this amounts to is that nobody
knows who is who; and it is this facelessness and anonymity that
led to the raid, state officials having exhausted other remedies.

The Northeast Kingdom Church has managed to slip through
the net of Vermont's civil and criminal laws — which drives the
townspeople crazy.

*"They've taken away all the normal means to detect child abuse. There are
no teachers to report scars — no doctors to report anything funny."* —
state trooper Cathy Cunningham

In a document dated July 17, 1984, John D. Burchard, Commis-
sioner of Social and Rehabilitation Services, Vermont Agency of
Human Services, defends the June 22 "raid": "The Island Pond
action was . . . a preventive action taken under the standards,
mandates and responsibilities of child abuse law . . . and taken
under the authority of the Court," and not without precedent: "In
the past three years there have been over 300 instances in Vermont
where SRS, because of noncooperation of parents, have obtained
assistance of law enforcement to gain access to a child alleged to
have been abused or neglected."

Before the June 22 action, the state "exhausted all less intru-
sive ways to ensure protection of children." The action of June 22
was, Burchard maintains, the culmination of "a long, complex,
and thoughtful process to protect the children." The state, according to Burchard, acted on these specific allegations, obtained during the course of child custody hearings and from affidavits from
former church members:

> A named four-year-old was hit fifteen to twenty times for imag-
> ining that a block of wood was a truck.
>
> A named seven-year-old was stripped naked by several persons
> besides her father for asking for more food; the spanking went
> on till her bottom bled.

A named thirteen-year-old female was spanked for not taking food from someone other than her parents; there were bruises on her legs and buttocks.

A named three-and-a-half-year-old boy was disciplined till his neck bled.

A named thirteen-year-old girl was stripped to her underpants and hit with a rod for being deceitful; she had as a result more than eighty welts.

A named eleven-year-old was hit with a two-by-four for laughing at an elder, receiving large blisters and bruises.

According to Burchard's document (which I have here paraphrased) sworn statements by witnesses and victims attest to these acts of brutality; in several instances, photographic evidence exists.

At one custody hearing, Judge Mahady, who later declared the action of June 22 unconstitutional, said: "At all material times while the children have been residing in this community they have been subjected to frequent and methodical abuse by adult members of the community in the form of hours-long whippings with balloon sticks. These beatings result from minor disciplinary infractions."

On May 22, 1984, Roland Church, a ferrier and a cult member, called Suzanne Cloutier, a former practical nurse at the New County Hospital in nearby Newport, Vermont. Church told Cloutier, who lives in Orleans, that his thirteen-year-old daughter Darlynn had been stripped to her underpants and beaten for seven hours by elder Charles (Eddie) Wiseman. After meeting with Cloutier, Roland Church issued a statement to the press to that effect. Two weeks after the beating, Cloutier saw "twenty-four marks — linear scars — on Darlynn's legs." SRS in Newport has pictures of Darlynn's scars; emergency room records at the New County Hospital confirm Church's story, and that of Darlynn and Suzanne Cloutier. According to Cloutier, Roland Church and his wife, Connie, drew diagrams of the bedrooms in communal houses in which children were beaten — information that Cloutier turned over to the state. Both Darlynn and Church's older daughter Rolanda told Cloutier of many other beatings they had witnessed. Both Darlynn and Rolanda, Suzanne Cloutier says, were "no more physically developed than a ten-year-old," presumably as the result of malnutrition. Another ex-cult member, Carol Fritog, told Cloutier of five young girls going into a bedroom and being told, by an unmarried church elder: "Take off your clothes, take off everything."

Children have been beaten, according to ex-members, for asking for one more strawberry; for refusing to take a nap; for wetting the bed.

Suzanne Cloutier's involvement with the Northeast Kingdom Church began when Juan Mattatall came to her for help in 1982. Mattatall, a member of the cult for seven years, sued for custody of his five children, who had disappeared into the maws of the church. He did eventually gain custody of the children — one of whom, one-year-old Lydia Mattatall, was found living in France with Elbert Eugene Spriggs. Before Mattatall gained permanent custody of his children, he recorded two of his daughters, eight-year-old Jennie and seven-year-old Annie, on tape:

"We want to feel decent," they say. . . . "Do something like spanking us or hit us. . . . Spank us. . . . Spank us or put us in the corner. . . . Do you rather put us in the corner, Papa? . . . If you love us . . . then you'll spank us. If you spank us, then you love us. If you don't spank us, then you don't love us. . . . That's what it says in the Bible."

Together with a special investigator, James Leen, and with state's attorney Phil White, and with the owner and editor of the Barton *Chronicle*, Chris Braithwaite, Suzanne Cloutier set the wheels in motion for the June 22 "raid."

Leaders of the Northeast Kingdom Church say all ex-members are liars, possessed of the Devil; they say Suzanne Cloutier works together with evil reporters for her own aggrandizement.

On August 5, 1984, Roland Church recanted. In a statement issued "at the request of Roland Church" by "the Church in Island Pond," Mr. Church said: "I've had a change of heart. I'd like to make that public so that I could have a free conscience and that Charles, or Eddie, Wiseman wouldn't be convicted of beating a child for seven hours — the ordeal went for seven hours, not the discipline. Now, if I had it to do over again it would never have

happened that way. I would learn to discipline my own child. . . .
I didn't quite agree to discipline myself, and I was weak in that
area. So I asked Eddie Wiseman if he would do it. And he did. . . .
I have nothing against the way they discipline — it is according to
scripture — it's the church. I'm weak in that area." Church claimed
to have been pressured by the "news media" and by Suzanne
Cloutier: "She called everyone in Vermont, I guess. . . . She's the
instigator."

After Roland Church recanted, Suzanne Cloutier — who has
four children of her own, and who says she spent five thousand
dollars of her own money in her fight to protect the children of the
cult — announced her intention to stop fighting. "I'll help individual members," she says, "but I can't go on beating my head against
a wall. I feel betrayed by Roland Church. He stayed in my house
on and off for eleven months after Darlynn was beaten. It bugs me
out. . . . You tell *me* why the state can't bring a case against these
people — they have medical and photographic evidence. . . . The
church members are going from house to house in Orleans to find
information to discredit me. They won't find any, but they dig
deep and hard. . . . This may sound crazy, but I have the feeling
that someday I'm going to be snuffed out. I'm not going around
looking over my shoulder, but . . . God forgive me, I almost pray
a child dies. Nothing will happen until then — and they're all
dying a slow death."

All appeals to the Vermont Supreme Court stemming from the
June 22 action have been dropped.

*"These roles are interchangeable: Pharisee, journalist, witch-hunter, re-
porter, murderer of the innocent. . . . All interchangeable in their spirit
and likewise in their reward."* — "Open Letter to the Editor of a Local
Paper from the Church in Island Pond"

*"We do not pray for the death of ex-members. . . . We only pray for
mercy. . . . For some, the mercy of the Lord is that they won't incur
greater judgment from the Lord by remaining on earth."* — "Open Letter to a Reader of the News from the Church in Island Pond"

Although I regard it as an unnecessary precaution, I have told
three people outside the church that I am going to Pleasant House

for dinner, townspeople having warned me that cult members are capable, in the space of less than an hour, of "debasing" people whom they choose to play mind games with, and — this came from Jeff Hare, a first-grade teacher and a member of the St. James Roman Catholic parish council — "making you doubt everything you've ever held dear, all your beliefs and values." Even Suzanne Cloutier, whose informed opposition to the cult has never been in question, says: "I wouldn't have believed their charisma — I found myself doubting my own perceptions; I snapped back when I saw the marks on the children and when I kept hearing the terrifyingly consistent stories of ex-members." My own experience tells me that anyone from an actress of sound and original mind to a public-defense lawyer to an idealistic and brilliant Harvard senior can suddenly start spouting the cant of the cults (or of the human-potential movement, from which cult language is sometimes indistinguishable); but I am arrogant: I do not think they can bend my mind (not if Isaac's conversation is a sample), which is stubborn, in one evening. Vickie Guthrie glares and blares: "Don't think they can't hurt you," she says; she will call the state troopers if I do not check in with her by ten P.M. I am not alarmed; I am warmed by people's concern, although it seems to me excessive.

In the event, Donna, whom I meet at the Common Sense, tells me that dinner will be at Belleview House; no reason is given for this change of plans.

There are two playpens in the large kitchen of Belleview, a rambling Victorian house with an unloved yard and garden. I am introduced, by Donna, to a score of people — all the men sport beards, all the women wear babushkas; the effect is of a small army in uniform. Donna disappears with my briefcase into her bedroom. The children — I count thirteen, including three babies — are objects of intense fascination to me, and I reproach myself for this: I do not want to regard any child as a specimen, yet it seems impossible not to. None of the children touches me or expresses any curiosity about me. A beautiful little girl comes in with a shoebox in which, she says, there is a bird. "I won't kill this one, though," she says . . . and then I hear a hissing — a sharp intake of breath — as all the adults in the kitchen freeze. After a silence in which the child trembles and looks beseechingly around her, Sandy, one of the women I've met at the Common

Sense, says: "They had a baby bird once and they touched its wing. The bird died. Now she knows not to touch its wings." The shoebox is removed from the child, the child is taken from the room. I do not see the child or the man who took her out of the room again.

Everyone — after some small talk about the threshing of rye, the making of wheat flour, the return of the commune to the "reality" of simple life — is seated at long refectory-like tables. The seating is choreographed; if I wish to see the children, who are seated behind me, I have to swivel, which I don't like to do (I feel, all at once, like an Englishman in the jungle — good manners seem, at this moment, almost crucially important to me). As we are served dinner — thin soup made of flour and water with bits of broccoli floating in it; plates heaped with good whole wheat bread; no napkins — a young girl falls off her chair and hits her head sharply (there is an audible *crack!*) on the wall molding. One strangled cry, she turns bright red and reseats herself. No adult comments. A baby in diapers makes the gurgling noise appropriate to a baby in diapers; the baby is hit on the hand and wails; after a second slap, the baby is taken upstairs. I hear, from upstairs, no sound.

I have been given a baby spoon with which to eat my soup. When I dribble soup on my dress, I apologize, and three people tell me that's "normal"; when I ask if I may have another piece of bread — "I'm greedy," I say — I am told that is "normal."

Donna hands me an embroidered handkerchief to use as a napkin. A man called Asher says he wants to "share" with us evidence of the Lord's miraculous intervention in his life that day; there follows a long story about a tractor that almost, but didn't, run him over. This is greeted with beaming applause. Asher has a particularly luxuriant beard; when I comment on this, I am told that it is "normal" for a man to have a beard — razors are not normal. A woman called Ruhama "shares" that when the children were being taught that day, they learned how Catholics persecuted heretics in the Middle Ages and how the Pilgrims persecuted those who did not share their religious beliefs. "And I never knew that!" she says, her face ablaze; "I never knew that, and I went to college! I was *leveled* in college, I was *leveled!* I wasn't *cognitive!*" Asher says: "Our children will inherit the earth. They will be called upon to speak before kings and judges. It is appropriate for them to know these things. They must be cognitive." During this time — the "sharing," punctuated by glad cries, has occupied thirty minutes — no child asks for more food or declines food; no child talks. An elder says: "Donna, is there any *reality* to Phoebe's having to help Joseph? She says there is." "There is no reality," Donna says; and Phoebe is led away. At seven thirty the children are led, in a group, to bed. Donna and Sandy talk with me about the raid — about their terror, and the children's; and I ask them to hit my hand with a balloon stick — a thin reed — with as much strength as they would use to hit a child. Donna immediately obliges with a sharp rap. "That's for disobeying," she says; "for lying it would be harder. Do you want me to hit you again? . . . You understand why the children can't fantasize? Because when the Lord calls our children, they have to be sure it's *his* voice, not the voice of *another*. They have to live in *reality*."

A black man called Theron, who is afflicted with a dreadful stutter, tells me that he comes from Manhattan and that he was a seminarian — but he wasn't "cognitive" then. Soon the men drift away to prepare for a meeting at the Common Sense. I am left at the table with Donna and Sandy and Ruhama. Theron reappears. His face is disfigured and clotted with rage. He screams: *"Doesn't anybody know there's a body in this house?"* His explosive rage unsnarls his speech: no stutter. "He means there's a meeting tonight," Donna says calmly. Ten minutes later, Theron appears on the lawn, where I am having a cigarette in the company of Donna and another "seminarian." "I want to repent," he says — his stutter has returned; "I want to repent for my anger and for giving a bad testimony." He is embraced. Donna says, "It's *normal*, Theron, that's *reality*. We all have different ways of expressing our anger. We're cognizant." Theron stands there, shuffling his feet, looking chastened, fearful — and somehow also pleased, as if a necessary cycle has been completed. Donna again invites me to stay in her house for three days; I am driven away by a man whose name I do not know.

I am enormously tired. I cannot sleep.

"Why do they throw dirt in my yogurt?" Hope asks. Hope Bowen is nine years old. She lives on Mount Pleasant Road, near one of the church's communal houses. She would like the children of the

church to play with her, but they will not. . . . "And in my chocolate pudding, too. One girl came to my house to watch television — her name was Spring — and the next day I saw marks all
over her. That's when she threw dirt in my yogurt. They don't
know how to please so much. They just grab. And sometimes they
go around in rags. I know one girl — her name is Know-It-All —
and sometimes she plays with me. She's pretty and she has such
nice hair. But they hurt little birds. Robins. All kinds of birds, I
don't know why."

Deborah Hefland, a church defector, has told of having seen
Spring Howell, seven years old, beaten all over her body by a
group of church men.

It was because of the dogs that Frank Forbes didn't join the church.
The beatings, which he has not witnessed, do not trouble him. His
mother beat him with a buggy strap, Frank says, and he grew up
okay. Forbes, an ex-Teamster, is fifty-seven, hearty, and sad. In
the space of one year his wife died of cancer and he was forcibly
retired and his own church, he says, let him down: "Methodists,"
he says; "that's one hour a week." The people of the Northeast
Kingdom Church, he says, "give it their life." And he — after his
wife died and time lay heavy on his hands — was "ready to give
them my house. This fella called Dante in the church . . . he said
they could use my cellar for growing marijuana in. See, they
needed money. A lot of it is misery and marijuana at that church.
But they're nice people. They talk to you when nobody else cares.
They do chores for you. But they wouldn't let me live with my
dogs if I joined. They said I'd have to get rid of them. And the
children — very well behaved, but they teased my dogs. They
threw stones at them. . . . Misery and marijuana," Franks says;
"but whaddya do when your life is empty?"

Elbert Eugene Spriggs, according to published sources, was married three times. According to Isaac at the Common Sense, Spriggs
was married "oh, about ten times" . . . the former wickedness of
their leader presumably being proof of his present goodness. Isaac
says the church had to leave Tennessee because "Chattanooga was
inhospitable to the people of God — they got us on entrapment:
drugs."

*

Sixty-five-year-old Al Bresciani has had complicated real estate (and complicated human and emotional) dealings with the church. He says he has sold four houses to the Northeast Kingdom Church, and given them one. Church offices and the church thrift shop are in a large, partially boarded-up building called Kozy Korner, which Bresciani gave them, he says, for "the remaining mortgage and back taxes." According to Island Ponders, Bresciani is a "hustler" who overextended himself financially and is in trouble with the IRS. According to Bresciani, church members are "extremely giving people." Bresciani's wife, Jean, is a church member, as are two of his children, Edward and Angela. Jean (like Dante, who flies regularly to France to see Spriggs, and who lives outside the commune with a nonmember to whom he is not married, and whose bullying sexual libertinism is widely excoriated) appears to be exempt from many church regulations: Jean wears a watch and carries a purse and lives with Al. Her daughter is said to be in France with Spriggs.

"When I came to Island Pond," Al says, "I was the only Italian in town, and I was hated for it. I bought a lot of property here, and they hated me for that — they said I belonged to the Mafia. Nobody else invites me to their house but the church people. My own church — Catholic — is good for nothing. When my first wife died and left me with three kids, the priest came in asking for a donation for a new roof. I said: 'I'm all alone with three kids — how about giving *me* twenty dollars?' and he said: 'Courage, my son, courage.' I got courage — courage to get out. . . .

"So what if the church people wanted my property? If you needed ten thousand bucks for an operation, they'd give it to you.

"I whacked my own kids. I'd brain them before I'd let them hang out on the street. The church people's kids have respect. I tell these punks in town, 'If you say one bad word about my daughter, I'll kill you. I'll cut your hands off. I'll murder you. My wife had to stop me from smashing a guy's Adam's apple. . . . *They're* not violent people. In World War II I smashed MPs in the guts with my elbows.

"The only reason I don't join the church myself is, I'm not ready to give them my whole heart and soul. I'm an easy guy. I like to go fishing."

*

Bernie Henault, the town's welfare agent, says: "One day two local guys were sitting on the steps of a store up the street. One of the 'Moonies' passed by, and one of the locals made a crack. The 'Moonie' gave him one in the head and one in the stomach and laid him out — cracked his head on the sidewalk. The local kid went to get his shotgun. I talked him out of using it."

"What scares me most is the silence." Marian Barnes lives alone on Birch Street, across from a communal house. Sometimes at night she hears a cry from one of the children, then an adult voice saying, "Don't you cry!", then nothing. Her summer nights have been punctuated by noises she has learned to dread — a deep-throated gurgling wail that fades into a moan. Several years ago, Randy Langmaid, a grandnephew of a onetime boarder of Marian's, a thirteen-year-old whose third escape attempt this was, came to her from a communal house on the hill, three quarters of a mile away. He was wearing layers of clothes — all he had — and he said: "Close the curtains, Marian, they'll see me and give me a licking. I'll kill myself if I have to go back," he said. Marian Barnes is seventy-one; churchmen and women greet her smilingly. "You're old, Marian," they say. "Aren't you afraid of living alone in that big house? Aren't you afraid something will happen to you?" Then they call her *Satan*.

On Sunday the Northeast Kingdom Church has its Celebration in a barnlike room above the Common Sense that smells of spices and human sweat. I enter to the sound of tambourines; the women are dancing heavily on the wooden floor, but their bodies are stiff, out of sync with the tambourines and with their own feet.

Kirsten, a young woman in her early twenties who has twice been deprogrammed, once by Ted Patrick, has been returned to the church, delivered by a man called Gladheart, who stands over her while she testifies, her head bowed. Kirsten's twin sister, Johanna — once also a member of the church, successfully deprogrammed by Ted Patrick — arrived in France, where Kirsten was living communally with her husband in Spriggs' château. Kirsten says she was all unsuspecting when Johanna — who refused to go to the château or to talk with church people — took her for a "walk on a rocky place where there were two men with walkie-talkies."

All unsuspecting, Kirsten was grabbed by her brothers, who were equipped with masking tape and rope. She was abducted in one car and followed by another. She was taken to Paris with a deprogrammer called Mary Alice, and then to Iowa, to a deprogramming "safehouse," from which she managed to escape, having called the Vermont church to say she'd wait for a rescuer at an appointed time in the town library. "I just played along with the deprogrammers?" Kirsten says, with the lilting inflection used by all the female members of the church; when they speak, every sentence ends with an invisible question mark. "I just really wanted to serve the Lord? So I told them, 'Oh yes, I just really wanted to get out, I'm so glad you kidnapped me.' And a miracle happened? The two things I said in my heart I wouldn't do would be to appear on videotape to show other kidnapped members my deprogramming? And I wouldn't eat pork? And the video machine broke down? I just really want to praise the Lord? And even some of the deprogrammers know we have the truth? Because when I told them the church teaches us that women are equal in grace but not equal in authority, one guy said, 'Where *is* that place? Take me to it.' And I just love Gladheart so much? He shaved his *beard* off for me, he'd do *anything* for the Lord. And I'm just so glad to be home? Back in the land of the living? And I was so grateful when I drank the wine of the new covenant? And all I want to do is be with my husband in France?"

No one is told (no one asks) how the deprogrammer and Kirsten's family managed to get her passport and to get her, a protesting adult, on an airplane. No one asks why, if she wants so much to be with her husband in France, she has been obliged to make this detour from Iowa to Island Pond, the obvious reason being that Kirsten is giving the church in Island Pond a buzz. Persecution always acts as a jell for members of cults; it proves to them, in the absence of history, liturgy, tradition, and doctrine, that they are God's chosen.

No one will tell me at what special meeting of the initiates the "wine of the new covenant" is drunk.

Kirsten has come to rejoice, but also to repent: she repents of having doubted her church elders' ability to rescue her — she had entertained the idea, she says, of becoming a cocktail waitress in order to make money for her fare back to the church: she should have known to wait for Gladheart — "And I'm just so sorry?"

After her first deprogramming, Kirsten lectured for two years, along with her sister, on the college circuit, talking about the dangers of the cults. I learn this later, from Suzanne Cloutier. Church members do not allow me to talk with Kirsten.

After Kirsten's testimony, I see a young girl describe an arc in the air with a large sweeping gesture: *Whack!* she says. *Whack!*

On Main Street, Al Bresciani is cruising in his pickup truck. He stops me: "See this?" he says. A shotgun. "Just in case there's a deprogrammer in town. Lucky I know you're not a deprogrammer, isn't it?"

Bill Smith, who claims to have been a Quaker seminarian, is the elder in charge of the children's education. When I ask Smith if the church believes in the Trinity, he answers: "Jesus . . . *not* Jesus, that's a curse word used by so-called Christians. . . . The Messiah's name is Yeshua. . . . Yeshua was an expression of God made flesh." Did God become man and die for our sins? "That's a disgusting idea," Smith says; "Yeshua sweated and defecated just like us." (The church has changed its spelling of *Yeshua* from one year to the next: *Yashua* was the preferred spelling last year; these minor changes come to the cults with the full force of revelation — much is made of them, as if to prove that there is something new under their doctrinal sun.) As for Mary: "We're just beginning to think about how to honor, not adulate, her. Without question she received grace. But when Yeshua went into the temple to cast out the moneychangers, she tried to stop him. Mary was the first deprogrammer." When I ask whether the drinking of the "wine of the new covenant" is a form of what the mainline churches call Communion, Smith says: "I hate that word — Communion. Christians use it." What does the wine symbolize? "We don't have that down to the last jot and tittle. . . . We're waiting. The Bible is a dangerous book."

The church is sure enough that we are living in the "endtimes" to be building an ark in Nova Scotia — in any case a ship. ("I'm just a child," the children sing; "how will it feel to be on a boat in Nova Scotia?") At the Common Sense, a young woman named Eileen sings and plays an autoharp (her sweet high voice, she says, has been given to her by the Lord — she couldn't carry a tune before she joined the church): "You have chosen your creation, woman, to bring restoration to man / What an honor, Holy Father, you have put upon her. / Never has there been a thing for a woman to encompass man. / Now we are free to willingly return our glory to man. / What a vision you reveal to those who wait upon you. / Days of old retold as woman submits to her man." They are sure that God has "a shadow government, a resistance government, a kingdom forming, an underground." Members of this "underground" do not wear clothing that "exposes genitalia." The church defines itself largely in relation to what it is not and what it does not: it is not "Christian — as you understand Christianity"; and "You can't trust America" . . . for which reason — so that the government, "the FBI, and the CIA can't keep track of us" — church members do not register for the draft.

Every member of the church talks of his or her previous misery: they had been drunks, they had had traumatic abortions, they had been "so depressed I couldn't even wash a dish," they'd been on drugs, they'd been suicidal, they'd killed. All had been full of self-hatred, a condition they describe as "emptiness." No one, apparently, came to the church relatively whole or happy. (And yet the sad parents of lost children — the parents who stand at the windows of the Osborne with binoculars looking for youngsters who have drifted into the cult — say that their children were like any other children; and some say the young people who are lost to the cults are the brightest and best.) Perhaps, as townspeople say, all this is a result of malnutrition and brainwashing and an inhuman work load placed by the leaders upon the led. Perhaps their present acquiescent state obliges the young people of the cult to redefine their blurred past. In any case, it is as if they have redefined original sin to mean psychosis.

The fact that they do not yet know exactly how to flesh out their simple apocalyptic beliefs does not prevent them from knowing exactly what it is their children do not need to know: Smith says he sees no reason for the children ever to have to read Henry James, Emily Dickinson, Shakespeare, Dickens, Chekhov, Tolstoy . . . no need, in fact, for them to read anything but material written for them by their elders. ("For example, we might make up a story about a child who was persecuted, or a child who needed to be disciplined for taking a cookie out of a cookie jar.")

Could the children play Ring Around the Rosie? "Never heard

of it." Recite "Humpty Dumpty"? "That was by Lewis Carroll, wasn't it? A verse disguising an attack on a scholar? No. Why should we teach our children about a cracked egg?"

I am sitting in the house of Diana Marckwardt, in East Charleston, a ten-minute drive from the center of Island Pond. With us are Cheryl ("I won't give you my last name because I'm scared of those 'Christians' and I don't want my head manipulated anymore") and a handsome thirty-two-year-old man called D.T. D.T.'s wife and two children are living with Dante. D.T. is "waiting to get it together" before he tries to get custody of his kids — "I'm just a poor asshole sitting in a corner," he says; "how am I supposed to fight them? I don't have any money for a lawyer." Although Isaac has told me that Dante is "in rebellion," a church member not in good standing, Diana and Cheryl and D.T. are convinced — as is almost everyone else in Island Pond — that Dante is a member of the church hierarchy who enjoys special status and privileges. Dante's ambiguous status bolsters their belief that the church has "runners" who pose as "civilians" in order to infiltrate the community and gather information. I have a hard time convincing them that I am not a "runner"; Diana's eagerness to talk, to discharge herself of the poisonous feelings she has been harboring, overwhelms her suspicion.

Diana is a person who needs to believe that her motives are good and that she is fair. Two years ago people she identifies as "runners . . . undercover agents" insinuated themselves into her life and assaulted her where she can least afford to be assaulted: they defeated her idea of herself as a good, sane person, a member of an extended, nonbiological "family," of which Cheryl and D.T. are a part. She has no proof — "I don't know how much of this is paranoia" — but for a year, during which time she helped Juan Mattatall in his search for his children, she looked askance at all her friends and neighbors, not knowing who was secretly serving the interests of the cult.

Diana is a woman of sound mind and pleasant spirit. Her own goodness resides in her belief — unshakeable till she came into contact with the cult — that all people are, given a fair chance, good. Since she came to Vermont seven years ago from Los Angeles she has helped to organize a transport system for the elderly and a food co-op. She is a single mother who lives, with her deliciously antic three-year-old, a boy named (by perverse coincidence) Isaac, slightly above the poverty line. She has never been to the only good restaurant in Island Pond; she does not have a color TV; she works part time for a cardiovascular surgeon; she makes do. Another baby is on the way. Another woman might have had an abortion; but Diana, who is not promiscuous ("just fertile — I can't say unlucky, a child is a blessing, though I never expected to be a single mother, even once"), welcomes life.

Her story is a complicated one. She is the first to acknowledge that nothing she has to say about the "runners" is susceptible of proof: "They started coming over to can with me, and they asked me a whole lot of questions about the Family — I know a lot of people. I gave them a lot of general information — nobody's secrets. I began to see that they were moving in on the Family." The Family is cash poor; among the scattered network, thousands of acres of land are owned. The Family, Diana says, is "a group of people, very diverse, who have in common the belief that we can work together and help one another and love one another and live decent lives without a whole lot of money. The runners," she says, moved in on her because "they thought I was vulnerable; I was more insulted by their perception of my extreme vulnerability than anything else. I was flat-out conned. I began to see that they used everything I gave them — they began to move in on all the Family members — and they suggested to me that people were committing adultery, stealing . . . these were people I loved and trusted. They divide people. And they rely on people not talking about their humiliation." In fact Diana — who reproaches herself for sounding incoherent — has not discussed the runners with an outsider before. "I feel like a jerk," Diana says. "This is so weird; how do you explain it? Juan Mattatall was in and out of here. The runners were keeping track of him through me. When they first came, they said Juan was a good guy. Within days they were saying that he'd raped a little girl in the church. They claimed to be part of an underground to get people out of the church; that's how they justified going to Celebrations and meetings. They played me every which way. And they moved into every single low-income, hard-pressed organization around here. They were so charmingly innocent, so sincere — and I realized that nothing that was coming at me was real. They pushed me all the way down to the bottom — I'm a patsy and they fed back to me that I'm a patsy — and it took me six months to feel that I was all right again. I believe they had designs on my Isaac. My expertise is that I'm good at growing gardens. They wanted that. Juan Mattatall's expertise is that he can tell you all the wild birds and edible plants here — he can tell you how to survive all year round here — and they wanted that. When I began to see how they were using us, I panicked, and I kicked them out. Then I started getting phone calls — Southern voices — threatening my life."

Cheryl, like Jan Montford, has been told by Isaac ("their sex symbol, their bait") that if she were to join the cult, she would be "an empress, a queen." Cheryl has spent time in a detox center; "but I'm too smart to get intoxicated by dumb Isaac," she says.

D.T. says: "What they wanted from me was my wife, my property — twenty acres — and my kids, and my books. Books about growing things, things you're not suppose to grow, know what I mean?" His books disappeared, he says; so did his wife and kids.

This sounds like crazy talk; and Diana knows it: "Either I am crazy or I am not, and I don't think I'm crazy," she says. It is because she knows she sounds crazy when she talks about the runners that she has kept this to herself; she is not crazy. "I believe their strategy is to divide and conquer," she says. "And I believe they had designs on my Isaac. He was sick a whole lot that year. Can I prove they were doing it? Of course I can't. But I've never eaten any of the peaches we canned together. I won't touch anything they touched."

Diana is so trusting one is afraid for her; she wishes to be of use. She locks her door now. She has a watchdog. She tries never to let her child out of her sight. She is moving away from Island Pond because three-year-old Isaac will be going to day school next year. Perfectly composed when she talks of anything else, she shakes when she talks about the cult.

Diana's complaint goes deeper: What they robbed her of was her goodwill, her easy faith in the goodness of others. She will never forgive them.

I never did get to speak to the people Diana and Cheryl and D.T. refer to as runners; they sent word out that they would not talk to me. Al Bresciani says they are "friends of the church — like me."

I don't know if all of Diana's fears are justified. I do know that she is a casualty, if not a victim, of the Northeast Kingdom Church.

Diana and little Isaac and I are sitting at the edge of the pond. "I will catch you a fish, Barbara," Isaac says. He is pretending a twig is a fishing rod. "I will catch you a chocolate-chip fish." He deposits the "chocolate-chip fish" in my lap — sweet little boy, I've just told him chocolate-chocolate-chip is my favorite ice cream — and then he catches a "fierce red fish," and then a "strawberry fish" (strawberry is *his* favorite flavor), and then we eat the fish, which have been cooked, he says, by "water magic." He hugs me. For this enchanting piece of business, Isaac, whose brown eyes gaze into mine with perfect trust, would, if he were a child of the cult, be beaten.

Not one of the cult children has called me by name. They are empty vessels, the cult children, with nothing to fill them but the insistent words of their elders — not even music: they may not listen to music with "worldly" lyrics or "demonic" themes. At the thrift shop, a church member named Barbara told me she vomited when she heard *The Sorcerer's Apprentice*. And that Beethoven's Ninth Symphony was just as bad. "How about Michael Jackson?" I asked. "Who's Michael Jackson?" she said. Adult cult members do not read newspapers or magazines or watch TV; those selected elders who are permitted to read edit and verbally present the news to their followers.

Bill Smith has a son named Abraham. When Abraham was one or two, he "ran a high fever for three or four weeks." It "wasn't in my heart," Smith says, "to take Abraham to the hospital." So he prayed, and put the child on a diet of grapefruit and eggs. Abraham lived. And if he had died? "Birth and death belong to God," Smith says. "They belong to God," he repeats. "Just wait — that Vickie Guthrie over at the Osborne, she'll die of her hatred for us."

I am scribbling at the Common Sense, and Isaac says: "Are you taking notes? We don't want you to. We don't speak to reporters, only to compassionate, caring human beings with good hearts. I don't want you to take notes. When was the last time you examined your conscience? I'm not talking about that hokey stuff in that black box, that corruption, that evil, the confessional, that garbage," Isaac (sex symbol) says. "Does your conscience tell you you are worthless and needy? *Needy.*"

I am saved from more lunatic conversation with Isaac by the entrance of a young Vietnamese. Church "walkers" — proselytizers — in Boston have given him literature that inveighs against homosexuality, the military, cold and uncaring hospitals, capitalism, communism, liberation movements, Walt Disney (and all the woes and complexities attendant upon the industrial and technological revolutions), literature that invites people with a deep sense of injury to separate themselves from the world and to leave "fear, death, loneliness and isolation" behind. ("All the gangsters and prostitutes and cult leaders are being controlled by Satan. . . . And so are the bankers, and the religious leaders, and politicians, factory workers, and little old ladies on Social Security.")

"Give him anything, anything he wants, everything," Isaac says expansively. What the Vietnamese is given is a bowl of popcorn and a glass of water.

"Isaac doesn't like me," I remark to the elder called Asher. Five minutes later, Isaac, whom I think cannot possibly have heard me, reappears. "I don't want you to think I don't love you, Barbara," he says. "I do. I love you very much. I want you to live our life."

The young woman called Sandy says brightly: "Are you still staying at the Twin Maples?" I am baffled. In my briefcase is a folder on which is stapled the name and address of a bed-and-breakfast place in Northampton. The name of the bed-and-breakfast is Twin Maples. It had occurred to me, of course, that Donna might look through my briefcase when she removed it from me at the cult dinner I attended; I chose to dismiss this thought as paranoid. From their point of view it makes sense. Why, after all, shouldn't cult members act to protect themselves from what they perceive to be worldly dangers? It's consistent with their belief that we are fodder for destruction, important only insofar as we persecute them. They see nothing wrong in lying to us or manipulating us — we are children of darkness, they are children of light, enjoined by Jesus to be "mild as doves and wily as serpents." Their vast sense of otherness and of differences permits them to deal with us in any way they choose.

When I leave the Common Sense that afternoon, Isaac sneaks behind me: *"Boo!"* He is stroking a jackknife. "I just like to play," he says. "Did I scare you?"

From this time on, whenever I make a phone call from the Osborne, someone from the cult stares in at me through the plate-glass window; whenever I have coffee with a townsman at Jennifer's Restaurant, a cult elder honks the horn of a vehicle that follows me everywhere — he is letting me know that I am under surveillance.

This behavior strikes me as more silly than diabolical, although concerned townspeople are telling me that I am pressing my luck.

On August 28, members of the press were invited to hear Roland Church publicly repent. He shared a platform with Charles (Eddie) Wiseman, the elder Church had previously alleged had beaten his daughter Darlynn till "she looked like a zebra." Church, who had also said that the church's troubles with Darlynn stemmed from unspecified sex games, repeated what he'd said in his published recantation: Darlynn had lied. She was beaten because she lied — neither he nor Wiseman would say in what way she lied — and she had lied when she signed a deposition to the court saying that she had been beaten. The "ordeal," Wiseman and Church said, had made Darlynn "freer and lighter"; the "scourging" and the "controlled severity" had produced "the fruits of the spirit." Why it had also produced a signed statement in which Darlynn claimed to have been beaten for seven hours was a problem Church — who, not to put too fine a point on it, looked and sounded like a zombie — could not resolve for the press. Wiseman showed us pictures of Darlynn's neck and back, on which there were no marks. He declined, with a great display of delicacy of feeling, to show us photographs of Darlynn's buttocks and legs. It was motive that counted, elder Wiseman insisted; most people beat kids when they were drunk or angry — Darlynn was chastized by a loving elder with love and Darlynn therefore knew love. When someone remarked that abused flesh was incapable of interpreting motive, Church said: "I don't know what you're getting at."

It was a sorry performance — Roland Church saying he'd be glad to spend fifteen years in jail for perjury if that was the Lord's wish, Eddie Wiseman bloated and cocky with the thrill of "repenting" for having exercised a father's prerogative, church elders gleefully awaiting an officer of the court to present them with a subpoena (which evidence of their status as the persecuted never arrived).

For the first time since I arrived in Island Pond, I allowed myself to express anger to members of the cult. I think it was Darlynn, so present in her absence, who provoked it.

The next day I was driven to the Common Sense by Father Conners, the pastor of St. James Roman Catholic Church. I thought, arrogantly, that I could tough it out. An elder I'd not met before stared at me, unblinking (how do they do this?) for half an hour and told me in many variations on a single theme all about the Lake of Fire, in which, if I did not change my evil ways, I would soon find myself. I don't remember his words. They were silly words. I remember what I felt — virulent hatred focused on me, the kind of hatred that is like an invasion of the body. I felt my heart being attacked. Nobody (pity the children) can stand being the object of such intense hatred. The women — their voices sweet — chanted about the Lake of Fire. The children watched.

Three hours later I was admitted to the New County Hospital for chest pains. Hugh Jenness, the Quaker doctor who examined me, must at first have thought — I am perfectly healthy — that I was crazy. "Do you often feel your body is flying apart? Have you had any suicidal thoughts in the last six months?" When I told him where I'd been and what I'd been doing, he said: "Well, why didn't you say so? You're not crazy. You're responding to craziness. You're lucky that it was your body that went haywire. It could have been your mind. I know those people. They're evil. You can't go back there."

Lise Grimaldi packed my bags and picked me up at the hospital the next morning. I did not go back to Island Pond.

When I looked through my notes — notes that I had left in my room at the Osborne — I saw that one entire section was missing: I have no written account of the night I had dinner on Pleasant Street, the night Theron said: "Doesn't anybody know there's a body in this house?" I cannot explain this, nor can Lise, nor can Vickie Guthrie.

What to do?

Bernie Henault, the coordinator of the Northeast Kingdom

Community Affairs Agency, says: "If they disciplined a child to death with love we'd never know it. The laws of this country stop at Island Pond and have stopped here for six years. . . . I've heard them call Spriggs *Lord*. When they say the Lord says this or the Lord says that, are they talking about God, or are they talking about Eugene Spriggs? If Spriggs is Lord, we've got a Jonestown in the making. Does the government have to stand mute while they do this? Island Pond is an indoctrination center. If they run afoul of the laws here, then can run up to Canada. . . . Look at that church: they've got two generations of people missing. Where are the old people? Where are the teenagers? . . . I'm burned out. I had seven people in my office one day, all needing to leave the church, all flippin' their cookies. They threaten me and my wife — 'You'll wake up some morning and find that the wrath of the Lord is upon your head.' They told my twelve-year-old daughter, who was severely emotionally disturbed when we adopted her a year ago, that my wife and I were the Devil. They told her to come and live with them. They watch. They play with the system, they mock the system. Their only responsibility is to the Lord. Who's that? Spriggs? . . . I had a fifteen-minute meeting with them once, and I thought *I* was going nuts. I was never so exhausted in my life. If you want to see *1984*, just go to the Common Sense, that Venus flytrap. . . . My grandfather was harsh and beat me with a strap. My grandmother was harsh and beat me with a high-heeled shoe. The difference is, they didn't do it methodically. And I'm not a zombie. . . . I don't even know if I want them to leave town. Jim Jones left San Francisco and went to Guyana." Bernie and his wife, Sharon, help people who come to them of their own initiative to leave the cult — "All we do is send out a very clear message that if you want to get out we will help you get out." They are afraid, not only of the cult, but of "the hotheads" in town who might precipitate a "bloodbath." Bernie keeps "running papers," a diary, "to be prepared for anything that might come down."

Bud Wade, town selectman, is "so damned mad I can't hardly talk about it. It's hard to keep getting beat. We've tried everything — but the state won't even act on its own zoning ordinances to get those people. And those civil-liberty lawyers are paid by the state to defend people who are just laughing at the state. . . . The church people say the windows of the Common Sense were shot at and their garden shed was burned. You've gotta ask yourself, Did they shoot their own windows for notoriety and publicity? What the hell — they can put in a new piece of glass. Nobody was hurt when the garden shed burned down — and they were the only ones working there. Nobody was turned over to the cops. If they're not persecuted, they're not happy."

One might think that the mainline churches would act to remedy the misery in Island Pond. And to an extent they do: Father Conners has put up young people who wish to leave the cult at the Osborne and seen them safely on their way out of Island Pond. But by and large, the mainline churches keep a low profile — to avert "bloodshed," Father Conners says; because the churches are afraid to act lest they be acted upon, more cynical voices say. In many quarters the silence of the churches is interpreted as a perverse form of "Do unto others. . . ." If the churches leave the cult alone, they too will be free of state intervention.

Reverend Jenks of the Grace Brethren Church says: "There is no organized effort to help. Part of that is because when people leave the cult, they're still sufficiently indoctrinated to believe that we're evil. I don't know what the answer would be," he says, "unless it's less publicity, less press: they rejoice in negative publicity." Reverend Jenks is conservative, he believes that to spare the rod is to spoil the child; his quarrel with the cult is that "there's nothing more dangerous than to believe you are the only one in possession of the truth." That claim to exclusivity — and the cult's "using the book of Acts as if it were a blueprint, not a history" — leads to thinking and behavior that "destroys homes and families," to a sense of superiority that is "destroying Island Pond. They say if you don't believe in Wiseman or Spriggs you're damned for life. They've appointed themselves judges." Judges can become executioners.

Reverend Jenks places some of the blame for the existence of the cult on the mainline churches: "We offer people a building. They offer people a life."

Some townspeople, like Jeff Hare, who is a member of the St. James parish council, believe that it is the role of the churches to bear witness, and the role of good people to maintain dialogue with the cult (not so easy in his case: after ten minutes with a cult elder, Hare says, he felt "worthless, debased").

But while the mainline churches literally occupy the horizon, graceful white steeples rising into the air, the presence of the churches is not easily felt. The parochial school to which generations of Island Ponders sent their children has been forced to close because of lack of money. One day — trying to place myself in the position of someone who needed help to leave the cult — I clocked five hours trying to reach priests and ministers on the phone: Reverend Jenks could not be found; Father Conners was on vacation; the pastor of the Congregational church did not answer his phone; the Episcopal priest is an itinerant.

Bearing in mind that a thousand years is but a blink of the Almighty eye, the devoutly religious are as prone to despair in Island Pond as are secular pragmatists, who believe that the only answer to the presence of the cult in Island Pond is for the State of Vermont to enact new legislation.

God works in mysterious ways; the wheels of justice grind slowly; there are no easy solutions. (It's easy to become fatalistically axiomatic in Island Pond.) As long as there are people who require the absolute simplicity of absolute authoritarianism, as long as the wounded, the defeated, the hopeless, the idealists-gone-awry exist, and as long as spiritual con artists hungry for power are around to authenticate them and to give them a life empty of choice and full of the business and spiritual double-talk that passes for meaning, the cults will thrive; as long as there are people willing to sacrifice their lives, and those of their children, for the promise of transcendency, the cults will thrive; as long as the bludgeoned and the bewildered and the brainwashed are willing to endure a drab present for the hope of an exalted future, the cults will thrive.

But what of the children?

Island Pond may learn to deal with its problem, and to deal — though this is far from certain — with the scars left by fear, paranoia, and loathing. But it is not Island Pond's problem alone. They are all our children; and if the Northeast Kingdom Church is forced to leave Island Pond, where will it go? Where will the children go; and what will become of them?

Postscript (1992)

◆ ◆ ◆

*V*ickie Guthrie is dead. The Osborne Hotel fell upon hard times and was scheduled to be auctioned in September 1990. There is now a twenty-unit motel on the main street. The Common Sense Deli has burned down. The town, Bernie Henault says, is "holding its own." He believes that a struggle for church leadership resulted in modifications: only parents can now "discipline" their children, church elders cannot. The children of the sect still do not go to public school. There is less emphasis on proselytizing now, perhaps because, as Bernie says, "the lean years are over." The spotlight has been turned off the church and the community. Bernie wishes I had not been so "profoundly angry and frightened." He wishes I had, instead, dispassionately investigated the cult's money and property dealings, their relationship to the IRS. We can only be what we are. Bernie now, by his count, has rescued — taken to safehouses — 218 members of the Northeast Kingdom Church. Hugh Jenness, the Quaker doctor who was so kind to me, died trying to rescue a child from drowning in an icy lake.

*M*y friend Margaret Steinfels, editor of *Commonweal*, asked me — and a lot of other people — to write a few words on prayer (otherwise I wouldn't have presumed). This is the kind of subject that can be written about only in fifty words or five hundred thousand. For once I was glad of the opportunity to write short; I did keep thinking I was presuming on the Almighty — and on Peggy, too. . . . *Can you smoke while praying?* No. *Can you pray while smoking?* Yes. That's one of the smarter things I've heard. Everything is a matter of emphasis.

Prayer (1989)

◆ ◆ ◆

IF I WERE TO FOLLOW a formula for prayer (which I do not), I'd find one in the acronym submitted by Evelyn Waugh to Nancy Mitford (whose work, piercing and gay, full of the joy of the mystery that permeates daily life, is a kind of prayer . . . if you ask me): ACTS — adoration, contrition, thanks, and supplication, in that order.

I should like very much to meet Evelyn Waugh and Nancy Mitford (who said that Waugh's description of the resurrection of the dead put her in mind of a bunch of guests madly scrambling for their coats at the end of a long and probably drunken party) in heaven.

I do not like to burden God with gratuitous information. For example, I am sure He knows I'd like to meet Evelyn Waugh and Nancy Mitford in heaven, so I don't tell Him that. One of the things that makes God God is that He knows everything (before I know myself, He knows me); so when I have wishes in regard to other people, I just say their names. I let Him fill in the rest. I don't think He requires résumés or detailed specifications. In any case, He seldom arranges people or events in a way that is consistent with my wishes — though all may be (how would I know?) in keeping with my needs. I just keep on saying the names of people I love.

Believing in their goodness, I pray for the happiness of my children; I also pray, as all mothers do, to bear their pain, but, on the evidence, God wants them to bear their own pain, more's the pity.

When I look at a painting I love (that of St. Paul by Caravaggio, for example); or a building I love (Brunelleschi's Santo Spirito, for example); or a cityscape that hammers at and enlarges my heart; or the familiar world transformed by snow; or, in particular, when, sheathed in shining water, buoyed, weightless, amazed, relaxed, I swim, waves of joy spread all over me and find expression in multiple silent *thank you*s, which I hope God interprets as prayer, for that is surely what they are. (Sometimes I fall asleep floating.) I am a baby-swimmer, but I can do two rather extraordinary things with ease — I can sit in deep water without treading water (I can read a book in this fashion), and I can stand perpendicularly in deep water; this makes me immensely happy, and I forget myself. Sometimes I think that just not thinking of oneself is a form of prayer, because one's thoughts fly upward.

I do not use prayer as a form of meditation. Perhaps I should. I say the Hail Mary only when I am overwhelmed with physical pain; it is soporific. On the other hand, I do make the sign of the cross a lot (shut up, make the cross, and go to sleep, my Calabrian grandmother used to say to me when I got above myself); for example, when I hear the siren of an ambulance, or when something terrible is on the television news. This is a form of superstition, and of nostalgia, and of faith, too.

Many years ago, I was full of hatred for a man who had had the effrontery to die — a man I'd lived with — and, not knowing that I believed in God, I asked God, as a last desperate measure, to take the corrosive, corrupting hatred away. He did, in the blink of an eye, enabling me to live. That made me His for life. (But I have never again gotten the whole candy store at once.)

White Curtains (1982)

✦ ✦ ✦

THE STREET on which she lived had two funeral parlors, two laundromats, a candy store, a small grocery store owned by a Ukrainian (her landlord's cousin), a coffee shop in which one could get Turkish coffee and peyote served ceremoniously by two tall light-skinned Negroes dressed in — she supposed — North African robes, roving armies of fat orange cats. From the moment she saw this street — the apartment she rented was the first one she'd looked at, in fact the first empty apartment she'd ever seen — it all seemed familiar to her; it seemed drawn to her specifications. This sense of belonging, which made her feel good, ordinary (words she used interchangeably), was diluted only when her aunts visited from Queens; then, seeing it through their eyes, it all seemed merely exotic. *Two* funeral parlors? *Two* laundromats? Excessive. (The aunts, of course, knew nothing about the peyote; the coffee shop was always closed when they visited — at six o'clock every other Monday evening — so they knew nothing about the light-skinned Negroes, either; which was just as well.) She loved this street.

She loved the billboard across the avenue, where the all-night Jewish delicatessen was: SLEEP WELL, YOUR NATIONAL GUARD IS WATCHING! She half believed the National Guard was watching over her, just as she half believed Carmelite nuns were praying for her through the dark hours of the night. Often she set her alarm for three A.M. in order to dress for the Jewish deli, where she ordered cheese blintzes and cherry blintzes and sweet strong tea.

Her aunts would have been horrified had they known this, but she was not thinking about her aunts when she ventured forth in the early hours of the morning. She was thinking only that this was her street, and that she loved it.

Her apartment, for which she paid seventy dollars a month, was on the first floor of a four-story walk-up. The kitchen was larger than the living room; this pleased her. No light came into the kitchen, which faced on to a dim and dirty courtyard; she liked this. In the sunny kitchens of her childhood, where the aunts had presided, she had never been happy, and she had never been alone. In her dark kitchen — brown burlap café curtains at the windows — she reigned entirely alone over her meager collection of pots and pans and secondhand dishes, preparing meals at odd hours, which, as often as not, she lost interest in as soon as they were cooked. She stocked her small freezer, and this too gave her pleasure. Over her bedroom windows she nailed plasterboard; and over the plasterboard she hung dark green corduroy drapes (she bought the fabric herself and sewed the drapes herself); and this wall of green — which in candlelight looked like rich velvet — inspired her with joy; she could not have said why.

She entered the dark rooms she loved through the tiny living room, which received light filtered through a Japanese reed shade. In this room was a rehearsal piano (she did not play the piano), a red studio couch with red bolsters, a black safari chair in which she never sat, and bookshelves resting on cinder blocks. From time to time she gave thought to painting the room black, but always in the end she decided that would call attention to it, and she preferred — except when the aunts visited — to regard it only as insignificant space to be traversed.

She lived here for a year, during which time — it was later pointed out to her — she wore only black.

Once a water bug crawled over her toothbrush. "There's a water bug on my toothbrush," she yelled into the courtyard from her bathroom window. "Call the ASPCA," someone shouted back. She removed the curtains from her bathroom window. She pasted typewritten poems over the glass; in those days, she read e. e. cummings. Whatever happened to silverfish? she wondered, thus reconciling herself to the water bug. In her aunts' house, silverfish darted in and out of all the shoes in all the closets, and in and out of her dreams. Of all living creatures, she disliked silverfish the most.

Once, coming home from work — she was a secretary in a downtown publishing house — she saw a man being dragged through the front door of her building by police. She looked conspiratorially at the old man (his head was bloody); he spat. "He throw rocks at air conditioners," her landlord said. "He not like noise." She had no air conditioner; she had nothing to fear. "A man killed here one time — second floor," the landlord said. "He jeweler, bring home money." "Yes," she said, asking no questions, having nothing to lose, nothing to fear.

On weekends, when the weather was mild, she sat in the backyard on a folding chair: A jazz trumpeter lived in the next building; listening to him practice, absorbing sound, alone, she laughed. The Half-Note was a block away; she never went there.

"Who are your friends?" the aunts asked. This was not a question she regarded as worthy of an answer; nevertheless, she answered it, with calm inventiveness. She had no friends. She had no need.

One morning she came home from the Jewish deli and found a man sitting at her kitchen table. At first she thought — it seemed entirely reasonable — that it was the man who had thrown rocks at air conditioners. It was not. It was no one she had ever seen. "Where is Diane?" the man — who was very young (her age), very clean, very soft-spoken — said.

"I know no one called Diane," she said.

"Diane died of cancer tonight," the man said; "she died at five thirty. Is it five thirty?"

"Oh," she said. "No." She knew — she had read somewhere — that the Carmelites stopped praying at five A.M. Perhaps, she thought, the man was confused.

"What now?" the man said.

One of the windows to the courtyard was open. She drew the curtains together. *What now?* she thought. "What now?" she said.

"It isn't five thirty yet," the man said.

"No," she said.

"Tell Diane I miss her," the man said.

She was obliging. "Yes, I'm sorry," she said. She knew — immediately she knew — that he did not believe her expression of sorrow. Did she believe it? This was a difficult question. It occurred to her that it had been a long time since she had asked herself a difficult question. She felt gratitude toward the man who was sitting at her kitchen table and forcing her to wrest a difficult answer from herself. It occurred to her that it had been a long time since she had expressed gratitude to a human being. ("Thank you, Aunt Kate, thank you, Aunt Mary" — these were ritual expressions, in any case lies.) "Thank you," she said to the man, who was scratching grooves in the kitchen table with a pocket knife. "Please don't," she said. She loved the grain of the wood.

"I know you," he said.

"Yes," she said, "I know."

"Well."

"Well."

"Is it five thirty?" he said.

"No."

The candles in her bedroom were lit. She did not remember having lit them.

For a long time she sat silently, regarding the man; it was like listening to the jazz trumpeter — one simply took it all in, one absorbed, one made nothing happen, therefore nothing bad could happen.

"I'll go, then," he said at last, placing the knife in her outstretched hand.

He passed through the tiny living room, which received the light from the streetlamp, pausing to say goodbye.

"Goodbye. Good night."

Soon after this, she moved.

Years later — when she was famous and feted; when she had become, quite astonishingly, beautiful — she was to describe that year as the happiest of her life. It was the happiest year of her life. There was nothing that she needed, nothing that she wanted or wanted for, nothing at all.

Sometimes she drives her daughter down that street. In front of that house she stops the car. "I was happy here," she says. And her daughter — who has read all the shimmering poems, the books — thinks of all the parties in all the spacious, cluttered, peopled rooms, imagines white curtains billowing outward, hears the music of trumpets, sees her mother playing the piano — Bach? Lovers, the daughter thinks; and, the daughter thinks, Someday I will have that life. They smile complicitously.

"I was happy here," she says.